Mentor Texts

Teaching Writing Through Children's Literature, K–6

By

Lynne R. Dorfman and Rose Cappelli

Stenhouse Publishers
Portland, Maine

KH

Stenhouse Publishers
www.stenhouse.com

Library of Congress Cataloging-in-Publication Data

Dorfman, Lynne R., 1952-
    Mentor texts : teaching writing through children's literature K-6 / by Lynne R. Dorfman and Rose Cappelli.
    p. cm.
    Includes bibliographical references.
    ISBN-13: 978-1-57110-433-5
    ISBN-10: 1-57110-433-X
1. Language arts (Elementary) 2. Children's literature–Study and teaching (Elementary)–Activity programs. 3. English language–Composition and exercises–Study and teaching (Elementary) I. Cappelli, Rose, 1950- II. Title.

LB1576.D657 2007
372.6–dc22   2006033463

Photographs by Lynne R. Dorfman, Rose Cappelli, Pat Cleveland, and Ralph Abbott
Cover photo by Pat Cleveland
Cover and interior design by Howard P. Johnson, Communigrafix, Inc.
Typeset by Howard P. Johnson

Manufactured in the United States of America on acid-free paper

13 12 11 10 09   9 8 7 6

7/5/11

To our mentors, professional
as well as personal,
who have taught
us the secrets of living,
writing,
and teaching.

There is no power like the gift
Of learning literacy,
Nor any greater purpose or
Responsibility.

This we bequest to rich and poor
And share with young and old;
How crucial is the charge we have
To light a child's soul!

Thanks to Lori A. Schmidt, a participant in our Writing and Children's Literature course offered by the Pennsylvania Writing and Literature Project. Lori used the syntax of Emily Dickinson's "There Is No Frigate Like a Book" to create this poem.

C O N T E N T S

ACKNOWLEDGMENTS

Many people have acted as mentors in our professional lives, helping to inform our thinking and shape the beliefs that guide our teaching. Some of them are personal friends and supportive colleagues with whom we interact on a regular basis. Others are people we have listened to at conferences and whose work we have read extensively. Both groups have left a lasting impression in our minds and hearts, and have provided us with insights, gentle nudges, and words of encouragement.

Regie Routman and Shelley Harwayne provided invaluable guidance through their written words as well as through personal conversations. Shelley helped us see the power of the anecdote in a professional book such as this. Regie showed us the power of a peer response group for feedback on clarity and purpose. Other authors such as Katie Wood Ray, Donald Graves, Ralph Fletcher, Barry Lane, and Lucy Calkins have influenced our teaching and our personal writing. Their voices are inside our heads, and as we wrote, they spoke to us. We believe you will hear them, too.

Thank you to literacy consultant Sue Mowery for your friendship and your enthusiasm as our biggest fan. Over the years your work provided a model for taking risks and trying things that we never thought were possible. Thank you, Bill Mowery, for your insight in bringing us together as a collaborative team. Our love of children's picture books was greatly fostered by friend and colleague Nancy McElwee. Thank you, Nancy. We think we finally have more picture books than you do!

Thank you to everyone involved with the Pennsylvania Writing and Literature Project at West Chester University, especially former director Dr. Robert H. Weiss, current director Dr. Andrea Fishman, and associate director Dr. Mary Buckelew. Our participation in the institutes and courses brought to life the idea of teacher as writer. The ideas shared in those writing communities challenged us to reflect on our teaching practices. We have rehearsed the writing of this book for the past seven years through our facilitation of Writing and Children's Literature, a graduate course we have offered every summer. This course was instrumental in bringing us together to share our thinking as we grew and changed. Our collaboration each summer produced the seeds of the ideas presented in this book. Through the years we have met a multitude of teachers from various districts as we present courses and inservices. Thank you all for trying out our ideas, giving us new ones, and sharing your classroom successes with us.

Our involvement in the Keystone State Reading Association has given us many opportunities to present our ideas at state conferences and local council events. We sincerely thank all the wonderful people in KSRA who have encouraged and supported us in our journey.

Several years ago we began meeting with Patti Sollenberger of Reading Matters to have conversations about picture books as avenues for helping students become more successful writers. As we sat around the table at the Reading Matters office, we all came to the realization that we had more to say. Thank you, Patti and the staff at Reading Matters, for your support and the introduction to our Stenhouse editor.

We consider ourselves fortunate to be considered Stenhouse authors. Our editor, William Varner, gave us solid advice and provided the right information at the right time to empower us as writers. Thank you, Bill, for your support, your kind and thoughtful words, and your belief in our message. Thank you also to everyone else at Stenhouse who has had a hand in shaping our book, particularly Erin Whitehead, Jay Kilburn, and Doug Kolmar. Thank you to the copyeditor, Laurel Robinson, and designer, Howard P. Johnson.

Finally, thank you to all the children's authors who write the amazing books that touch the lives of the students we teach. They are the mentors who stand beside us every day in our classrooms and enable us to create successful writers.

From Rose:

A few years ago I received a Christmas card from a friend and colleague. Along with the appropriate holiday sentiment were the words *Write the book*. I kept that card in my desk drawer, rereading it when doubts about my ability to finish this manuscript surfaced in my head. Somehow, it served as a reminder of the many people who supported, encouraged, and believed in this project. (Thanks, Joe.)

Thank you to all the teachers at Fern Hill Elementary School in the West Chester Area School District, West Chester, Pennsylvania, especially the K–2 team: Pat Aubry, Patty Cleveland, Mary Jane Corabi, Heather Curtin, Shawn Dzielawa, Connie Harker, Jeannine Langlois, Heather Lovelace, Susan Lucy, Christine Miller, Barbara Norton, Kim Parise, Sue Phifer, Peggy Ridgway, and Linda Trembath. Thank you for welcoming me into your classrooms and working alongside me as we discovered more about the development of writing in young children and the possibilities they can achieve.

Thank you to Cheryl Ash, former principal of Fern Hill Elementary, for your constant encouragement and belief in me. Thank you also to current principal Dr. Robert Culp for sharing professional beliefs and understandings.

Thank you, Lynne. Without your vision this book would never have been. I always eagerly anticipate our discussions and our work together. You have taught me how to keep looking forward.

Thank you to my family. To my sister, Margaret DeAngelis, for memories of reading aloud and for demonstrating the writerly life. Thank you to my children, Brian and Ann, for inspiration you never knew you gave. And, last but not least, thank you to my husband, Allan, whose love, support, and friendship sustain and fulfill me.

From Lynne:

I want to begin by thanking all the teachers and students of the Upper Moreland Intermediate School in the Upper Moreland School District, Hatboro, Pennsylvania. How lucky I am to have had your constant support and inspiration! A special thanks to Maribeth Batcho, Sue Coram, Mark Curtis, Marlajean Fay, Sandra Fedele, Teri Gearhart, Valerie Hawkins, Lisa Labow, Teresa Lombardi, Cathy McParland, Michelle Moore, Sue Powidzki, Kathy Randolph, and Barbara Wright for letting me try out so many Your Turn lessons, conduct writer's cafes, and refine the use of writer's notebook in your classes. A big thank-you to friend and colleague Bruce Bloome and his son Matthew. All I can say is, Bruce, you're next! Matthew, thanks for sharing all the wonderful children's books and your insightful discoveries.

My heartfelt thanks to Dr. Joseph Waters, principal, colleague, and friend. I love working for you. Linda Young, you are a gem, and I hope we continue to work together for a long time to come. Thank you to Jenny Lehman and Dr. Robert Milrod for supporting my position as a writing coach and giving me opportunities to grow as a literacy leader.

To Sister Anne Marie Burton, thank you for helping me develop writing stamina. Thanks to you and all the professors at Immaculata University who have touched my life and helped me challenge my thinking.

Thank you, Dave. You always said I should write. You nudged me through a master's thesis, supported me through a dissertation, and continued to urge me to publish. Thank you, Shinners family, for always believing in me and giving me the joy of having a wonderful goddaughter, Alexandra Paige. Alex, Brooke, and Caitlyn, you are always in my heart wherever I go.

Fran, Mary, and Diane, you are my friends, colleagues, and the best of listeners. Thank you for always being there for me. And Ralph, you never doubted that this book would be published from the very start. Thank you, Sandy and Diane, for your belief in my ability to write this book.

Even though you are not here to read these words, thank you, "GaGa," for giving me all those wonderful memories so I would never run out of grandfather stories to write about in my writer's notebook. When I write about you, I feel as though you are still here with me.

Finally, a big thank-you, Rose. I could never have written this book without you, Rosie. Our collaboration in course work and as a writing team has been one of the best things that has ever happened to me. I have learned so much.

CHAPTER 1

Reinventing the Writer with Mentor Texts

With you as a guide, and literature as the landscape, you can open young writers' eyes to the full range of possibilities before them.

–Fletcher and Portalupi, *Writing Workshop: The Essential Guide*

What Are Mentor Texts?

Patricia and Emily MacLachlan's book, *Painting the Wind*, tells the story of a young boy who loves to paint the water and sky and special places on his island home. But one thing he has never been able to do is paint the wind. The boy eagerly awaits the long days of summer when his friends, the painters, will return. They are his mentors—his teachers who willingly share their craft. The boy sets his easel alongside each one and learns how to paint flowers and faces and still lifes. One day he accompanies the landscape artist to the beach. The artist paints his dog, Meatball, running along the beach with his ears flying in the wind. The boy, feeling the wind on his face, begins to paint the bent trees. Later, the two view their paintings as they hang side by side, and the artist points out to the boy that he has accomplished what he has longed to do—he has painted the wind. The boy responds, "'He is right. On my island, surrounded by water and light, I have done what I could not do before. I have painted the wind.'"

We all need mentors in our lives—those knowledgeable others who help us learn how to be teachers, mothers, musicians, artists, athletes—who help us do what we could not do before on our own. So, too, do our young writers need mentors. Although it is impossible to have our students open their notebooks and write alongside Cynthia Rylant or Jane Yolen just as the boy was able to paint alongside the island artists, we can bring the literature of these authors and many others into our classroom communities to serve as mentors. Writing mentors are for everyone—teachers as well as students. Katie Wood Ray (2002) describes the importance of feeling the presence of authors in our classrooms as we go about our daily teaching of writing:

> *I often think that when I watch a really good teacher of writing, it's almost like there are life-size cardboard cutouts of authors all around the room. Jane Yolen is standing up by the chalkboard and Eloise Greenfield is just by the door to welcome students as they enter . . . With a room full of authors to help us, teaching writing doesn't have to be so lonely. (150)*

Mentor texts are pieces of literature that we can return to again and again as we help our young writers learn how to do what they may not yet be able to do on their own. Although some teachers use the term *touchstone texts* to describe books that serve as models for students, we take a slightly different view. A touchstone can be a word such as *dog* to help a reader remember the sound of *d*. It can be a phrase such as "furrow followed free" from *The Rime of the Ancient Mariner* to remember alliteration. It can be a book that uses one word to organize a story such as *Suddenly* by Colin McNaughton. To us, a touchstone text is remembered for a specific purpose.

We believe a mentor text is a book that offers myriad possibilities for our students and for ourselves as writers. Katie Wood Ray (2002) tells us; "As we develop teaching relationships with authors and their work, we will find that certain texts seem to surface as very important to teaching. These are texts that are just full of curriculum potential"(147). Mentor texts are books that are well loved by the teacher and known inside and out, backward and forward. Sometimes they have been used so often that they can be rendered almost without looking at the pages. They have been revisited many times to help students examine an unusual sentence structure, find the poetry in prose, connect with their own memories, think about how a setting creates a mood, or find the places where an author shows instead of tells. In other words, they become our coaches and our partners as we bring the joy of writing to our students. And we, as teachers of writing, will never be alone again if we have mentor texts stored in our classrooms. Mentor texts serve as snapshots into the future. They help students envision the kind of writer they can become; they help teachers move the whole writer, rather than each individual piece of writing, forward. Writers can imitate the mentor text and continue to find new ways to grow. In other words, mentor texts help students and teachers continually reinvent themselves as writers.

The "fingerprints" of the authors' craft found in mentor texts often become our own. Mentor texts are as comfortable as a worn pair of blue jeans. Their familiarity allows us to concentrate on writing skills and strategies—we know the text that well. They ignite the writer's imagination and determination to create high-quality text that mirrors the mentor text in many ways. Mentor texts help writers notice things about an author's work that is not like anything they might have done before, and empower them to try something new.

Often students, and sometimes even teachers, think that it is not okay—that it is almost cheating—to borrow an idea from or imitate the writing style of an author. But this is how we learn to walk, to talk, to do almost anything: we imitate what we see others doing. The important thing to remember here is to find stellar literature that will inspire students to "copy" the author's style, focus, or organization. Peter J. Lancia (1997) calls this imitation *literary borrowing*. He goes on to say that literature was a most effective model for writing in his classroom.

> *The literature-rich environment in combination with an interactive workshop enabled this mentorship to blossom. The children made natural connections between their reading and writing through their daily interactions with books as well as their conversations with fellow authors. (475)*

Mentor texts serve to show, not just tell, students how to write well. They, along with the teacher, provide wonderful examples that help students grow into successful writers through supportive partnerships.

Throughout this book you will find many titles that can be used to teach a particular skill or strategy. Some books may be touchstone texts, but you will discover other titles that are used over and over. These books serve as our mentor texts—books that we know well and love deeply. We offer many titles for you to explore in the hopes that you will make your own decisions about which mentor texts will best serve the needs and purposes of you and your students.

Choosing a Mentor Text

How do you go about choosing a mentor text? The first criterion is that you must connect with the book and love it. You might be drawn to the subject matter, the author, the illustrations, or the genre. Then you'll want to look through the book to find examples of author's craft such as powerful language, effective repetition, predictable patterns, use of imagery, or rhythm and rhyme. Next, think about how the book serves your students' needs and connects with your curriculum. Is this a book that your students could relate to and/or read alone or with a partner? Does it provide examples of the kind of writing you want from your students? Can it be revisited often for multiple purposes, providing opportunities for lessons across the traits of writing? In choosing mentor texts it is always good to have a balance of genre such as fiction, nonfiction, memoir, and poetry. In addition, teachers should choose some texts for cultural diversity and because they demonstrate lessons for living in a social world. Choosing a mentor text is in many ways a personal decision. It is our hope that the titles we offer as mentor texts provide a foundation for you to build upon.

Introducing Mentor Texts

We firmly believe that young writers should be introduced to mentor texts first as readers. They need to hear and appreciate the story and characters as well as the rhythms, words, and message. Only then can they return to a well-loved book and examine it through the eyes of a writer. We teach students to read like writers when we use mentor texts in our classrooms. When teachers bring literature to serve as mentor texts into the writing workshop, they demonstrate the power of the reading-writing connection. Shelley Harwayne (2005) reminds us,

> *Writers take their reading very seriously. When they read, they discover topics for their own writing. They become interested in new genres and formats. They study authors' techniques to learn how to improve their own writing. They develop mentor relationships with their favorite writers, aspiring to be more like them. (121)*

That is what we do with mentor texts. We introduce them as read-alouds, appreciating and responding to them as readers. Then, we revisit them through the eyes of a writer. It is with these writing eyes that we use mentor texts to help us (teachers and students) set goals over the course of the year.

Shelley Harwayne (1992) talks about her visits to reading and writing workshops. On the back of the clipboard she carries is a line she borrowed from a magazine: *I wonder if I can do that.* She tells the young writers she works with that "those words remind me that it's okay to be jealous of the books I read. It's okay to fall in love with a writer and try to do what that writer has done." Sometimes this happens quite unexpectedly, as was the case one afternoon as Rose worked in a first-grade classroom. She had just shared the book *Barn Savers* by Linda Oatman High. This book is about a boy who helps his father dismantle an old barn and save the parts for reuse in building new barns and houses.

It is filled with rich language used in interesting ways. The students were discussing what they liked or disliked about the book and Rose asked them to think about the words. Chase's hand shot up immediately. "I didn't like all the chicken words," he commented. Because Rose wasn't quite sure what he meant by *chicken words*, they returned to the text for some examples. Sure enough, there were several places where the author referred to chickens:

> *Papa plops the tools in the trough, and dust floats like chicken feed.*
>
> *Darkness falls soft and silent like chicken feathers around the barn.*

Then Becky pointed out that perhaps the author used the *chicken words* because chickens live on farms and the book is about barns that you mostly find on farms. Rose and the children then noticed that there were other references to things that were farmlike:

> *Finally, the darkness fades to dawn, and the sun rolls before us like a wagon wheel.*
>
> *I stack and stack, and the sun sinks low in the sky like a sleepy, red-faced farmer.*

Could these first graders be on to something? Rose observed that as usual, Becky had been writing about her soccer game in her journal that day. "Becky," she said, "what exactly about your soccer game were you writing in your journal today?" Becky explained that she had been writing about the goal she scored and how far she kicked the ball. "So," Rose continued, "if you were to compare how far you kicked the ball to something else in sports, then you would be doing what Linda Oatman High did." Brian chimed in, "I know! A home run goes really far. You could say you kicked the ball as far as a home-run hit." It was an unplanned, teachable moment. Without really understanding similes, this first grader had noticed a particular craft and was able to copy it—to do what she could not do before. *Barn Savers* was becoming a mentor text in that first-grade classroom.

It is not only the craft of writing that we learn from our mentor texts. We also learn that they are places from which writers gather ideas.

Many authors write about names. Kevin Henkes writes about the joy and sadness of having a unique name in his book *Chrysanthemum*. Lois Lowry echoes these sentiments in *Gooney Bird Greene*, as does Patricia MacLachlan in *Journey*. In *House on Mango Street*, Sandra Cisneros writes a series of vignettes that describe what it is like to grow up Latino. Lynne used the vignette "My Name" as a read-aloud in a fourth-grade classroom. She encouraged the students to share what they knew about their own names. After reading aloud, Lynne displayed the text on a visualizer. The students read it with her, taking turns, and then as a choral read. She wanted them to internalize the cadence of the text and understand the power of the words. She suggested that they, too, could write about their name just like Sandra Cisneros did. Here is one example:

My Name

by Beatrice

My name is Beatrice.
My boy name would be Robert Bruce.
I don't like my name for I could not
Spell it until third grade.
I only like one part about it—
I was named after a princess!
If it were up to me my name would be Bridget.
My Native American name would be Little Creek,
A nickname from my Indian Club.

And so I go by my middle name;
It has a pretty ring,
So my family and friends call me Grace.

Rose used a chapter from Lois Lowry's *Gooney Bird Greene* to inspire a group of second graders to think about their names. Zoey wrote in her journal:

I got my name for three reasons: Zoe from *Sesame Street*, because my grandma didn't want another J (my sister's name is Jaz), and because no matter what my name was Jaz would call me Zoe. Zoe was spelled with no "y" but my mom added it.

Mentor texts help students find ideas and breathe courage into their writing by helping them take risks and think outside their "writing box." In conferences, teachers collaborate with mentor texts to help their students solve problems with drafting and revision. Mentor texts are the "benchmarks." As mentor texts become part of the writing community, they inspire students and teachers to set goals that will help them continually reinvent themselves as writers.

Picture books make great mentor texts because they can be read and reread many times within the course of a school year. Students can easily hunt through them to find the craft idea they are hoping to imitate. Furthermore, these books provide examples in every genre, are culturally diverse, and serve as a model for the kinds of texts we want our students to imitate. They are a manageable size and help students understand that length is not always a criterion for good writing. In addition, picture books are rich in wonderful illustrations that layer the text and pull in our more reluctant readers and writers. Although most of our mentor texts are picture books, you will find that we sometimes use excerpts from chapter books and young adult literature. They add another layer to the use of literature as mentor texts.

The Teacher as Writer

Central to our beliefs about how to help students become successful writers is our understanding that a teacher of writing must be a teacher who writes. "Teacher as writer" drives everything else we do in writing workshop. Like the hub of a giant wheel, it helps us connect the spokes of all our other teaching practices. In fact, teacher as writer is the core belief we must articulate to our students, our colleagues, and ourselves. We do this by allowing our belief to guide us in our daily teaching practices. Spandel (2005) addresses the importance of teacher as writer:

> *Almost nothing does more to sustain a culture of writing than a teacher who writes with students, thereby underscoring the importance of writing, and also allowing students to see the process—one writer's version of it—as it unfolds. (42–43)*

The benefits of "teacher as writer" are far-reaching. When teachers share and model with their own writing, they stand with their students as members of the writing community and as fellow writers instead of as "the writing teacher." The writing community needs a teacher who is willing to take risks in the composing process and face the same peaks and valleys that his or her students do. When teachers take the responsibility for providing the high-quality support our students need to move forward as writers, we commit ourselves to leading a writerly life.

Writing for our students is part of the explicit instruction that we do for them. It allows us to make our thinking visible—to explain the thinking behind the choices we make as they watch us draft and revise. We have established ourselves as part of the writing community, so when we model in front of the students and get stuck, they help us get unstuck, freely offering suggestions for revision. This offering of suggestions then also becomes part of the explicit instruction as teachers decide if they will use the suggestions or not. We constantly model what we do as writers.

Bruce Morgan (2005) models writing by gathering his students in the "Oval Office," where he sits in a comfortable chair with all the materials he needs: chart paper, markers, and picture books. He gathers his writers together because he believes it strengthens the writing community and helps him monitor students' engagement and attentiveness. Morgan does this daily so that students can observe him thinking aloud as he models with his writing. He talks about his writing process—the things that are going right, the things that are going wrong, and where he's stuck. During this time, Morgan expects his students to listen with both ears so that they can, in turn, try to approximate what he is modeling. He asks his students for their help because their responses help him assess their understanding. It also raises students to a conscious understanding that they, too, are writers.

When we write ourselves, it helps us engage in the same struggles as our young writers and the same problem-solving strategies we want them to use. It helps us be more fluid and flexible through experimentation with specific targeted skills and strategies for specific writing situations. Therefore, it becomes easier to help our students in teacher/student conferences. In other words, it would be difficult to teach someone how to swim if you didn't do it yourself. Trying it out yourself makes you privy to all the little secrets of the craft. You can more easily find the places where your students went wrong and make helpful suggestions to them.

Additionally, writing will help us provide clear guidelines of what we expect from our students. We need to believe that students can do better and can use the strategies that we offer them. We should not be afraid to show them things that we think may be just beyond their reach. According to Russian psychologist Lev Vygotsky (1978), children learn best when they are in the "zone of proximal development" and can work in collaboration with a more knowledgeable other (teacher, student, and/or mentor text) to help them reach their full potential. Through modeling and shared and guided experiences, they will eventually be able to try out new strategies and skills on their own.

Writing for ourselves and for our students will help improve our own confidence, competence, and self-esteem. Although writing in front of our students is the best model, allowing us to teach more effectively in less time, sometimes we need to take smaller steps toward that goal. Lynne is very comfortable writing on her feet, but Rose found that she had more confidence when she did a little planning first. With practice, she discovered that jotting down some short notes or engaging in oral rehearsal before the actual lesson helped her write in front of her students with ease. Now when the teachable moment arises, she is more comfortable writing without rehearsal. You may be fearful to write in front of your students because you think your models aren't good enough. You will find, however, that your students will applaud your efforts, and even if by chance they create some better pieces of writing than those you've modeled, your teaching was successful! According to Regie Routman (2005), "If you have never written in front of your students before, take the plunge: They will appreciate your risk taking, and you will have a much clearer idea of what you are actually asking them to do" (25).

When we write our own memoirs, poems, and essays and share them with our students, we learn to enjoy writing, and at the same time, we become more real to our students. Morgan (2005) writes, "We write to capture our lives, and that's what our students need to see us model" (62). Writing will inspire our students, develop a classroom synergy, spark curiosity, and create passion for writing. We join our students as a player in the classroom writing community instead of standing apart as a spectator. Vicki Spandel (2005) reminds us, "Writing comes from who we are; modeling must begin with sharing ourselves and what interests *us* . . . Let them see who *we* are first, and how that translates into what we write" (81).

To treat our students like genuine authors, respect their abilities, and understand their struggles, we need to write so that we can call ourselves "author." Because we are part of the writing community, our writing efforts should be included in hallway and classroom bulletin board publications, and as part of classroom writing anthologies. Our writer's notebook should always be available to record our thoughts and observations. Writing for our students and for ourselves continually immerses us in the fundamentals of writing craft and process.

Remember, "Practice makes perfect." Arthur Ashe did not become a great tennis player solely by sitting in the stands of Wimbledon and watching other athletes play. Lance Armstrong did not become the renowned cyclist who won the Tour de France seven consecutive times because he sat in front of his television set and watched other cyclists compete. We improve in writing because we write.

So, if you are feeling a little afraid or even if you do not like to write, take a deep breath and purchase a writer's notebook. Write about the things that are happening all around you. Read professional books like this one to let other people's thinking into your mind and into your heart. The Your Turn lessons in this book are for everyone, including you, the teacher. Try them out on your own to build confidence before you write in front of your students. And read the experts, the children's authors themselves, to find interesting sentence structures, powerful leads, vivid language, useful scaffolds, and ways to play with time. Not only will you see your own writing improve, but you will notice that your students' writing is improving, too. If we truly want to have a writing workshop where all children are encouraged to find their own writing voices, we must first find our own.

How Mentor Texts Fit into the Curriculum

Ralph Fletcher and JoAnn Portalupi (2001) describe the writing workshop as a place where students acquire the necessary skills for writing, develop a feel for the power and purpose of writing, and have the opportunity to see themselves as writers. From Fletcher, as well as others such as Donald Graves, Lucy Calkins, and Katie Wood Ray, we have learned about the essentials of creating a writing workshop environment. We have learned how to use purposeful language as we present focused mini-lessons and offer suggestions to our growing writers. Powerful writing comes from students having the opportunity to choose their writing topics and lots of time to put words on paper. It comes from specific feedback that helps them reflect on what they have done well and the direction they need to go in order to move their writing forward.

It is important to help students become strategic learners. To do this, teachers should make the strategy visible to the students. How can we become strategic teachers? We point out how authors use the strategy during read-alouds, literature circles, or even content-area discussions. We name the strategy up front and we model it. For example we might say something like this to our student authors:

> 66 *We have been working on how an author reveals his character to his readers, and I want to show you how I use this knowledge as I write.* 99

Teachers should model the strategy they hope to eventually see their students use in their own writing as many times as necessary and find examples of mentor texts where the author's purpose for using the strategy is clear. It is also important to mention that only a small section of text is needed to model the strategy. Therefore, returning to a mentor text does not mean the entire picture book or chapter of a novel needs to be reread. Nonfiction texts should also be used as early as the primary grades so that students can start to understand the strategies needed for writing in this mode.

Traditionally, the format for the writing workshop has included a short focused mini-lesson. This short lesson is an opportunity for the teacher to demonstrate a particular skill or strategy and for students to try it out briefly in a supported environment. It is followed by a sustained period of time in which students work on individual projects or confer with their teacher or peers. The workshop ends with a sharing session in which students can read the work they have done that day in small or whole groups. Fletcher and Portalupi (2001) compare this format to the busy atmosphere of an industrial arts class in which students are all working on individual projects. Occasionally, the teacher will pull the students together to demonstrate the use of a particular technique. Most often, the teacher roams about the room offering encouragement and suggestions, or conferring individually with a student on the use of a technique.

Because the majority of time in the workshop should be devoted to students' writing, the mini-lesson must of necessity be just that: highly focused and short. A technique or strategy is demonstrated, and students have the opportunity to try it out with support. Sometimes this model presents enough information and practice for students to apply the technique in the work they are doing that day. If the technique doesn't lend itself to direct application to their independent writing that day, they can store it away for use later. But for many students, this short lesson isn't enough.

Using Your Turn Lessons

Sometimes students need extended time to really try out a technique before it can become part of their repertoire of strategies. In our work in classrooms, we have found that the mini-lesson format does not always provide enough time for students to understand the strategy and make it their own. The demonstrations as well as the shared and guided experiences need to be expanded before students engage in independent writing. If students have the opportunity to experiment or to play around with the technique offered by the lesson, often collaboratively with teacher guidance, they get a feel for how it will fit into the context of their own writing. Here mentor texts play a key role. Their rich, distinctive features enable student writers to say, "I see what he's [the author] doing and why he's doing it. I can try this, too." During these times, the workshop might look and feel more like a laboratory. Everybody is experimenting with the same thing—perhaps not in the same way or in the same context, but working toward the same result. Like true experimentation, it takes time for students to study something in depth. The writing they produce may or may not become a finished piece, but because students have had the opportunity to delve a little more deeply, they may be more likely to remember the technique when they need it. This is the format we refer to as the Your Turn lesson. The Your Turn lessons described throughout the book are not specific to any grade level. They can be adapted for use with all students. They are not intended as recipes. Rather, they serve as guides to help all teachers try out writing experiences to grow as writers themselves and to lower their level of concern about writing with their students.

The Your Turn lessons incorporate a gradual release of responsibility model: a demonstration of the strategy, a shared and/or guided experience in which students can learn and practice together, followed by an opportunity to try the strategy or technique on their own. During the demonstration, the teacher is in control, modeling and engaging in explicit teaching. In shared and guided experiences, students take on some of the responsibility with the teacher there to offer help and encouragement as needed. As Regie Routman (2005) explains,

> *In shared writing, the teacher and students compose*
> *collaboratively, the teacher acting as expert and scribe*
> *for her apprentices as she demonstrates, guides, and*
> *negotiates the creation of meaningful text, focusing on*
> *the craft of writing as well as the conventions . . .*
> *Shared writing is the context in which the students gain*
> *the skills and confidence to "have a go" on their own,*
> *with guidance. (83, 84)*

Shared writing experiences can be conducted with the whole group, in small groups, or in pairs. This is probably the most important part of the lesson, because it is by trying things out collaboratively and with guidance that true learning takes place. Routman goes on to say,

> *One of the most powerful aspects of shared writing*
> *(or reading) is that it is here that many students begin to*
> *figure out how written language works. Much of that*
> *learning occurs through the collaborative opportunities*
> *and social interactions that take place, not just through*
> *our explicit teaching. (84)*

In guided writing experiences students take on even more responsibility, as they are most often working alone but still receiving help as needed from the teacher during conferences. Although there are some differences between shared and guided writing, the goal is the same: to provide the opportunity students need to try out a skill or strategy with support. For this reason, we include them together in the Your Turn lessons. The important thing to remember is that this step is crucial to all learning. Sometimes we need to have several shared or guided experiences before we move on to independent work. Don't worry if you can't finish a Your Turn lesson in one day. If your students need more practice, it might extend over several days. Just make sure they are doing some kind of writing (shared, guided, independent) every day. We can't expect students to understand what we want them to do by simply demonstrating. They need opportunities to experiment, try things out, and play with language with our guidance to build the confidence they need to write independently. This part of the gradual-release-of-responsibility model is what helps all students achieve success.

When we make use of the Your Turn format, we isolate one skill or strategy to better understand how to use that skill as we write our own pieces. Sometimes, we choose to isolate a skill or strategy because we are introducing it to a majority of students in our class. Sometimes we choose a strategy because it is important to the mode of writing we are talking about and trying out. We need to provide authentic reading experiences (mentor texts) first, and then model the target strategy with our own writing, making sure our students have an opportunity to try it out in shared or guided writing. Therefore, the Your Turn lessons are for everybody—teachers as well as students. Your Turn lessons will help classroom teachers become writing teachers who write.

Reflection Time in Your Turn Lessons

Unlike the traditional mini-lesson format, the Your Turn lessons provided at the end of each chapter in this book build in time for reflection. Students are encouraged to notice things about their writing and ask questions about how a particular strategy, craft, or organizational format worked for them—how it improved their writing. They have the opportunity to stand back and think about their writing through the eyes of a writer. Writing involves creating text and critiquing what was created. Reflection gives students the thinking time they need to envision other possibilities for a strategy. When teachers simply tell or feed students information, they don't own it or remember it. Students need to try something out several times and then ask themselves how it worked and how they could use it again. This kind of thinking will lift the quality of the writing and will move the writer forward, not just the individual piece of writing.

The reflection component is an integral part of the Your Turn lesson design. Although we know it is tempting to omit this part because of the ever-increasing curricular demands on our time, we believe that in the end it will save teachers precious time. It is important to slow down the process and help students become aware of themselves as writers. How did the use of the strategy or skill work for them? How did it improve their piece? How will they revise the use of the strategy or add their own personal touch? A reflective writer is one who understands the whys and hows of writing and can transfer strategies to future writing situations. Therefore, teachers will not find it necessary to reteach the same skills and strategies over and over to the majority of their students. Reflection also helps students and teachers during writing conferences. The reflective writer comes prepared with key questions for focused revision work, instead of handing a piece of writing to the teacher with the idea that she will fix it. Reflection, the most powerful form of revision, reaches far into the future. It helps our writers imagine and create even before their pencils ride across the pages of their notebooks, trotting out their thoughts. Students need opportunities to help them understand what it is that they can do well, and what it is that they still cannot yet do on their own.

Writing takes time. As Katie Wood Ray (2001) tells us, "There is no quick, easy way to get to good writing instruction, no one place we can go to find out all we need to know. That may, in fact, be one essential characteristic of being a good teacher of writing—that you have to love the learning journey" (120). To that we might add, you have to *live* the journey as well, learning along with your students as you write and reflect together every day.

Our Hope for This Book

In creating this book, we draw on our experiences as teachers of writing and lovers of children's literature. In addition to our work with students, we have had the privilege of working with many teachers through the Pennsylvania Writing and Literature Project at West Chester University. We've noticed that teachers are at various levels in their understanding of how to teach writing. Some teachers have simply assigned it as class work and/or homework. Some teachers have tried to offer explanations or strategies based on how writing was taught to them. We have helped these teachers reach another level, putting into practice a vision for writing workshop that includes the partnership of the teacher as writer and mentor texts to provide rich models of quality writing. According to Peter Lancia (1997),

> *In a classroom where students have the opportunity to interact with books and authors every day and to practice writing in an environment built on support and encouragement, authorship becomes real as they imitate their role models and write their own stories. Literature inspires, influences, and instructs young writers by providing examples needed for effective learning. (475)*

Furthermore, we have demonstrated to teachers how their students can become more independent if they are taught to read like writers, recognizing that mentor texts can show them how to take their writing to new limits. We have encouraged teachers to take time for reflection, helping students understand how they are growing as writers. Finally, we have taught our colleagues how to reexamine their classroom libraries and personal collections of children's literature with new eyes, looking for mentor texts that can provide a host of lessons for teaching the traits of writing. It is our hope that through this book we can share these ideas with you, helping you discover the authors and literature that will serve as experts for your classroom—experts that will help reinvent you and your students as writers.

Mentor texts will guide the way
Using powerful picture books to make connections
Creating lifelong learners
A classroom full of fantastic readers and writers

Using powerful picture books to make connections
Third graders excited about Communication Arts
A classroom full of fantastic readers and writers
Poetry—capturing students' imaginations

Third graders excited about Communication Arts
Readers theater makes it fun
Poetry—capturing students' imaginations
Developing writing craft

Readers theater makes it fun
Creating lifelong learners
Developing writing craft
Mentor texts will guide the way

An Endless Step Pantoum written by David Marks, a third-grade teacher from Pequea Valley School District, Gap, PA.

Digging for Treasure: Discovering Personal Stories by Connecting with Read-Alouds

Literature triggers thoughts, unlocks memories, and
helps children realize they have something
important and interesting to say. We want children to
remember the powerful memories they often forget
when they sit down for writing time.

–Shelley Harwayne, *Lasting Impressions*

If literature is to become an essential part of the writing workshop, it must first become part of the classroom community. Before we teach students how to read and think about literature through the eyes of a writer, we must first show them how to make meaningful connections to the story. Students should always be introduced to a new book first as a reader. They need to get beyond the content of the story before they can focus on the craft of writing the story. Students need to let the story take them to a new place, introduce them to new friends, or help them understand some aspect of their world. Ellin Keene and Susan Zimmerman (1997) taught us the importance of making connections to deepen comprehension. These connections can also help children unearth a treasure chest of memories that will provide them with topics for writing in the writing workshop. When students connect to literature on a personal level, they can begin to understand that they have similar experiences or feelings. This allows them to understand that the everyday occurrences in their lives have meaning and are worth sharing. When young writers are encouraged to tell the stories of their lives and are made to think those stories are important, it won't be long before they are eagerly writing them. This is the power of the read-aloud and the first job of the mentor text. The books that our students connect with on many levels are the books they fall in love with and want to return to for many reasons. These are the books that become mentors for our writers.

Welcoming Responses to Read-Alouds

Because students have different backgrounds and experiences, their responses and the connections they make to a book will vary. *Fireflies!* by Julie Brinckloe tells the story of a young boy who catches a jar full of fireflies with his friends on a summer evening. Eventually he realizes that to save the fireflies he must let them go. One student might connect to this book by thinking of a similar experience catching fireflies, another might be reminded of a summer evening game of flashlight tag with a group of friends, and yet another might connect to that feeling you get when you think you might have done something wrong. By allowing students to share their personal connections to read-alouds in whole-group discussions, we create a reservoir of new meanings from which our students can discover topics to write about. Harwayne (1992) reminds us that we must carefully choose the texts we use to help students find topics for writing. We need to choose texts that are "rich, enticing, and full of flavor" to evoke a variety of personal responses among our students. Books rich in stories about families, children, animals, and special places, to name a few, are the kinds of books we should introduce to our students as read-alouds. In addition to being the kinds of books students can easily relate to, they provide models of the type of writing we expect our students to do. When literature becomes a part of the classroom community, when books are shared throughout the day and across the curriculum, it will naturally spill over into the writing workshop.

There is no one way to respond to a book, and reactions can trigger all sorts of memories and go in different directions. For instance, hearing Jane Yolen's *Owl Moon* read aloud might elicit the connection "I saw an owl in the zoo." Children might also take an insignificant part of a story and tie it to something they know. "My sister has red boots like Lilly's" does little to help connect with the feelings and situations that are important to comprehending *Lilly's Purple Plastic Purse* by Kevin Henkes, but may help a young writer unearth a topic for writing. Upon hearing the same story, other children might think about an important teacher, or perhaps a time they felt bad about something they did. These memories triggered by the books we read aloud to our students are the topics we hope they return to when it is time to write.

Filling Our Treasure Chests

Writers should always have a place where they can record their writing ideas so they are not lost when it comes time for writing workshop. For younger students this may be in the form of pictures, short phrases on sticky notes, or lists that they keep inside a writing folder or perhaps a daily journal. Teachers can help by creating lists on chart paper through a shared writing experience and posting them in a writing center so they can be revisited often. As students get older, writer's notebooks become their treasure chests. They write their observations, anecdotes, connections to literature, and discoveries about authors' craft. They write the tiny stories that record the history of their lives. Lists also find their way into the writer's notebook and can be collected in one place, perhaps the back, for easy reference when needed for finding a new writing topic.

Books such as Jane Yolen's *Owl Moon*, Eve Bunting's *The Wednesday Surprise*, or Lester Laminack's *Saturdays and Teacakes* tell stories about times spent with special people. Connections with books such as these could evolve into a class list of "happy times" or "special people" and include such things as visiting Grandma or going hiking with Dad. From these general lists writers can narrow their topic further so that it becomes more specific and personal.

Sensory images are powerful tools for evoking memories. *Night in the Country* by Cynthia Rylant is about the sounds heard outside on a quiet night. Connections to this book might lead to lists such as "The Sounds of Christmas" or "Things That Go Bump in the Night." Richard Paul Evans demonstrates how smells can call up a childhood memory with vivid detail in *The Christmas Box*.

> *I remember once, in grade school, we made Christmas ornaments by poking whole cloves into an orange. I can remember how wonderful it smelled for the entire season. I can still smell it. And then there is the smell of perfumed candles, and the hot wassail or creamy cocoa on a cold day. And the pungent smell of wet leather boots after my brothers and I had gone sledding. The smells of Christmas are the smells of childhood.*

After using this excerpt in her class, Lynne's students buzzed about all the gifts they had ever made for important people in their lives. They remembered the smell of peanut butter on their hands as they made bird-feeder gifts. Some talked about the smells of the holiday season such as the wreaths, Christmas trees, buttery sugar cookies baking in their grandma's oven, the clean smell of the air after a first snow, and scented pine candles. Together, Lynne and her students listed the smells of the holiday season on the board. Some students created individual lists in their writer's notebooks and expanded their thinking to include other senses or other holidays. Later, they returned to these lists to compose poetry and stories from the memories called to mind by the imagery found there.

Even though *The Christmas Box* is not a children's book, it demonstrates how teachers can bring the books they are reading into the writing workshop. Read-alouds do not always have to be whole books. They can be one or several passages from a chapter of a more lengthy text, including those intended for older audiences, as well as excerpts from magazines, newspapers, catalogs, and travel guides. When teachers share the things they have been reading for pleasure with their classes, they demonstrate that they, too, are readers. Being a reader is a necessary ingredient to becoming a confident and successful writer. As our reading world expands, so does our writing world.

Some books such as *Imogene's Antlers* by David Small, *George Shrinks* by William Joyce, or *Matthew A.B.C.* by Peter Catalanotto show how possibilities for writing might occur simply by asking the question "What if. . ." These books can inspire a class "What if . . ." list. Other list possibilities that we have used are "Trouble," "I Wonder . . . ," "Excitement!," and "Pet Patrol." (*Patches Lost and Found* by Steven Kroll is a great spark for stories about pets.)

Writing treasures are often unearthed in the way a book is introduced. In *Crab Moon* by Ruth Horowitz, a young boy named Daniel experiences the spawning of hundreds of horseshoe crabs in the middle of the night. In the morning he finds a marooned crab and helps free it. Although not all children who hear this story have had that exact same treasured experience, they can be led to connect to it and find their own similar treasures in the way the read-aloud is introduced.

One fall Rose was working with a group of first graders on digging for those treasured moments of their lives. The children each had an outline of a treasure chest inside their writing journals. As stories were read aloud and thoughts were shared in conversation, Rose encouraged the children to use their treasure chests to jot down ideas or experiences they could write about later. She explained that their notes could be in the form of a few words or a small picture. The notes were made on sticky notes and placed on the treasure chest. On one particular afternoon, Rose introduced the class to *Crab Moon*. During the previous weekend the Northeast had experienced a spectacular meteor shower—one of those extraordinary events that happen once or twice in a lifetime. Rose knew that many of the children had awakened in the darkness of the early morning hours to experience the meteors just as Daniel's mother in *Crab Moon* had awakened him to watch the crabs lay their eggs. In her introduction to the read-aloud she asked the children if they had ever gotten up in the middle of the night or very early in the morning to see or do something special. Of course there was much excited talk about getting up to see the meteors, what they looked like, how many they saw, and how long they stayed up. But the conversation went beyond this event as other memories were triggered. One child recalled getting up very early to go fishing with her grandfather. Another child talked about starting the long drive to their vacation spot so early that it was still dark. By beginning to introduce the story in this way, the children's connections for the stories they could write were not limited to the scope of Daniel's experience in *Crab Moon*. Rose didn't want these young writers to lose their tiny treasures of time, so they took a few minutes to jot them down on sticky notes and add them to their treasure chests of writing ideas.

Next, Rose asked them to think about how they felt during those times they had recorded in their treasure chests. Helping children connect to the feelings of the characters in the books we read aloud, rather than just the events of the story, can help foster new connections and unearth even more writing treasures. The students then had the opportunity to talk with partners about their recorded events and the feelings connected to them. Discussion partners play an important role in writing workshop. Partnering gives all students a chance to be heard and encourages 100 percent participation. In addition, when students share ideas, they learn to appreciate the rich diversity of thinking in the writing community. Students monitor their own thinking to make sure they are on the right track and often find new ideas—unexpected treasures—triggered by their partners' ideas.

As Rose prepared to read *Crab Moon* aloud, she told her students that the story was about a boy named Daniel who gets up in the middle of the night to see something special. She asked them to think about what he might be feeling as they listened. She wanted the children to connect with Daniel's feelings not only to deepen their comprehension of the story, but also to extend this understanding to their writing lives. Together they isolated three parts of the story to identify Daniel's feelings and discussed how the author's words helped them do it.

Surprise:
The path felt cool under Daniel's feet. As the beam of their flashlight swept the beach, he drew a sharp breath.

Excited:
In the morning, Daniel raced back to the beach. The tide was low now. The crabs were gone. Curly black seaweed was strewn on the sand, like streamers left over from a party.

Afraid:
He carefully lifted the crab. As her body left the ground,
her claws started to snap. Daniel put her down fast. Then
he took a deep breath and reached for her again.

Next, they created a web of these feelings. The children were then invited to record on a small slip of paper a time when they, too, felt surprised, excited, or afraid. Some continued the idea they had originally added to their treasure chest about the meteor shower or fishing outing, but for others it may have been a new experience they recalled as the read-aloud and the talk surrounding it took them deeper into recalling the moments of their lives. Their treasure chest of writing topics was becoming richer. On subsequent days during writing workshop, many children returned to these recorded moments and extended their thoughts into a small, focused piece. (See Figures 2.1 and 2.2.)

An Angel for Solomon Singer by Cynthia Rylant is the story of a lonely, elderly man who lives in a New York hotel for men. He wishes for the wheat fields of Indiana where he once lived, and for other things that would help him be more content with where he lives now. He never wishes for these things out loud, but he gradually finds the contentment he seeks. At first it seems that it might be difficult for a young child to connect with a book like this, but again, we can plant the seed for a

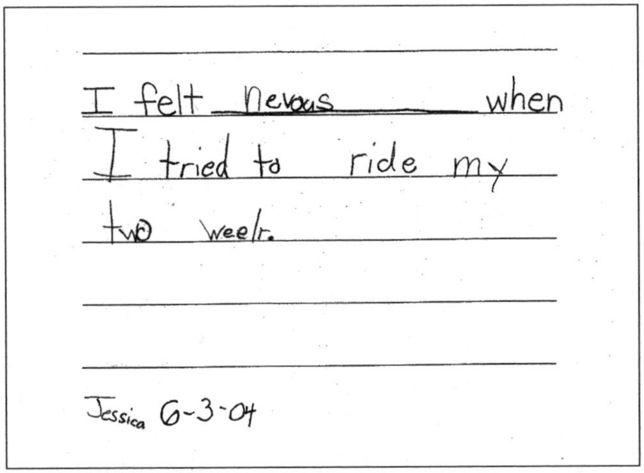

I felt nervous when
I tried to ride my
two weelr.

Jessica 6-3-04

FIGURE 2.1 Jessica writes about a time she felt nervous.

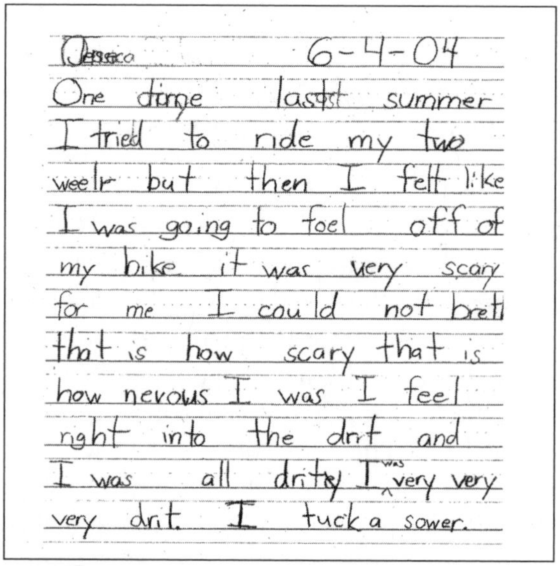

Jessica   6-4-04
One time last summer
I tried to ride my two
weelr but then I felt like
I was going to foel off of
my bike it was very scary
for me I could not breti
that is how scary that is
how nevous I was I feel
right into the drit and
I was all drity I was very very
very drit. I tuck a sower.

FIGURE 2.2 Jessica's expanded piece.

deeper connection in the way we introduce a book. When Rose reads this book aloud to young children for the purpose of connecting for understanding and digging for writing treasures, her introduction goes something like this:

> 66 *Think about celebrating your birthday. Think about how after the candles on the cake are lit, everyone sings "Happy Birthday" and then you get to blow out the candles. Before you blow them out, you make a wish, but you don't say it out loud. In this book a man named Solomon Singer makes wishes. They are called dreams, and he never says them out loud. Think about how some of his wishes come true and how maybe some of your wishes come true.* 99

Such an introduction often leads to talk about secret wishes, but just as often it might lead to connections to birthdays. Through conversation children can be led to thinking about why a certain birthday was special. Was it the place, the people, the wishes that came true? This thinking will not only help students understand the book on a deeper level, but can provide the writing treasures that may find their way into a writer's notebook. *An Angel for Solomon Singer* is a book that can be returned to again and again for discussion to deepen comprehension as well as help young writers unearth more writing treasures such as the special people in their lives, favorite places, hopes for the future, and home.

Book illustrations are another way for young writers to discover writing treasures by connecting with the feelings or actions of the character. Peter Catalanotto is a master at evoking thoughts and feelings through the images he creates. In *The Painter* we are brought into the world of a young girl who loves spending time with her father. Although the text moves the story along in the simple language of a child, it is the powerful illustrations that let us in on the character's feelings. We see the little girl sitting alone on the hearth, eyes cast downward, her chin in her hand, and we can immediately feel her disappointment at having to wait until her father is finished with his work before they can do something together. We share her excitement as we see her, paintbrushes in hand, with a huge smile when she is finally allowed to spend time painting with her father in his studio. Writers can list similar times they felt disappointment at having to wait for something, or excitement at finally being old enough to do something. *Emily's Art*, another book written and illustrated by Peter Catalanotto, is the story of a young girl whose spirit is crushed when her artwork is judged by its content instead of by its creativity. The judge of the art contest is about to award Emily the prize because of her wonderful detail and use of color, but the teacher tells her that the painting is of a dog, not a rabbit.

> *"A DOG??!!" screeched the judge. "I was attacked by*
> *a dog once! Nasty thing ripped my favorite dress!*
> *UUUUGHH! I hate dogs!"*
> *Emily's heart twisted.*

In the powerful illustration that accompanies this text we see Emily with her head down. She appears to be almost invisible as the background of the painting shows through her. If we allow children to linger on the illustrations during a read-aloud, returning to them for conversation after the final words are read, or perhaps even the next day in writing workshop, we can help them make the connections that will lead to meaningful writing. In this case they might have experienced something that made their "heart twist" just as Emily's did. The best books for reading aloud are those that can be returned to for many purposes throughout the day, and especially in the writing workshop.

The Memory String by Eve Bunting is an excellent source for digging up the writing treasures of older primary or intermediate children. In this story a young girl, Laura, is having difficulty adjusting to having a stepmother. She has a memory string of buttons, each of which represents a piece of her family's history. The most precious of these buttons belonged to her mother, who has died. When the string breaks and a button is lost, Laura's new stepmother, Jane, is there to comfort her as her mother would have. But it just isn't the same. Although not all children can relate to having a stepparent or a parent who has passed away, a deeper understanding of the feelings and actions of the characters can be brought about by the talk we create in our book introduction. An introduction to *The Memory String* might go something like this:

> 66 *Have you ever had to find room for someone or something new in your life?*
>
> or
>
> *Did you ever say something to someone deliberately to hurt him or her and then wish you hadn't?*
>
> or
>
> *Did you ever have the feeling of being "choked up"?* 99

After the teacher poses a probing question, students can take a few minutes to do a quick write in their writer's notebooks before having a group discussion. These entries can then be returned to later as possible topics for an expanded piece of writing. Teachers could also create the list of memories that each button in the memory string represented for the main character, Laura, about her mother. Students could then be encouraged to do the same in their writer's notebooks. Lynne chose her mother to model a set of memories before she asked her students to try it out for themselves:

Memory String for Mom
reading the *Cat in the Hat*
coloring in coloring books when I was home sick
walking with my sisters and me to the library
eating at Barson's restaurant
teaching me how to drive
shopping at Gimbels for college clothes

In Sharon Dennis Wyeth's *Something Beautiful* a little girl takes us on a journey that reveals the ugliness that exists in her world. When her teacher talks about the word *beautiful* in school, she writes in her notebook:

Beautiful! I think it means: something that when you have it, your heart is happy.

She searches through her neighborhood and finds that everyone has "something beautiful," like the smooth worry stone that Mr. Sims keeps in his pocket, the tasty fried-fish sandwiches that Miss Delphine serves up, or Jamaal's new shoes. In the author's note Wyeth reveals that as a young child she asked her mother for something beautiful to take away some of the ugliness of her world. Her mother gave her one of her wedding presents—a small pitcher—that the author still keeps next to her bed. Like the author, we all have memories tied to objects, places, and people. We all have our own treasure chest of "something beautifuls" and only need the help of a good book and a good writing teacher to unearth them. After reading this book with a group of fourth graders, Lynne wrote the following notebook entry:

> Memphis, my wonderful tri-colored Welsh Corgi, is my something beautiful. He always has been a cuddle-bug since he was little. I love the way he jumps up on the couch and throws himself against me so I can wrap my arm around him while I watch the morning news and sip my tea. He loves his walks and helps me get some exercise. I think without him I would weigh at least ten pounds heavier! I love his company. Every day he is there waiting for me at the big picture window as I drive onto the driveway and burst through the door with my big ton of books. Whenever I'm away I start to miss his snuggles and cuddles, my silly Corgi with one ear up and one ear down—Mr. Personality Plus!

After sharing her entry, Lynne asked the students to make a quick list of the things they considered a something beautiful in their lives, then turn and talk with their partner. She reminded them of the definition of *beautiful* that the little girl in Wyeth's book wrote in her notebook. The students were asked to choose one thing from their list and create a notebook entry about it. They were also told they could draw a picture to go along with their entry. (See Figure 2.3.) For some students, drawing helps trigger ideas and details about those ideas. For others, it is a culminating activity. The power of the read-aloud, combined with the teacher model, inspired all the students to find the words to write about their something beautiful. Celina, a fourth grader, remembered her mother:

Memories

I hugged my bear as tears of sorrow crept down my cheeks. I remembered all the stories she had told and all the cookies we had baked. But most of all, I remembered her smile. I could still feel the mushy cookie dough in between my fingers as I shaped it like soft clay into perfect round pieces. I remembered all the lovely dresses she wore, and all the giggles we had playing games in the Giggle Berry Fair held inside at Peddler's Village. I just couldn't stand the thought of my mother being buried. I turned to face the pillow and I cried and cried until I felt I had no tears left.

After hearing books like *The Memory String* or Mem Fox's *Wilfrid Gordon MacDonald Partridge*, students are often inspired to bring in objects from home that represent stories from their lives. They can then make real treasure boxes full of tangible things—a soccer trophy, a hair ribbon, a shiny pebble—that will help them discover those tiny treasures of time that are so important to their writing. A good read-aloud for introducing children to the idea of writing around an object is *Aunt Flossie's Hats (and Crab Cakes Later)* by Elizabeth Fitzgerald Howard. In this book two young girls visit Aunt Flossie every Sunday. Aunt Flossie has a trunk full of hats, each with its own story, which she never tires of telling. Rose sometimes has children bring in a favorite hat as a preparation for this read-aloud. She contributes an old straw beach hat and tells the story of how one day she was sitting in her backyard, totally engrossed in a book, when she suddenly felt something tugging at her hat. In an instant, it seemed, the hat was lifted from her head and dropped to the ground several yards away. She peered cautiously and noticed a small bird pecking at a loose piece of the straw. She then encourages the children to share the stories connected with their hats. At first there are often those superficial connections, such as, "Well, it's just

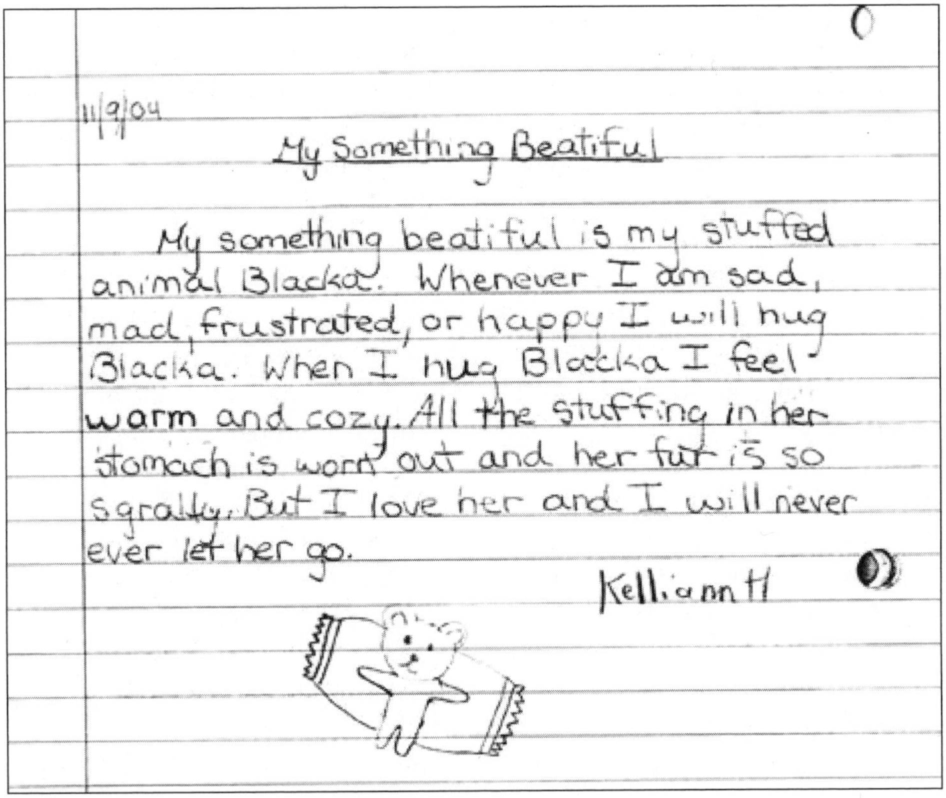

My Something Beatiful

11/9/04

My something beatiful is my stuffed animal Blacka. Whenever I am sad, mad, frustrated, or happy I will hug Blacka. When I hug Blacka I feel warm and cozy. All the stuffing in her stomach is worn out and her fur is so sqralty. But I love her and I will never ever let her go.

Kelliann H

FIGURE 2.3 "Something Beautiful" notebook entry by Kelliann, grade four.

my baseball hat!" But with some guided questioning, children can find the stories behind them. After reading and discussing the stories behind Aunt Flossie's hats, the children are asked to think about the places or the people that their hat may remind them of. Before long, talk about the day the team won their first game and everyone threw their hats up in the air, or the time the coach gave everyone a special "big league" wool hat on picture day fill the classroom. These are the almost-forgotten treasures of time that become the seeds of writing projects.

Some authors use photographs to reveal their treasured moments in time. In *My Rotten Redheaded Older Brother*, Patricia Polacco skillfully includes pictures of her and her brother inside the front and back covers of the book. We see them as children on their grandmother's farm in front of the garden, happily celebrating birthdays, and engaged in playful poses across various settings. The stories behind these photographs are the stories the author tells in the book. Polacco uses a similar technique in *My Ol' Man*. In the pictures included on the end pages in this book, we meet the characters whose thoughts, feelings, and stories she poignantly brings to life. Photographs also play a major role in *Journey* by Patricia MacLachlan as the main character, Journey, searches for answers to his life in the photographs taken by his grandfather. Books such as these can inspire students to bring in photographs and tell the stories behind the pictures. Lynne models this technique with a set of pictures all taken at the stable where she once worked as a riding coach. It was the middle of January and Lynne was on top of the manure pile with one of her students, attempting to flatten it by using a pitchfork to spread the manure. A parent snapped photos of the riding students making snowballs in the courtyard and firing them at Lynne and Jody, the student. Lynne ended up falling over backward into the manure pile and disappearing from view. After she shared her story, she encouraged her students to ask her more questions about what had happened—the who, what, where, when, and why behind it. Later during writing workshop, Lynne drafted the story and shared it the next day. Before long, some of the students were tucking photos inside their notebooks and using them to spark story ideas.

In the first-grade classrooms that Rose visits, she often lingers on the displays brought in by the "student of the week." Many of the displays contain photographs used to introduce family members or pets. Rose often engages the student in a guided conversation, leading him or her to tell the story behind a picture in the display—the who, what, when, where, and why behind it in order to bring to mind the rich detail. She then encourages the student to jot down the memory, often in the form of a short phrase, in his or her writing folder, journal, or notebook. The story behind the picture becomes a writing treasure that can be returned to during writing workshop.

When using photos as a vehicle for finding writing topics, it is important to model for students that the story must be theirs, not one told to them by someone else such as their parents or grandparents. For elementary classrooms, taking these stories through the entire writing process to publication is a worthwhile project. Stories with photos are often read and reread by the wider school community when hung in the hallways or classrooms.

As in *An Angel for Solomon Singer*, read-alouds can also help children uncover the memories connected with special places. In *All the Places to Love* by Patricia MacLachlan we read of a small boy who is thinking about the places he loves best on the farm where he lives.

What I saw first were all the places to love:
The valley,
The river falling down over rocks,
The hilltop where the blueberries grew.

Eileen Spinelli's *In Our Backyard Garden* takes us to a special place where memories are unearthed with each passing season. We can encourage young authors to dig up writing treasures associated with the special places in their lives: a vacation spot, a secret hiding place, a favorite park. The Your Turn lesson at the end of this chapter describes a technique that involves sketching and conversation to encourage young writers to dig up the stories connected to special places.

An Outdoor Writer's Café

Finding topics for writing can be difficult, especially as spring arrives and students begin to think about summer vacation, Little League games, and weekends at the shore. State testing takes a great deal of energy from both students and teachers. One year Lynne thought it was time to renew her students' love and enthusiasm for writing, and she thought a writer's café would be the perfect way to do it. She talked with a fifth-grade class about her ideas for an outdoor writer's café. They had been working on a poetry cycle and using scaffolds to create poems. The weather promised to be unusually warm for April, so Lynne wanted to take advantage of it. "Tomorrow we're going to do exactly what writers do. We are taking our notebooks and pencils and going outside for about forty minutes. I want you to write about the things you see, smell, hear, taste, and feel. I am going to ask you to write from at least four different vantage points. Don't stay in one spot for too long. And the first time we go outside, I don't want you to talk with anyone—not even your teacher or me. Just write. Don't evaluate whether or not the stuff you are writing is good or bad. Just write it down. Don't let any ideas escape. Capture them in the white-lined cages of your writer's notebook. But first, today I want to share a beautiful picture book with you titled *Call Me Marianne* by Jen Bryant. The author imagined a story about the poet Marianne Moore. Bryant based her imaginings on actual details from the poet's life." Lynne gathered the students closely and read. When she read the following words, she paused and asked the students to turn and talk to their discussion partners about how it might apply to their writer's café:

"For me, being a poet begins with watching. I watch animals. I watch people. I read books and look at photographs. I notice details—little things that other people miss.

At the end of Bryant's book, the poet hands Jonathan his very own writer's notebook and encourages him to stay and write about the tiger. He remembers the poet's words—that being a poet begins with watching. Lynne looked at her students' faces and knew she had captured their interest. "Let's go outside for a quick tour today and think about what could be possible topics for writing and where we might want to be to observe those things." Outside Lynne modeled her writing by talking out loud as she wrote. "Here I'm going to take some notes about the school." She wrote these observations and shared with the class:

> shiny windows
> squares neatly stacked
> brown brick rectangles
> sun reflected on windows
> empty slides and basketball courts
> yellow school buses waiting to take kids home

Then she turned her attention to the church and its steeple:

> slender steeple
> whiter than clouds
> a simple cross
> a strong message
> keep the faith

She asked the students to suggest topics. Steven said he could write about the basketball that was left outside. "I could be the ball. I'd feel lonely and forgotten." Some students chose the pine trees, or the slender, young trees with delicate pink blooms, or the light post in the church parking lot, or the baseball diamond. Lynne was satisfied that they would find lots of things to write about. "Now remember, sometimes a poem will just spill onto the page. Other times, you may need to make a quick sketch and/or write down some words, phrases, and sentences. There's no right or wrong way to do this. We all have our own writing process that works best for us."

When they returned to the classroom, Lynne wrote her notes on the board. Then she created a draft of two poems from the notes she had made. The following poem is about the school.

Shiny-clean windows,
squares neatly stacked
while brown brick rectangles
march along like a Cub Scout troop.

But inside, cold and silent,
as empty as the slides and
basketball courts on
Friday afternoons
when children leave
on yellow school buses . . .

Looking out the shiny-clean
windows of the school bus
and dreaming of home-run hits
and pedal-fast bike rides
and sleepy Saturday-Sunday
mornings when alarm clocks
are strangely silent.

Lynne encouraged the students to talk about her poem. They noticed that some of the things she added to her poem did not appear in the original list. "That's exactly what you will do. You'll come up with something you never imagined before. That's because you'll be doing what writers do . . . noticing little details that other people miss, like Jennifer Bryant suggested Marianne Moore might have done . . . looking at ordinary things but seeing them in extraordinary ways."

The next afternoon the class took their notebooks and went outside to write for forty minutes. Their teacher wrote, too. Lynne wrote. Everybody was writing. When a third-grade class came out to play kickball, the game just became another topic to write about. Here are Amber's notes from her notebook, untouched:

I'm brown and hard and smooth and fell off of my father and alone in the grass.
—branch

I smell beautiful with a soft top and a strong stem and green leaves.
—flower

People leave footprints on me
And when rain comes,

I turn into mud
And dry in the sun.
—dirt

I'm dying for water, some of me is green and
some of me is brown, some of me is soft and some is rough.
—grass

Kurt wrote about the empty baseball diamond that borders the playground behind the school and imagined the following poem from his notes:

"The Pitch"

The sun beats down on us
As the whole world waits, silent
For the one final pitch.
The dust tumbles as
I bend my legs in the shape
Of a crooked nine.
The crowd hollers as
The red and white ball flies through
The open-aired field.

Maria observed the pine trees and wrote several poems about them. This was a class favorite:

"Pine"

Pine tree.
Sweet pine scents filling the air,
Not like the other trees that stand empty and bare.
Lined with prickles on every side,
By a school and a church standing tall and wide.
Overgrown grass all in its middle,
Green needles dropping little by little.
Pine tree.

The kids were amazing! Barbara (their teacher) and Lynne were speechless. They wrote and wrote, and when it was time to go back inside, they came in slowly, as if a film had been set at slow motion to notice every detail. They kept stopping to kneel down to write one last thought. They scanned the field, the playground, the sky . . . hungry for more. When Lynne asked if anyone wanted to share, the students took turns coming to the podium to read notes and poetry. Their words rushed and gushed in rivers and whispered in silver streams, and the air was filled with writing by students who believe that they are writers. When their teacher (who is quite fond of mathematics) announced that she had several poems to share, they listened eagerly and burst out in enthusiastic applause when she was finished. Lynne had to pull herself away to go to her next class, and as she left, the students were still sharing their writing.

Shelley Harwayne (1992) captures the value of response to literature as a resource for writing topics: "Literature helped recreate very powerful moments for students, those that they often forget when they sit down at their school desks for writing time" (79). One of the techniques she describes is using sticky notes on which children record their responses. These notes can be posted, honored, and shared, then added to a notebook or treasure chest of writing ideas. We have used this technique many times with various sizes of sticky notes. When very small sticky notes are used, children may respond with just a word or short phrase. Later, during writing workshop, they can return to this and extend their thinking—as Harwayne (1992) says, "write to get to the bottom of it." Although responses often lead to the writing of personal narratives from the unearthed memories, students sometimes try out other formats: poetry, persuasive pieces, letters, even recipes. *Mud* by Mary Lyn Ray is a delightful book that describes the "season" of mud—when winter is waning, the earth is defrosting, and mud is overflowing. After reading this, Rose asked a group of second graders to respond on a small sticky note. Sarah wrote "mud pies." As we shared responses, she told about making mud pies with her sister and brother in the hollow of a large tree in their backyard. A few days later she drew the tree in her writer's notebook, along with a recipe for making mud pies. (See Figure 2.4.)

Carol Gay (1976), in writing about the importance of reading aloud to children, reminds us of the inescapable link this practice has to the development of writing:

> *Reading aloud is inseparably linked with learning to write.*
> *If elementary school teachers fail to read aloud to their*
> *students often, regularly, and for reasonably long periods*
> *of time, those students are going to be severely handicapped*
> *in learning to write. (87)*

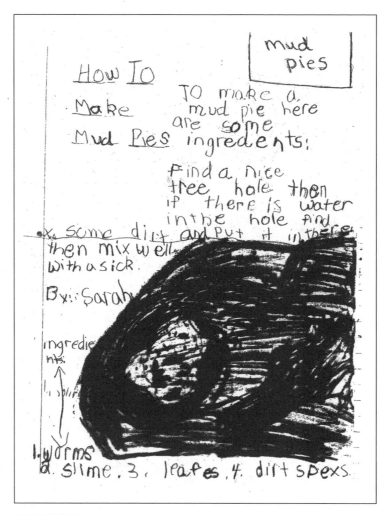

FIGURE 2.4 Sarah's notebook entry is a recipe for making mud pies (grade two).

The read-aloud is an important part of writing workshop and establishing a community of writers. Through careful selection of read-alouds as mentor texts rich in experiences that are both personal and magical, we can provide our student authors with a treasure chest of opportunities to find writing topics. As Carol Gay says, "Only by hearing good literature can a child come to realize what it is and to understand what writing has to offer him—an opportunity to describe, define, and perhaps understand his world" (93).

Drawing and Talking to Find Topics

Through sketching and conversation, writers dig up memories connected with objects or events from a special place. Variations of this lesson are endless, as the setting could be a backyard, a park, the playground, a vacation spot, a field trip, and so on. Try this out on your own so that you have a model to share with your students.

Hook: Read one or two excerpts from *In Our Backyard Garden* by Eileen Spinelli. Through whole-group conversation invite students to make connections to events that happened in their backyards. Be sure to participate in the discussion and share your own connections. Options include *In My Momma's Kitchen* by Jerdine Nolen or *All the Places to Love* by Patricia MacLachlan.

Purpose: *Writers, just like Eileen Spinelli told many stories about things that happened in a backyard, today we will learn how to use a familiar setting to help dig up memories and find topics and stories for our writing.*

Brainstorm: Ask students to create a list of favorite or familiar places such as their backyard, the playground, or a vacation spot. Have them turn and talk with a partner to share their lists and add or revise as needed. Ask students to circle or star one place they would like to sketch and write about.

Model: Distribute a strip of plain drawing paper (approximately six by twenty-four inches) to each student. Instruct them to fold back approximately one-third of the strip. Share the sketch you have prepared, thinking aloud and talking about each object or relating small stories that you are reminded of as you explain your drawing. Ask students to sketch their place on the two-thirds portion of the strip. You may have to demonstrate what a sketch is so that students don't spend too much time on the drawing.

> *Writers, close your eyes and think about the place and the experiences you have had there. Think about the objects in this place. Sketch this place on the long part of your strip. Remember that this is only a sketch and that a sketch takes only a few minutes.*

Allow students some time to sketch, then ask them to talk and share.

> Now turn to your partner and talk about the different things in your sketch. Tell the stories that you remember when you think about or talk about each part of your sketch.

Continue to model by choosing one object that evoked a special memory or story. Sketch this again on the small folded part of the paper strip, this time elaborating and adding more detail.

> This tree in my backyard has so many special memories attached to it, but one thing I remember is the time I watched a robin build a nest for her eggs, then take care of the babies and teach them how to fly. So on this part of the strip I'm going to zoom in on that tree and add the detail of the robin's nest.

Invite students to do the same.

> Think about the one thing in your sketch you had the most to talk to your partner about. Zoom in on that and sketch it again on the small part of your strip. Add as many details as you can. You can list words or short phrases that come to mind as you sketch.

Shared/Guided Writing: Talk to the students about your detailed sketch. Model for them how you might jot down words or phrases that you can use. Then begin to draft your piece. Invite students to do the same.

> Turn and talk again with your neighbor about your detailed drawing. As you talk, create a list of words or phrases that describe your object or memory. Share your list with your partner.

Circulate and listen in, often asking clarifying questions to guide the thinking.

Independent Writing: Invite students to write a small story or notebook entry on the memory from the sketch.

Reflection: Invite students to reflect on the strategy.

> Did the sketching help you focus your thoughts? How?

> When could you use this strategy?

Students can first share in pairs, then share ideas with the whole group. After reflecting on the strategy, ask students to reread their writing and think about the things that they do well as a writer. What revisions could they make? Some students might choose to continue to work on their piece during subsequent workshops.

2

Finding Topics from a Memory Chain

A memory chain is a prewriting experience to help writers find topics and ideas to write about. It is a wonderful strategy to use when students are experiencing writer's block. A memory chain is a collection of ideas that are sometimes related and sometimes unrelated. It is a menu that helps a writer make good choices for a writing piece.

Hook: *Letter to the Lake* (Susan Marie Swanson) is an excellent book to demonstrate to writers how objects can spark memories. Talk about how different objects in the book remind Rosie of things she experienced at the lake in the summer—the raspberry jam she has for breakfast reminds her of the time she picked raspberries, the rock shaped like a bear reminds her of finding the bear tracks, the speckled rock reminds her of watching the dragonflies catch bugs. Other options include *Night Tree* by Eve Bunting, or *Bigmama's* by Donald Crews.

Purpose: *Writers, sometimes objects or words can remind us of things that happened to us or things we wonder about, just like Rosie is reminded about the lake. Today I'm going to show you how to create a memory chain. When you are having difficulty finding a topic for writing, a memory chain can help you unlock some ideas.*

Brainstorm: Together with the class, brainstorm objects in the room, words, ideas, seasons, or holidays that could be a starting point for a memory chain. For example, bulletin board, desk, flag, playground, window, winter, Thanksgiving, and so on.

Model: Choose one of the words from the brainstormed list and write it on the board or overhead. Continue to think aloud, recording ideas that are generated as a stream of consciousness. Here is an example from Rose's notebook:

snow

$\downarrow$

blizzard at the farm

$\downarrow$

ice skating on the pond

$\downarrow$

ice skating at Italian Lake

$\downarrow$

the whip—skating over my finger

$\downarrow$

hot chocolate at Christina's house

$\downarrow$

Daddy making hot chocolate before school

Try to make your memory chain as long as you can so you have lots of ideas to choose from. Then go back to the list and circle one idea that you think you could write about today. Orally tell the story, or write the story on chart paper.

Shared/Guided Writing: Ask students to choose a word and try out the technique in their writer's notebooks. Sometimes it is interesting to have the class all start with the same word, then see how many different ideas can come from it. After students have completed their chains, have them share with a partner. Partners can give feedback on what story they would like to hear more about. They can then circle those ideas and tell their stories to each other, providing oral rehearsal.

Independent Writing: Invite students to complete a notebook entry on the memory they circled.

Reflection: This strategy can work very well but can also hit a dead end—it all depends on where the ideas take you. Try it out several times, and begin this part of the lesson discussing with students how the strategy has worked for you. Then ask students to share their ideas on how the strategy worked for them.

How did the strategy work for you?

When would you use it again?

What changes would you make?

3

Finding Topics and Using Senses to Create First Memories

First memories of an event, place, or even a person are usually vivid because they are associated with several senses and have strong emotional appeal. They offer young writers an array of starter topics. Students can use them as writer's notebook entries, eventually finding seeds of ideas for narratives, poems, and even informational pieces.

Hook: Read *The Seashore Book* by Charlotte Zolotow. Discuss how Zolotow awakens the senses in her readers and helps them visualize the seashore—its sounds, smells, sights, and the feel of the sand. (Options: *Crab Moon* by Ruth Horowitz, *Hello Ocean* by Pam Muñoz Ryan, *When This Box Is Full* by Patricia Lillie.) Create a web of ideas organized around the senses. Refer to the text for specific language. Ask your students the following questions: How did the mentor text inspire you? What words and images from the text stayed with you?

Note: Geographical location may be important to think about here for first memory topics. Lynne used books about the seashore because most of her students vacation at the New Jersey shores. If your students live in Arizona or New Mexico, you might use books by Byrd Baylor.

Purpose: *Writers, often we can recall with extraordinary detail and powerful feelings, the people, places, and events of our first impressions—our first memories. They are etched in our hearts and our minds, and when we begin to write about them, our words often spill onto the page. Today I will show you how to use your senses to create a first memory for your writer's notebook.*

Brainstorm: Together with the class create a list of possible first memories. Some examples may include learning to ride a bike, sledding down a hill, riding a horse, surfing or Boogie boarding, watching a sunrise or sunset, seeing the ocean for the first time.

Model: Choose one of the ideas from the brainstormed list and create a first memory with strong appeal to the senses. Lynne's example:

> *I am standing on the beach and curling my toes into the warm, grainy sand. My grandparents stand on each side of me and hold a hand tightly. They know I want to run toward the water. I close my eyes and breathe the salty air into my lungs. When I gaze out onto the blue-meets-blue-horizon, I catch a glimpse of a gull floating high above me. I think to myself, "I wish I could be that gull and never leave here." The waves roll in and out, in and out . . . a pulsating rhythm that beats like my heart. It reminds me of life itself. I watch the water stain the sand a dark beige color. The foamy fingers waltz out again to continue their dance from the sea to the shore. My grandparents smile at me, and I cry out to them and the whole world, "It's so beautiful . . . it's so very beautiful!" I catch my breath as the wonder of it all wraps around me like a warm blanket.*

Shared/Guided Writing: Students note the appeal to the senses used in the teacher's model and think about its effectiveness. Ask students to choose an idea from the list and try writing about it in their writer's notebooks. Some students may need to start with a prewriting experience such as the graphic organizer that makes use of the senses. Circulate to encourage, ask questions, and give feedback. Students may share with a partner or in small response groups, noting powerful words and phrases that appeal to the senses.

Independent Writing: Invite students to complete a first draft from their notebook entry or choose a new topic and write another notebook entry.

Reflection: Students examine their first memory piece. During individual conferences, whole-group discussion, or partner sharing they can guide their thinking with the following questions:

> *How did the use of the senses strengthen your writing?*
>
> *What writing strategies did you use to help the reader "be there" with you?*
>
> *What other first memories could you write about?*

Every Picture Tells a Story

Whereas some authors write personal narratives from photographs that spark memories, others use pictures or artifacts to create fictional accounts. This lesson will show your students how to create stories from pictures. To prepare for this lesson, collect pictures from magazines or newspapers that are rich in detail and that might inspire places, characters, or events for stories.

Hook: Introduce the use of photographs to reveal moments in time by reading *Journey* by Patricia MacLachlan or *Best Friends* by Loretta Krupinski. *Best Friends* is an example of how a fictional story can be built around photographs or artifacts. Other options: *Dirt on Their Skirts* by Doreen Rappaport and Lyndall Callan or *Teammates* by Peter Golenbock. These books use photographs of real people to tell their story.

Purpose: *Sometimes authors build stories around pictures or photographs. Sometimes the stories are personal memories sparked by connections made to the photographs. Sometimes the pictures provide the ideas for settings, characters, or events for fictional stories. Today I will show you how to build a story around a picture.*

Brainstorm: Choose a picture from a magazine and display it on an overhead or visualizer. Ask students to think about the characters, setting, problems, story events, and so on that the picture makes them think about. Elicit as many ideas as possible and make a web on a chart or whiteboard. This brainstorming can be repeated for several pictures. An alternative for older students is to place a picture on the center of a piece of chart paper. Create several of these charts and display them around the room. Students can do a "gallery walk" (walk around the room looking at the pictures as they would in an art museum) and jot down ideas for characters, setting, events, and so forth.

Model: Begin to map out or outline a story idea by choosing from the list of brainstormed suggestions. Use thinking aloud to let your students in on how you chose the ideas—how you think of the things that might work best for you. Your outline can be written on a prepared story map outline or simply listed.

> Characters:
>
> Setting:
>
> Problem or Goal:
>
> Events:
>
> Resolution:
>
> Ending:

Talk through your story, demonstrating how it might sound when you start to compose.

Shared/Guided Writing: Create another outline or story map from the brainstormed list, using a shared writing format. Invite students to tell the story orally. Students can also work in pairs to create story outlines that can be posted.

Independent Writing: Ask students to begin a story in their notebooks. They can choose to write one of the stories that the class already outlined, or they may want to choose a new picture and begin to jot down a new set of possibilities. Offering students several choices can help differentiate among those who may still need more guidance and those who are ready to try it on their own.

Reflection: Using pictures to create stories involves lots of thinking and decision-making. Your class may want or need to spend several days working with this strategy. Encourage your students to find pictures that spark ideas. These can be put in a writing center or kept inside a notebook. Remember to focus on the strategy by guiding discussion around the following points:

> *How did the pictures help you think of story ideas?*
>
> *Did any of the pictures spark connections and lead to writing personal narratives?*
>
> *What type of pictures work best?*
>
> *Did the sharing of ideas help? How?*
>
> *Did the pictures spark ideas that led to revisions on previous work?*
>
> *When might you use this strategy again?*

What Are You Really Writing About? Discovering the Inside Story

Good writing will come from finding fresh
new things to say about a topic and from knowing
how to write about the topic in different ways
for different audiences.

–Katie Wood Ray, *Wondrous Words*

Exploring Writing Territories

Where do writers find their story seeds—the kernels of rich ideas that can grow and blossom into narratives, poems, letters, and articles? In looking closely at the works of authors, we can often begin to find evidence of what Nancie Atwell (1998) referred to as writing territories, the treasure chests of their hearts and minds where they store precious memories about people, places, events, and objects. Cynthia Rylant, for instance, grew up in the hills of West Virginia with her mother and grandparents. Her extended family of aunts, uncles, and countless cousins played an important role in her life, and served as a territory from which she could farm the ideas for books such as *When I Was Young in the Mountains*, *The Relatives Came*, and *Night in the Country*, among others. In *Best Wishes* (1992) Rylant says that as she was growing up, she liked to roam around the town where she lived. This wandering gave her the opportunity to meet many people, watch what they did, and listen to the kinds of conversations they had with each other. It helped her begin to develop her "people" territory. Rylant also met many animals as she roamed, such as a big dog named Mudge, who eventually became a central character in the *Henry and Mudge* books. We can find other evidence of her "animals" territory in books such as *The Whales*, *The Great Gracie Chase*, *Dog Heaven*, and *Tulip Sees America*.

Sometimes authors include a note in the front or back of the book. This section has value for young writers, often revealing the seed of an idea that was plucked from a larger territory. Judith Byron Schachner is another author, like Cynthia Rylant, whose territories include family and pets, writing territories young authors can easily relate to. Schachner's Siamese cats are the subjects of *The Grannyman*, *Skippyjon Jones*, and *Skippyjon Jones in the Doghouse*. In the afterword of *Mr. Emerson's Cook*, Schachner provides some background information on Ralph Waldo Emerson, and also explains that her great-grandmother Ann, the main character in the book, actually worked as a domestic in the Emerson home. *Mr. Emerson's Cook* is based on stories passed down to Schachner from her father. In *Yo, Vikings!* we learn of how an authentic Viking ship found its way into the Schachners' backyard. This story is found in the background information provided about Vikings in the author's note, as well as in the information on the dust jacket (another good source of information about the origin of story ideas).

Mentor Texts: Teaching Writing Through Children's Literature, K–6

Lynne usually begins her discussion of writing territories by talking about authors such as Allen Say, Patricia Polacco, and Gary Paulsen. These authors are interesting to upper elementary and middle school students because they deal with themes the students find interesting, such as friendship, courage, divorce, death, separation, and family traditions. Students read biographical excerpts about these authors on Internet websites, in newspaper book reviews, in dedications and about the authors information in books, as well as in the author's notes previously mentioned. In *Bat Loves the Night* by author/zoologist Nicola Davies, the reader learns that the author enjoys being out under the stars and watching bats. As a matter of fact, she happens to live in a cottage with pipistrelle bats (the subject of the book) residing in the roof. Lynne talks to her students about how heavily the writer draws from personal experiences—the people, the places, the events, and the objects that bring about an emotional response and clear, crisp memories. If we are alert to discovering the inside stories (the stories that only the authors know and can write) in the writing territories of the authors we introduce in the classroom, we can help our students identify their own writing territories and the stories that are contained within them.

Students Discover Their Territories

Once students are familiar with the concept of a writing territory, they can more easily begin to explore their own. In a fourth-grade classroom, early in the school year, Lynne wrote her list of writing territories on an overhead transparency. A smart board, chart paper, or blackboard would also do; however, it is important that the students see the teacher's brainstorming process. Although Lynne had saved countless lists of writing territories, she demonstrated the writing of the list as if it were being written for the first time. The list she created looked something like this:

special events	Girl Scouts	The first time I . . .
relatives	surprises	best friends
grandfather	trouble!	bullies
parents	sisters	sad times
holidays	teachers	happy times
summer fun	animals	hairdos
horses	Christmas	sports
pets	school tales	car stories
church and	embarrassing	angry times
synagogue	moments	when I was afraid

Next, Lynne asked her fourth-grade students which territories they thought they could write about. Most students included friends, school, holidays, pets, and animals as writing territories. For this particular list, they also added vacations, parties, and times they needed to be brave. Todd volunteered, "How about weather? My big German shepherd turns into a chicken during a thunderstorm." That created a ripple effect, and the class buzzed with talk about weather stories.

Marie asked, "What about family traditions?"

"Do you mean traditions that revolve around holidays?" Lynne questioned.

Marie explained that she was thinking about the Irish dancing that her grandmother had passed on to family members. It took on a special meaning when the class learned that Marie had lost her grandmother the year before. Lynne clarified, "Two territories for Marie could be 'grandmother' and 'family traditions.'" She helped her students understand that the territory "relatives" can be listed as well as a separate territory for one or two special relatives. In addition, certain holidays having special traditions and celebrations can be listed separately. Sometimes the same story seed can arise from two or three different territories, as did the Irish dancing story for Marie. The point is, it's not the territories themselves that are important, but the use of them as trigger words that spark the memories for the inside stories. Lynne talked about "horses" as one of her writing territories to show her students that territories can lend themselves to persuasive and informational writing as well. She talked about creating an essay on how to prepare a horse for competition or why horseback riding is a great sport for children. Finally, Lynne's students listed their territories in the back of their notebooks where they could refer to them often.

A territory can spark a notebook entry, a prewriting experience, a drawing or graphic organizer, a poem, or a first draft. The notion of having many, many stories about a territory is important for students to reflect on. They need to know that they don't have to tell *everything* about their grandfather in one piece of writing. With this understanding in place, students can eliminate the practice of writing "bed-to-bed" stories or writing five to ten pages or more about a single topic with no real direction. Once students understand the difference between a territory and a specific topic, they can understand that every piece will have a point or sharp focus. The writer knows why his or her piece is memorable or important and can effectively communicate the purpose to the readers.

Moving from a Territory to a Specific Topic

Of course, the hard part begins once a territory is chosen. For Lynne, a huge territory is her maternal grandfather. To help the students visualize the depth and breadth of a writing territory, she wheels a cart containing a set of World Book encyclopedias into the classroom. She hands the books out to the students so they can feel the weight of the books and examine the number of pages. She explains to her students that she could write a set of A to Z encyclopedias about her grandfather because he was her friend, her confidant, and her hero. "What shall I write about him today?" she muses. "Should it be the story of how he took my Raggedy Ann doll to work every day? What about the Easter when he brought home three live chicks? Or maybe it should take the form of a poem about our walk in the woods and the rescue of a fir tree I named Little Pocono." Lynne models how she narrows her territory using an inverted triangle to help her zoom in on the one story, poem, or essay she plans to write today during writing workshop. She thinks aloud in the form of a continuum from general (territory) to most specific (topic) while recording her thinking on an inverted triangle on a chart, board, or overhead.

> 66 *Writers, today I've chosen my grandfather as the territory I'd like to explore. As I'm looking through my writer's notebook, I see that I have many holiday entries that include thoughts about him. We spent every Easter together. Now I'm remembering one special Easter when Grandpa made me very happy but made my Grandma very unhappy. He came home with a cardboard box containing three small chicks—one dyed blue, one dyed red, and one dyed pink.* 99

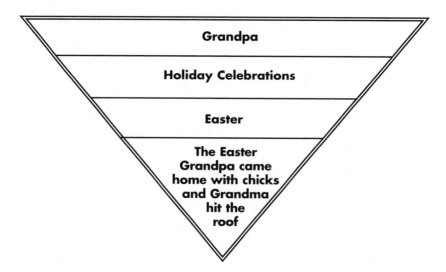

Without revealing any more information, Lynne asks the students if they would want to hear the entire story. By doing this, she demonstrates the importance of writing for a target audience and understanding what they would like to read or learn more about.

One of the Your Turn lessons at the end of this chapter models the use of the inverted triangle. This graphic organizer can be placed on chart paper and laminated so that both the teacher and students can use it over and over. By hanging it in a writing center and encouraging students to take turns using it on a daily basis, teachers can help young writers quickly internalize the process for this strategy. An additional advantage is the sharing of ideas. Writers who are having difficulty identifying their territories can begin to make connections to similar experiences that arise from the territories of their peers. Students can also begin to recognize that similar territories, for example, "summer vacations," can yield a wealth of stories.

It is important for students to understand that a writing territory is far too large to tackle. Often, it takes two or three steps to lead us from a vast territory to a specific writing topic we can handle. Nathaniel Tripp effectively demonstrates this process of narrowing the topic to a manageable size in *Snow Comes to the Farm*. This book tells the story of two brothers experiencing a snowstorm. Although the brothers have most likely experienced many snowstorms, the book is not about all of them, but rather about one special snowstorm—the first one of a winter season. This idea is stated in the opening paragraph:

Our farm is in a valley, all by itself.
    It is like living on an island, surrounded by woods and sky.
In the autumn the wild geese fly overhead.
    Their song is both happy and sad, and I begin to wish for snow.

There is one snow I'll always remember.

Along the same vein, Eve Bunting's *Night Tree* isn't about all the events of Christmas Eve, but rather about one special event where Luke's family goes into the forest and chooses a tree to decorate with goodies for all the wild animals. What a great example for students who want to write about a special holiday! They can use Eve Bunting's story as an example of how to shrink their topic to a manageable size.

Nicola Davies, in her book *One Tiny Turtle*, includes a foreword that explains to the reader how she narrowed her topic:

About Turtles

Sea turtles are related to tortoises and terrapins. They are all reptiles. Sea turtles are great wanderers, traveling thousands of miles each year, often far from land. This makes them difficult to study. So scientists are only just beginning to find out about their mysterious lives. There are seven species of sea turtles. This book is about the loggerhead turtle. Loggerheads live in seas all over the world.

This foreword can easily be represented in an inverted triangle as an example for young writers on how to narrow a topic in a work of nonfiction.

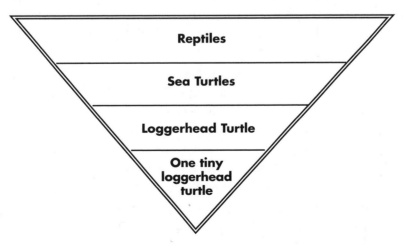

Usually, a territory can be voiced in one or two words, whereas the specific topic of a writing piece is written as one complete thought. A specific topic is something a writer can wrap his or her arms around. It is a topic that enables a writer to complete a high-quality first draft within one or several workshop settings.

Heart Mapping to Find Writing Topics

Georgia Heard (1999) talks about helping writers find topics for poems. She tells them that poets write from their hearts about the things they care deeply about. She shares with them that her poems come from the memories she has of her family, of growing up in Virginia, and of the people she meets as she travels. To help them understand this, Heard asks the students to make maps of their hearts. Heard has found that this visual display of the important people, places, and memories in these young writers' lives helps them write with depth and feeling. In our work with writers, especially our youngest writers who may still be struggling with spelling, we have used the technique of heart mapping as an alternative to listing writing territories.

In some of the primary classes Rose works with, writing workshop often takes the form of journal writing. Students write about themselves in small bound notebooks. These young writers often struggle with finding topics for their entries. Using "safe words" (words they know how to spell or are comfortable with), they write lists of things they like, or tell about something they did or somewhere they went in one sentence.

I love my mom and dad.

I like sal [school].
I like poomrn [pokemon].
I like me.
I like my tegr [teacher].

I went too my ferid hous.
[I went to my friend's house.]

In trying to help these writers better understand the concept of territories and discover the small moments within their territories, Rose uses the technique of heart mapping. In one particular first-grade class, early in September, she gathered the students together on the rug to introduce them to journal writing. She explained that a journal is a place where you can write about things that happen to you, people and places that are important to you, or things you might wonder about. She told them that because writing comes from one's mind and one's heart, she would show them how to make maps of their hearts so that they would always have something to write about. Rose then shared her heart map—a simple outline of a heart shape divided into sections. Each section had an illustration, sometimes accompanied by labels, of places in her heart where her writing stories come from—her family, her yellow lab Casey, vacation spots, her backyard, and music. Some of the sections were intentionally left blank. She wanted these young writers to understand that they could return to their heart maps and add ideas as new places opened up to them. Perhaps later in the year they would start to play baseball or take dance lessons. These big ideas could then become places where many stories could be found. Before the students made their own heart maps, Rose engaged them in conversation and sharing until she was sure they all had some ideas. This scaffolding is described in the Your Turn lesson at the end of the chapter.

The following day, Rose demonstrated how to find a story from a place in their heart maps. She returned to her map and looked at the section with the picture of her yellow lab Casey. "I have lots of stories about Casey," she explained. "I remember when Casey was a puppy she used to dump all of her toys out of the basket until they were all over the room, then she would play with the basket. One time she ran in circles in the backyard trying to catch a bee, and one time she locked herself in the bathroom for a whole day. I think that's the story I want to write about today—the time Casey locked herself in the bathroom." Rose went on to describe the story in great detail—how the bathroom was really just a powder room and she thought Casey went in to poke around the trash can and accidentally knocked the door closed as she was trying to turn around. She described how she couldn't find Casey when she came home from school that day, but that she could hear a muffled whimpering from somewhere in the house. Rose wrote in front of the students, but she wrote only as much as she thought they might be able to write from a

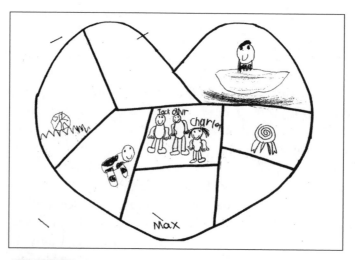

FIGURE 3.1 Max's heart map (grade one).

story like that. She wanted to give them a model for their own writing so that they could say to themselves, "I think I can do that!"

> One day Casey locked herself in the bathroom. She jumped and she scratched at the door. She couldn't get out. Poor Casey was so scared!

Rose then asked the students to pick a place on their heart maps where they thought they had a story that they might like to write about, share that idea with a partner, then write it in their journals. (See Figure 3.1 for an example of a heart map.)

During sharing time Mark showed the picture of the hermit crab on his heart map and shared his entry. "My friend has a hermit crab," he read.

"Can you tell me a little more about the hermit crab?" Rose probed. "Is there something about this hermit crab that caught your attention or something that happened with it when you went to visit?"

Mark replied, "Well, he lives in a cage and he drinks water from a sponge."

Rose nudged, "Tell me more."

Mark thought for a moment, then said, "Sometimes he's a little scary. One time I saw his big, huge claw come out of the shell and he started to climb up the side of the cage and I thought he might get out and jump on me!"

"Aha!" Rose exclaimed. "There's your story!"

Sometimes students need a little more guidance to find their inside story. In this case, Mark learned that he could let his readers know much more than just the fact that his friend had a hermit crab. He could make the point that sometimes the hermit crab is a little scary.

Of course heart maps can also be used with students in all grade levels. Older students can draw their maps freehand instead of using a template. They also tend to use words in addition to pictures. (See Figure 3.2.)

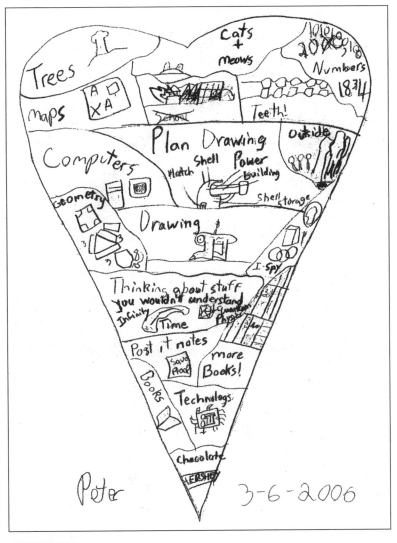

FIGURE 3.2 Peter's heart map (grade five).

The conversations surrounding the heart maps, territory lists, and triangles are as important as these organizers themselves. You can move among the students conducting roving conferences, or hold guided conversations in front of the whole class. In this way, you are helping your young writers discover the stories they want to tell as well as the reasons for telling them—topic and point.

The Point vs. the Topic

As literature is introduced throughout the day, consider taking a few moments to pause and guide students in thinking not just about the topic, but also about the point that is being made. What is the author's purpose for writing this piece? What thoughts or images did he think should linger on the reader's mind long after the book was finished? Arthur Howard's *When I Was Five* tells the story of a young boy, Jeremy, who is looking back on the things he enjoyed as a five-year-old. Although he has many different favorite things now that he is six, Mark remains his best friend. With simple language and colorful illustrations, Howard helps young readers discover the point of his writing—that although many things in life change, there is comfort in knowing that some things remain the same. The last line crystallizes the point: "Some things never change."

Sometimes the point can be found in the title, as in *Chameleons Are Cool* by Martin Jenkins, *Birds Build Nests* by Yvonne Winer, or *That Magnetic Dog* by Bruce Whatley. Jose Aruego and Ariane Dewey introduce readers to unlikely relationships in the animal kingdom in their book *Weird Friends*. Through a series of small vignettes that describe the behavior of some strange animal pairs, the reader comes to understand that certain animals pair up for survival. Helping students discover the point of an author's work means young writers will begin to understand the importance of making a point in their own writing and the many ways in which it can be expressed.

Closely connected to point is the idea of point of view. Books such as *The True Story of the Three Little Pigs!* by Jon Scieszka, *Hey, Little Ant* by Phillip and Hannah Hoose, and *Voices in the Park* by Anthony Browne help students understand that a story can be told from many sides. Madeleine L'Engle, in her picture book *The Other Dog*, begins by telling the reader that the French poodle wrote the story. The book goes on to discuss how the dog views the arrival of "the inferior canine Jo," the new baby. Ultimately, the poodle changes her point of view and not only accepts the new arrival but also grows to love her. Just as in Howard's book *When I Was Five*, L'Engle has her narrator (the French poodle) directly state the point: "in every home there should be at least two dogs." Incidentally, this book contains a lengthy author's note that reveals the story seed for the picture book, a story that comes directly from the author's life. The book provides an interesting avenue for students who would like to write about a topic from an unexpected point of view.

Some books such as *Sierra, Mojave,* and *Heartland* (all by Diane Siebert), *My Light* by Molly Bang, and *Atlantic* by G. Brian Karas are written from the point of view of an inanimate object, bringing a certain intrigue to the reading of the text. Portalupi and Fletcher (2001) call this technique "writing through a mask." At the end of Chapter 6 you will find a Your Turn lesson designed to help students understand how to write in the persona of another.

To discover the inside story, writers must begin by finding those treasures locked away in their hearts and minds that might make good topics for writing. Big ideas, or territories, need to be reduced to very specific topics. Authors must be able to wrap their arms around their topics and hold on tight. They must be able to discover what it is they really want to say about the topics—the stories that only they know and can tell. With this in mind, they write with clarity and purpose. Their points are not mysteries to the reader. Mentor texts can serve as wonderful models to young writers as they begin to understand how to sharpen their focus and make their points.

Using an Inverted Triangle to Find a Specific Writing Topic

Hook: Read *One Lucky Girl* by George Ella Lyon as a read-aloud or any other personal narratives that invite students to think about territories for writing such as weather/storms, relatives, friends, or school. Options: *When I Was Five* by Arthur Howard, *I'm in Charge of Celebrations* by Byrd Baylor, *Dad and Me* by Peter Catalonotto.

Purpose: *When you are trying to find a topic to write about, sometimes it is easier to start with a big idea and work to make it smaller and smaller until suddenly, there it is—the "inside story," the one only YOU know and can write. It's like starting with a slab of marble or block of wood and chipping away until your sculpture is revealed to your audience. Today, writers, I'm going to show you how to start with a writing territory and find your specific topic by using an inverted triangle.*

Brainstorm: Think about the big ideas—your writing territories—and the seeds of ideas you might be able to use to grow stories, poems, letters, and essays around a specific topic. Revisit your list of territories and add new ideas you might have after hearing *One Lucky Girl*. (Students typically add weather or storms.)

Model: An inverted triangle is a useful graphic organizer to help you refocus your camera lens from wide angle and zoom in on a specific subject. After reading Lyon's story, here is a possible example:

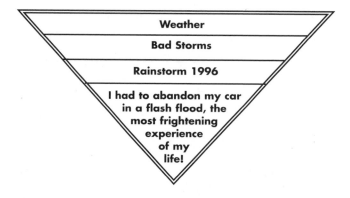

Follow with a few more examples. From *Night at the Fair* by Donald Crews, here is another model:

Shared/Guided Writing: Students try out the inverted triangle to take a territory and find a specific writing topic. Students use transparencies to share one of their efforts that led them to a suitable topic. Make sure that the students have not stopped at the "general" topic, but have moved to a specific statement to flesh out the "inside" story about their writing topic. The statement can help the writer focus on both topic and point (the point is why the author wrote the piece or what is most important or memorable about this topic). Ask students to talk about their point if they end up with only a topic statement. Here, you may have to model on chart paper or on the board with two or more examples from your territories list.

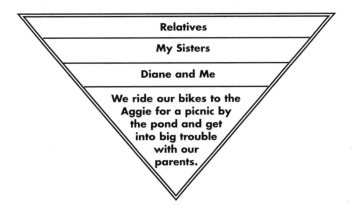

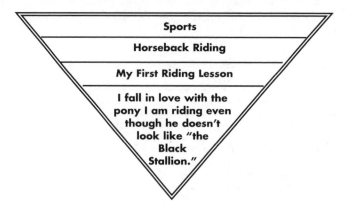

Sports

Horseback Riding

My First Riding Lesson

I fall in love with the pony I am riding even though he doesn't look like "the Black Stallion."

Continue to practice on the laminated chart paper each day where one student places his or her information in the spaces of the inverted triangle. Each student writes with a transparency pen that can be washed away the next day. The chart should be placed in a writing center or on a bulletin board where it is accessible to all students.

Independent Writing: Students can continue to use inverted triangles to narrow a territory to a specific topic across different modes. When they have found an appropriate topic, from one of their inverted triangles, invite students to create a first draft, notebook entry, or prewriting experience for the specific topic they wish to develop during workshop time.

Reflection: After completing a notebook entry or first draft for a poem, letter, narrative, or essay, allow time for students to "turn and talk" about the use of the inverted triangle to find a specific writing topic or about how the laminated chart paper containing new examples each day helped them find new topics or create specific topics for writing.

2

Creating a Heart Map

Hook: Return to any personal narrative read-alouds you have used in the classroom and talk about where the author might have gotten the idea for the story. Encourage your writers to think in terms of "big ideas"—family, school, and so on. *When I Was Little: A Four-Year-Old's Memoir of Her Youth* by Jamie Lee Curtis works well to help primary students understand writing territories. Students can easily identify many writing territories for the child in the book, such as people she knows, family, things she likes to do, and school. Options: *Goin' Someplace Special* by Patricia McKissack, *In My Momma's Kitchen* by Jerdine Nolen, *Song and Dance Man* by Karen Ackerman.

Purpose: *Sometimes it's hard to think about something to write about. This happens to all writers. It's important to remember that writing comes from your mind and your heart. Today I will show you how to make a heart map. A heart map is a way to remember what is in your mind and your heart so that you'll always have something to write about.*

Brainstorm: Think aloud about the big ideas that are in your mind and your heart that might give you lots of stories to write about—family, school, a hobby, and so on. Quickly relate some stories within those categories. It is important to demonstrate that these are big ideas, not small moments of time that capture a single event. Ask the students to share some of the things they might put on their heart maps. These ideas can be listed on the board or simply shared orally.

Model: Share your own heart map. You can either have this created ahead of time or quickly sketch it in front of the students. At this point, the heart map does not have to be completely filled in. Choose a section and relate a small story that comes from it. Write a short entry on the board or overhead.

Shared/Guided Writing: Invite one or two students to the front of the room to share their ideas in a guided conversation. If they start to relate single-event stories, for example, if they say something like "One day my brother and my dad and I caught ten fish," ask them if they have any other stories about their brother or dad. Lead them to the understanding that the place they might put on their heart map for these stories would be a place for family. Questions such as the following can help guide their thinking:

Who are the special people in your life?

Do you have any pets?

Are there any places where you go that hold special memories for you?

When you are at home, where do you spend most of your time?

What are the things that you like to do?

Again, ask students to quietly think about some of the things they might include on their heart maps, then ask them to turn and share with a partner. Encourage students to ask questions as you did in the guided conversation to help their partner formulate ideas.

Independent Writing: Allow time for students to create their own heart maps. We have found that with young writers it is easier to provide a heart template, but students can certainly draw the heart outline on their own. When the heart maps are completed, ask students to think of a small story from one of the areas on their heart map, turn to a partner and share, then write a short entry in their journals or notebooks.

Reflection: After students share their entries with partners or in small groups, ask them to think about how the heart map they created can help them think of things to write about. Questions such as the following can help guide their thinking:

How can a heart map help you find a writing topic?

What will you write about next?

What are some stories you have about_____? (Choose a section from the map.)

Did listening to others share their heart maps give you ideas for yours?

Note: For very young children, the above lesson can be split and taught over two days. On the first day, just have the students create the heart map. On the second day, demonstrate how to choose a story from a section on the map and write it.

3

Creating a Hand Map

In *Writing as a Road to Self-Discovery*, Barry Lane describes the use of a hand map as a prewriting technique to help writers bring memories to a conscious level. We have adapted this technique for use with students.

Hook: Find a favorite personal narrative that has a large emotional impact on your target grade level. The first chapter of *Charlotte's Web* by E. B. White works well for intermediate grade levels (3–6). Students can easily name Fern's emotions and/or character traits that are revealed through her dialogue and actions. Options: *Crab Moon* by Ruth Horowitz, *Shortcut* by Donald Crews, *Fireflies!* by Julie Brinckloe, *I Remember Papa* by Helen Ketterman, "Mrs. Buell" in *Hey World, Here I Am!* by Jean Little.

Purpose: *Do you remember when we read* Fireflies!*? What was the character feeling at the beginning of the story? How did he feel when he realized the fireflies would die if he didn't release them? What was he feeling at the end of the story? (List the emotions on the board as the students name them.) Can you see how much of this story depends on the emotions of the main character and how they changed during the telling of it? When we are trying to write about specific topics, sometimes it is easier to find an important topic—something you really want to write about—if you start with an emotion or one of your character traits. Today I am going to model how to use a hand map to find a specific topic.*

Brainstorm: In whole group, students make a list of emotions after they have had a chance to "turn and talk" with a partner. This list can become part of a writing binder or a writer's notebook entry. At some point in time, create a list of character traits. A hand map can use emotions or character traits or a combination of both. It is probably easiest to start with the emotions.

Model: Share your own hand map with your students. (See the model for the hand map in Figure 3.3 that Lynne shares with her students.) Start with basic emotions such as anger, fear, sadness, happiness, and excitement. Place one on each finger after tracing your hand on the board or on chart paper with fingers spread wide apart. From each finger, extend lines to connect to examples of times you felt that way. Try to think of one example for each emotion, but tell

Chapter 3 • What Are You Really Writing About? Discovering the Inside Story

65

students that they can concentrate on one at a time or move around. Hand maps are writers' tools like thesauruses and dictionaries and should be returned to often to add ideas or use an idea to explore a writing topic. Finally, choose an example from your hand map and write it in your writer's notebook.

This notebook entry came from Lynne's hand map where the emotion "happiness" led her to think about Saturday breakfasts. Each entry in her notebook is always dated and has a title to help her know what the entry is about. No more than one entry is written on each page. This format saves time when a writer is searching through his or her notebooks to find common threads or entries about certain topics.

September 24, 2005

Special Saturday Breakfasts

I loved Saturdays because Mom made special breakfasts. My favorite was when she made perfect pancakes—round, golden brown, light, fluffy, and filled with fresh blueberries. I loved to watch the·pat of butter slip-slide its way down the stack onto my plate. I drizzled maple syrup on the top and added more as I ate. Yummy! My sisters, Mom, and Dad always shared this breakfast together. Maybe that's why the food tasted so good!

Shared/Guided Writing: For this particular lesson, students create a "whole group" hand map, choosing from the list of emotions and/or character traits and volunteering ideas that are stated as complete thoughts. It is important to insist that students work in phrases or complete sentences when they create their own hand maps.

Examples:

scared—We drove home from the shore late one night during a bad storm.

happy—My parents finally let me get a puppy!

nervous—first time I played a solo in a school concert

While students are creating the group hand map, they should have their own hand maps in front of them. If they hear a good example for an emotion that applies to them, they can add it to their map. Continue to have students work on hand maps and share in small groups while you circulate around the room to observe, ask questions, and offer suggestions.

Independent Writing: Have students pick one description (example) from their hand map and write a short entry about it in their writer's notebook or begin to draft. They can return to their hand map to choose a different example if the first one does not work. Teachers should work on their own hand maps for the next several sessions, modeling that they are not finished in one sitting and should be reviewed and added to throughout the year. Students can create more than one hand map, especially to try out different emotions and character traits.

Reflection: Students examine their writer's notebook entries, work-in-progress folders, and portfolio pieces to find examples that started with seeds of ideas from their hand map(s).

> *How effective is your hand map as a tool for finding a specific writing topic?*

> *What kinds of writing seem to spring from your hand maps?*

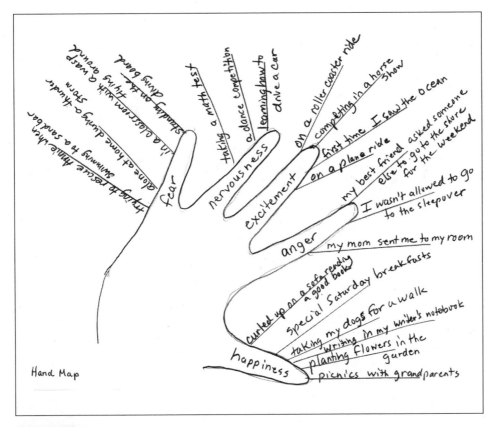

FIGURE 3.3 Lynne's model of a hand map.

CHAPTER 4

When Writers Use a Magnifying Lens

When we write, our entire lives are like the stretch
of mountains and we can choose where to dwell.

–Barry Lane, *After THE END*

In *All Those Secrets of the World*, Jane Yolen's character Janie learns a secret from her cousin Michael that helps her better understand the world. She learns that when you are far away from something, it looks small. When Janie's father returns from the war, she looks big to him, because finally he is close by again. It's the same thing when we write. We need to help our students bring their writing in closer so that we can see all the fine details that make it big. In *Nature Spy*, authors Shelley Rotner and Ken Kreisler help us understand that when we look closely at things in nature, we notice many more interesting details such as patterns in leaves, a turtle's shell, or the center of a sunflower. It's like putting something under a magnifying lens: we focus in on something small to make it big and bring out all the details. By examining mentor texts, we can show our students the techniques authors use to add the details that make their writing big.

Slowing Down Time in Writing

What we should point out to children is the need to develop their ideas first—the content—by writing about small moments of time. Schuster (2003) tells us always to put content first and second when we respond to student writing. After all, content is the most important writing characteristic. When high-quality ideas are developed, readers can visualize, make connections, use their senses, and dream the possibilities. To "take a reader's breath away" we must first start with specificity. We must encourage young writers to uncover the real story they want to tell as they write and stop telling us what we already know or can easily find out about. They must put their writing under a magnifying lens and look for those small moments that can be enlarged to take their readers there, wherever that might be.

Young writers struggle to create a movie in their readers' minds whether they are writing in the narrative, persuasive, or informational modes. They often hurry through the text they are creating for their readers, and it looks like good writing—after all, isn't it two or three or even four pages long? But when we read it, we are disappointed. Often it reads like an agenda or time schedule, moving from event to event in a blurring whir that leaves us scratching our heads and wondering what the piece is really about. As readers, we can't make any connections or form any pictures. The writing is a list (sometimes a very long list, but a list, nevertheless). Does the following piece of writing sound familiar?

I went to the aquarium with my class. I was really happy we were going on a field trip because I am going to be a scientist one day and study ocean animals.

We saw lots of fish. I saw a hammerhead shark. Then I saw beluga whales. Next we went to see tropical fish. They were neat and all different colors and sizes. We were hungry so we had lunch. I had a peanut butter sandwich and an apple. My mom didn't pack anything to drink so I had to use the water fountain. Then I had to use the bathroom because I drank so much water. We saw some seals. Then we saw some manta rays. They were cool. Then Tommy and Jimmy started fighting. My teacher said it was time to go back to the bus. We bought some souvenirs. I bought a candy bar because I was still hungry.

The bus trip was long. We sang songs. Tommy fell asleep. My teacher looked sleepy, but she stayed awake because she has to. I needed to use the bathroom as soon as we got back. It was almost time to go home, so my teacher read us a book about whales and then the bell rang and school was over. It was a pretty good day.

third grader (November)

We need to find mentor texts that we can use to show students how an author slows down a moment in time to look at an important event, examine a feeling, or reveal a character. We need to slow our writers down. If you look back at this young writer's piece, can you find a place where he could linger and put a small moment under a magnifying lens? Perhaps it is where he chooses to talk about tropical fish. He says manta rays are cool. Maybe this spot is ideal. Elementary school children write just like they do everything else—quickly. They live in a fast world, packed with schedules, video games with action figures, outdoor sports. They need to learn to slow their writing down at a special place. An author does this by taking a "small moment" (Calkins 2003) and putting it under a magnifying lens to enlarge it, just the way scientists use microscopes and magnifying lenses to look at something very small and make it much bigger so they can observe all the details.

The details are essential to good writing. Specificity is what makes it interesting for the writer to write, and it's also what moves the reader (Fletcher 1993). Slow scenes usually include longer passages built with such things as dialogue, sensory details, anecdotes, and other strategies from an author's craft. Sometimes authors add the thoughts of a character.

Barry Lane (1993) calls this strategy a thoughtshot. We find the places in the text that help slow down a moment in time and point them out as examples of powerful sentences, giving a piece both clarity and depth. In *Storm Angels* by Barbara Reese, the author describes a thunderstorm. Andrew's mother has compared the rumbling and crashing to a symphony. The author adds this thoughtshot: "'Yes,'" he [Andrew] thought. He could see it. "'Drums, definitely drums. And perhaps a trombone or two. Maybe a piano playing those very, very low notes.'"

In *Mice and Beans* by Pam Muñoz Ryan, Rosa María remembers that she has forgotten to fill the piñata. However, when the children break the piñata and the candy spills, we hear her thoughts: "'How could that be?' Rosa María puzzled. 'I must have filled it without even realizing!'"

In *Tiger of the Snows*, Robert Burleigh uses italics to set off the thoughts of the main character, Tenzing Norgay. Tenzing's monologue with the mountain shows his thinking as he becomes the young man who eventually realizes his dream of climbing Mount Everest.

> *Mountain,*
> *Mountain*
> *I cast my small shadow against your eternal skyscape.*

Sometimes authors don't use the exact words of the character's thinking but just tell us what they thought, as Bottner and Kruglik do in *Wallace's Lists:* "Wallace awoke to the sound of rain plinking on his window. He thought that on such a dreary day he might like to share some nice onion soup with Albert."

Authors also use dialogue to open up a scene, adding interest and details. We often learn more about the characters from what they say, how they say it, or what others say about them. In *Sugarbush Spring*, Marsha Wilson Chall intersperses description with dialogue as the little girl waits for the sap to turn into syrup. We can feel her anticipation and excitement in her words:

> *Already the sugarhouse smells like pancakes.*
> "*Is it syrup yet?*" *I ask Jim.*
> "*Too soon,*" *he says, and taps the thermometer. "Should be two hundred nineteen degrees. Seven degrees to go."*
> *I keep my eye on that thermometer: two hundred fifteen . . . two hundred sixteen . . . The bubbles creep higher, swelling to the top of the pan. "There she blows!" I yell.*

As the main character in Sharon Dennis Wyeth's *Something Beautiful* roams the neighborhood in search of *her* something beautiful, she enters into many conversations with those she meets about *their* something beautiful.

How much more interesting it is to the reader to hear the words and conversations of the characters! Lester Laminack includes a sprinkling of dialogue in *Saturdays and Teacakes* through the use of italics instead of the traditional quotation marks. The italicized words are not a conversation, but rather only the words of the boy's grandmother (Mammaw). We believe Laminack wrote the book this way because it is about his grandmother. Her dialogue reveals the era she was part of, her caring, gentle spirit, and her love for her grandson and their special Saturdays together, as well as her sense of humor:

> *Come on then,* Mammaw said, heading toward the door. *Let's get in this kitchen and see if we can't make us a mess.* [sense of humor]

> When it felt right Mammaw said, *Look in the Frigidaire* (that's what she called her refrigerator) *and find me two sticks of Blue Bonnet.* [sense of era]

> *Is that all you want, buddy? You be sure to eat all you want. We made them teacakes just for you.* [sense of love and caring spirit]

When discussing the effective use of dialogue with students, however, it is important to help them realize the reasons authors use it, and that even though a conversation can serve to add interest and details, too much dialogue may make the piece tedious or difficult to understand. Dialogue should be sprinkled the way we season our food with salt. We don't open the top of the shaker and pour it on. Rather, we sprinkle just enough to bring out the flavor without masking the taste.

Studying Descriptions

Readers are a lot like scientists. They like to "study" the events, feelings, and actions of characters, lingering a little longer to make connections and visualize in their minds. That's what good readers do. They can't do it without the help of the author. Fletcher (1993) tells us that Donald Murray calls readers "bottom feeders" who like to gobble up all the details like scavengers on the oceans' floors. We need to provide them with descriptions of our setting, characters, and even important objects by both telling and showing them.

The story in Kevin Henkes's *Lilly's Purple Plastic Purse* revolves around Lilly's obsession with the things (particularly the purse) she bought on a shopping trip with her grammy. Students can visualize the purse and its contents by the descriptions Henkes provides:

> [S]he had a brand new purple plastic purse that played a jaunty tune when it was opened . . .
> And the purse played such nice music, not to mention how excellent it was for storing school supplies.

Jen Bryant also builds content around an object—a tricorner hat worn by poet Marianne Moore in her book *Call Me Marianne*:

> Something tumbles in front of me. It looks like a piece of black cloth or a shingle that's blown off a roof. It rolls along the sidewalk and bashes against a bush.
> I see it's not a cloth or a shingle, but that lady's black tri-cornered hat. I pick it up and brush it off. It's made of felt and smells like roses. Inside, I find the initials MM.

Patricia and Emily MacLachlan describe the work of the still life painter in *Painting the Wind* with a list: "She painted until dawn—the peppermint plant in the window, the glass bowl of tulips, their green stems crisscrossing in water." It is important to give students opportunities to practice writing rich descriptions of people, places, animals, and objects. After all, description is found in every mode of writing. Writers often describe specific time periods as Margot Theis Raven does in *Angels in the Dust*:

> [O]ur sky, so big and blue, turned dark and fierce in the middle of the day. Great dust storms came blowing. They came with the drought that took hold of the land. No rain fell for a long, long time. Mean new winds came blowing, too, scorching hot and stiff as a dragon's breath. They withered our corn. They withered our wheat. They baked our land bone-dry until it looked as cracked and old as Mama's white milk pitcher. Soon nothing grew in Papa's fields except great piles of dusty earth.

Appealing to the Senses

Description also helps students understand how to be more specific since they are writing about just one thing. But they don't have to stop with simply describing what they see. Writers use all the senses to give us a concrete, physical experience. The act of reading and comprehending what we read is fairly abstract. If we want our readers to remember what they've read, to linger over passages where they can close their eyes and imagine what it would be like, how they would feel, what they would do, what they *will* do, then we must provide them with details to give them this concrete experience to balance with the abstract act of thinking about and comprehending text. In Chapter 2 we discuss the use of strong sensory images to help writers unearth memories for writing topics. Appealing to the senses is also a powerful way to add details to writing, bringing the reader in closer. In *Up North at the Cabin*, Marsha Wilson Chall uses specific sensory details to help anchor images in our minds where they linger long after we have closed the book. Maybe she closed her eyes and imagined the scene through her senses:

> *Grandma serves up my sunnies with fried potatoes and corn-on-the-cob. We eat at a long table on the screen porch, sitting next to one another on the same side so we can all watch the loons dance down the sun.*

Can't you just taste the delicious meal and imagine the butter from the corn on the cob dripping down your chin? Do you feel the hardness of the bench, or the warmth of the sun on your face? Can you hear the soft flutter of the loons as you watch them lightly splash down on the lake as the sun slowly sinks from view?

Jane Yolen masterfully uses the senses to add details to her description of an outing of a father and child in *Owl Moon*. Through her words we see the brightness of the moon reflected in the whiteness of the snow; we hear the song of the train whistle and the crunching of the snow; we feel the cold air and furry wetness of the child's scarf. These details bring us in closer and make us feel as if we are there. In *A House by the River*, William Miller lets us know that a storm is approaching by telling us what the main character sees, smells, and hears:

> *One morning, as she was getting dressed for school, Belinda smelled the rain in the air. The sky outside her window was low and dark. The rumble of thunder rolled down the river road.*

Nathaniel Tripp uses the senses to describe a first snowfall of the season in *Snow Comes to the Farm*:

[Snowflakes] were bigger now, too.
We could hear them whisper as they brushed
against the branches, and see their shapes
like little stars on our sleeves.

In *Twilight Comes Twice*, Ralph Fletcher helps us experience the dawn by appealing to our senses:

Walking at dawn is a special kind of walk . . .
The air is still moist from the cool of the night and your own
skin feels all tingly clean . . .
Outside the bakery the smell of doughnuts makes your stomach
rumble and growl.

By lingering on these passages as we read these mentor texts aloud, we can begin to help our students understand the importance of using the senses to add details to their writing. A wonderful mentor text that we often use to introduce use of the senses to students is *Hello Ocean*. In this rhyming text, Pam Muñoz Ryan describes the ocean through each of the five senses. After students are familiar with the book, we might return to it to record the images on a visualization chart such as in the following:

I see	amber seaweed
	speckled sand
	bubbly waves
	glistening tide pools
I hear	rushing water
	boats
	screak of gulls
I feel	a wet embrace
	tickling tide
	squishy, sandy, soggy ground
I smell	salty wind
	suntan lotion
	reeky fish
	musty shells
I taste	tears
	sandy grains

The next step would be to brainstorm some familiar places common to all the students such as the school cafeteria, the playground, or even the classroom, and fill in a visualization chart together. Sometimes we add an additional box for thoughts and emotions. This adds another layer to the details. The students can then use the chart to describe the place either orally or in a shared writing experience. Finally, the students can try it out on their own.

It is important to show students that authors use specific words to describe the things they experience through their senses. For example, Pam Muñoz Ryan talks about "speckled" sand and "musty" shells. It is also important to remember that some young writers need lots of modeling and chances to work together before they are ready to venture out on their own. Rose remembers working with a second grader who was very excited to try using a visualization chart to help him describe one of his favorite summer hangouts, the community swimming pool. Within minutes of getting started, Ryan raised his hand signaling that he was finished. "That was easy!" he said. "Listen: I see the water. I hear the water. I feel the water. I smell the water. I taste the water." With a little more encouragement, Rose helped Ryan add the specifics he needed to extend his thinking and help bring the swimming pool in close to his readers.

Using Anecdotes to Reveal Details

Another way to help students add details to their writing is through the use of anecdotes, or short accounts of an incident. Anecdotes can be used to reveal something about a character or event, or simply to add interesting or entertaining information to a piece of writing. In *My Brother Martin: A Sister Remembers Growing Up with the Rev. Dr. Martin Luther King Jr.*, Christine King Farris uses anecdotes to help her readers envision what her brother Martin was like as a child. We read about how Martin, Christine, and their younger brother, Alfred, enjoyed playing pranks as children. In the afterword of the book, the author tells us that she wanted to share some true and funny stories about Martin's earlier life so that her readers could get to know him as a regular boy growing up. Through the use of anecdote, Farris adds the details that bring us closer to Martin Luther King, Jr.

Mother to Tigers by George Ella Lyon tells the story of Helen Martini, the Bronx Zoo's first woman keeper, who initially raised baby tigers in her apartment. An anecdote about the tigers jumping into the tub reveals their mischievous side:

Once, washing clothes in the bath, Helen heard Raniganj crying.
His head was caught behind a pipe. While she ran to the rescue,
Rajpur and Dacca discovered the tub. Crouch . . . leap . . . splash!
Tigers love water.

In another anecdote from this book, Lyon reveals how determined Martini was to achieve her goal of starting a nursery at the zoo. These small stories add details that make the characters seem more real.

A true mentor text for anecdotes is *Talkin' About Bessie: The Story of Aviator Elizabeth Coleman* by Nikki Grimes. The fictionalized-but-based-on-fact story tells the life of Bessie Coleman through the memories of twenty mourners who have gathered after her death to honor her. They represent people from all aspects of her life, and their anecdotes about her reveal the true Bessie Coleman—her struggles and successes, her shortcomings and her strengths, her hopes and dreams. In the following example we find Willie Coleman telling the mourners that Bessie was quite a storyteller:

> *My sister-in-law shoulda been a writer since her was always tellin'*
> *tales. Enhancin' the truth was her specialty. Drummin' up publicity,*
> *she called it. Hear her tell it, she was bosom buddies with the Red*
> *Baron, had flown a German sea plane, and was near 'bout born*
> *with wings. Told the* New York Times *she went to France with the*
> *Red Cross during the war, and that she had one of them brigade*
> *officers teach her how to fly. Now, you tell me if that ain't stretching*
> *the truth!*

In a fifth-grade class the students were working on hero essays in order to write to an audience other than the classroom teacher. These essays were about people the students knew very well, and they were going to mail their essays to their intended audience when they were finished. Lynne talked with them about how anecdotes could add some interesting or humorous content to their writing while revealing character traits or quirks about their subjects. After sharing many examples from mentor texts, Lynne shared an anecdote about her grandfather:

> When I was little, my grandfather taught me how to swim. I
> remember the time we were at Sailor's Lake. The water felt cold even
> though it was the middle of July. Grandpa put his strong arms under
> me and told me to paddle with my arms and kick with my legs.

"Reach as far as you can, Lynnie," he told me. Grandpa showed me how he cupped his hands to pull through the water, keeping his fingers together. He practiced going under the water with me, too. We held hands and dunked our heads over and over again. One time, I took such a big gulp of air before going under, that I made Grandpa laugh. Grandpa laughed so hard that he swallowed some of the lake water. He made me laugh, too. Suddenly, I wasn't afraid anymore! And before I knew it, I was swimming through the water on my own.

She explained how adding this to her hero essay about her grandfather would demonstrate what a wonderful teacher he was and how he helped her work through her fears. She explained how powerful anecdotes are across the modes (narrative, persuasive, and informational). Later on in the year, Eleanor was writing a narrative about a bike-riding trip and included a humorous anecdote about her dad:

When we arrived at the river, it was jam packed so we barely got a parking place. My daddy started to yell at a guy who opened his door and slammed it into our car. Mommy and I whimpered in the corner as Daddy and the guy had a shouting fight. Finally, Daddy won and when the guy left he gloated in triumph. "Did you see me? He was nothing compared to me!" And on and on about it. (You know how guys are . . . when they win something, they never stop talking about it!)

After students have the opportunity to try out a strategy such as using anecdotes to build content, they will try it out again when the strategy seems appropriate or necessary. It is important to revisit strategies and key Your Turn lessons so that students can embed the technique in their repertoire of writing strategies.

Focusing on a Moment

Once students have learned several strategies for developing the content of their writing, they can combine some or all of them to talk about one very important moment in time. Barry Lane (1993) talks about "exploding a moment" by using powerful tools such as snapshots, "thoughtshots," appealing to the senses, and lots of detail to write in slow motion. When we are finished modeling and guiding students with mentor texts, they can move to independence by returning to the picture book to try out a strategy without having us there.

Consider the picture books of Robert Burleigh. In *Home Run*, he introduces his main character, Babe Ruth, in the first several pages, setting us up for the small moment he places under his magnifying lens—a moment that lasts from the pitcher's windup to the home-run trot around the bases. How long would that moment take? Certainly no more than a few minutes, and yet, Burleigh slows the action for us so that we feel we are there, watching "the Babe" hit another home run. Consider only a piece of this beautifully written moment in time as Burleigh takes us to the ballpark to watch a legend:

> *He watches the pitcher lean. Rotate. Rock back and forth. The leg wheels out. The arm whips over the head. Babe narrows his hunter-like gaze and strides into the pitch that is now only a tiny speck of whirling whiteness. This time. He swings big. His bat comes down and around. Powerfully. He swings "through the ball." Always "through the ball."*

In his book *Flight*, Burleigh describes Charles Lindbergh's Atlantic crossing. He does not attempt to tell his reader about the entire life of Lindbergh, only the most important event in the aviator's life. We feel like we are crossing the Atlantic with him when he writes:

> *He moves through the dense, curling fog, lit ghostly by the moon. He suddenly enters a huge stormcloud. The plane shimmers, moving up and down in the uniform blackness. He wonders: Can I fly above it? Slowly, he soars to 10,500 feet. Here it is clear, but very cold. He extends his arm outside the cockpit and feels "stinging pinpricks." He clicks on his small flashlight and peers out: Heavy ice has formed on the plane's wings. He cannot risk his instruments icing up. He points the Spirit of St. Louis back down. The wings quiver as they slice through the turbulent air. The fog continues, but now, at least, the air is warmer. The ice begins to melt and Lindbergh roars ahead.*

Ruth Horowitz creates a "slow scene" at the end of the middle of her narrative *Crab Moon*. The scene begins when Daniel finds a horseshoe crab he believes may be dead and uses a piece of driftwood to nudge her. The author describes every detail as Daniel plucks up his courage to turn over the horseshoe crab marooned on the beach and by doing so, saves her life. Horowitz would not have captured her readers' interest if she had simply written, "Daniel picked up the tail and turned the crab over." Through detailed description, the author slows down the action, placing us on the beach with Daniel:

> *Daniel reached out one nervous finger. The tail felt stiff, but not sharp. He carefully lifted the crab. As her body left the ground, her claws started to snap. Daniel put her down fast. Then he took a deep breath and reached for her again. This time, he quickly turned the crab over, and gently set her down.*

In *The Girl on the High-Diving Horse*, Linda Oatman High lingers on the moment the horse descends into the tank below. By appealing to the senses, the author slows time to help the readers feel that they are part of the crowd watching this astounding feat. We see the horse's mane blowing in the wind; we hear the water splash and the crowd whistling and cheering.

At the end of *A Taste of Blackberries*, Doris Buchanan Smith's powerful story, the main character returns to the blackberry patch to pick berries for his mother and for Jamie's mother. Jamie has died from an allergic reaction to bee stings, and his best friend is remembering him as he picks his way through the patch. Smith's words bring us right to the blackberry thicket, and we can see, feel, taste, and smell everything with the main character.

> *I hunched and picked my way into the thickest place . . .*

> *Steadily, steadily my basket filled. My fingers were stained red-violet. I smell bubbling blackberry pie already. I balanced one on another up and over the top until I was afraid I couldn't carry the baskets without spilling.*

> *Then I took one plump berry between my thumb and forefinger. It was so full-to-popping that juice eased out onto my finger. I let the berry stay on my tongue a moment before I pressed it to the roof of my mouth and let the juice trickle down my throat.*

Before beginning a unit of study on narratives in her fourth-grade classes, Lynne reads excerpts from previously shared read-alouds such as *The Girl on the High-Diving Horse* by Linda Oatman High and *Crab Moon* by Ruth Horowitz. When the students have found a topic and are ready to write, Lynne focuses their attention on the middle of these narratives to look for fast and slow action scenes. As the students discover the small moments that the authors have placed under their magnifying lenses, they turn and talk with a partner or small response group to try to understand what made the writing effective. They reread the passages from *A Taste of Blackberries* to find key strategies that helped the author slow down a moment in time. In whole-group sharing at the close of writing workshop, students discuss strategies from the various books Lynne has used and any other books they have read. Then Lynne charts these strategies so that the students can use them to create a slow scene and/or revise it during their next workshop time.

For teachers of upper elementary and middle school grades, an excellent reference is Barry Lane's *After THE END: Teaching and Learning Creative Revision*. An entire chapter is devoted to playing with time, a technique used by writers, play directors, photographers, artists, musicians, and cinematographers to create mood, rhythm, and strong emotion. The first thing a writing teacher needs to do is share these small moments that are expanded into larger moments in a text. Find three or four good examples and try it out yourself. Think about what strategies you used to develop one moment in time. Examine these moments for author's craft. How did you create a moment in time where the reader could climb into that moment and walk around? Lynne's third and fourth graders included these strategies in their lists:

- Show, not tell
- Appeal to the senses
- Thinking of the character
- Dialogue
- Strong verbs
- Vivid adjectives
- Unexpected words (such as adjectives created by a string of words connected with hyphens such as *full-to-popping*)
- Striking color words
- Exact nouns
- Humor or another emotion
- Effective repetition
- Metaphor

- Simile
- Personification
- Alliteration
- Details
- Description of setting, character, or an important object
- Writing in the present tense
- Anecdotes

Instead of writing an entire story, ask your writers to brainstorm a list of small moments with you. Recently, we worked with teachers representing first grade through eighth grade in a graduate class for the Pennsylvania Writing and Literature Project. Together, we compiled the following list of possible scenarios for small moments that our students could choose to expand:

- Flower girl/ring bearer walking down the church aisle
- Standing on the sidelines waiting to be picked for a game
- Trying to get rid of a bee that has entered the classroom
- Called up to the stage to receive an award
- Waiting for the curtain to open as you stand on stage to perform
- Final lap of a race
- Seeing or holding your baby brother/sister for the first time
- Right before a bicycle or car crash
- Being stopped by a policeman
- The long walk to the principal's office
- The first-time stories (like jumping off a high dive)
- Agreeing to a dare
- Sitting in the dentist's chair
- Tryouts
- A surprise party
- Losing a tooth
- Plane takeoff or landing
- Walking into the classroom on the first day of school
- Finding money
- The moment you are caught doing something you are not supposed to be doing
- Seeing the tree on Christmas morning

Of course, we always share a small moment of ours first with the students. In Lynne's class, she had her third graders think about what they do in the springtime and gave them some sentence stems to help them get started. They used "Spring makes me happy because . . ." and "Spring reminds me of . . ." Next, they created an idea splash on a big piece of chart or construction paper. The students drew a picture and labeled their small moment. Then they wrote words, phrases, and sentences around the picture to help them vividly recall that moment in time. Lynne's small moment was the first time she jumped a four-foot stone wall on a horse named Chances Are. Lynne drew her picture on the whiteboard and placed her words around it while she was thinking aloud. (See Figure 4.1.)

> I remember thinking that the wall looked as big as the Hoover Dam! My heart was climbing up my throat, and my hands were so sweaty that they kept sliding all the way back the well-oiled reins to the buckle. I gripped the saddle with all my might and silently said a little prayer. Please don't let me fall off in front of all my friends! Then I leaned forward, grabbed some mane, and looked right between my horse's huge ears. Suddenly, he rocked back on his hind legs, and then we were flying! It was a small miracle. Somehow I managed to stay on. I was victorious!

Lynne pointed out all the words and phrases she had written on the board.

> Here I already have a wonderful simile that actually fits my story. Over here there are quite a few "show, not tell" phrases. Can you tell me what emotions I might be feeling? Let's look for strong verbs and exact nouns. I am ready to write. I know what the most important moment in my story is going to be and how to develop it.

When the students were finished discussing Lynne's model, they used large pieces of construction paper to plan their small moment. We do not have the students use this strategy every time, but it is especially helpful to struggling writers who need to draw and engage in more extensive prewriting to stay focused and develop their ideas. Once your students have created their word splashes, they can begin to draft. You might give them a checklist of writers' strategies they can try out when they reach the revision stage. Be sure to ask some of your young authors if you can have a copy as exemplary models for your future classes. Here are some small moments that were expanded into larger moments:

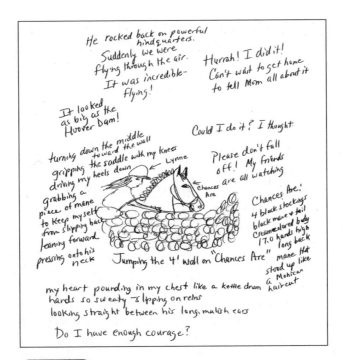

He rocked back on powerful hindquarters.
Suddenly we were flying through the air.
It was incredible—flying!

Hurrah! I did it!
Can't wait to get home to tell Mom all about it

It looked as big as the Hoover Dam!

Could I do it? I thought

turning down the middle
toward the wall
gripping the saddle with my knees
driving my heels down
grabbing a piece of mane
to keep myself
from slipping back
leaning forward
pressing onto his neck

← Lynne

Please don't fall off! My friends are all watching

← Chances Are

Chances Are!
4 black stockings
black mane + tail
Cream-colored body
17.0 hands high
long back
mane that stood up like a Mohican haircut

Jumping the 4' Wall on "Chances Are"

my heart pounding in my chest like a kettle drum
hands so sweaty & slipping on reins
looking straight between his long, mulish ears

Do I have enough courage?

FIGURE 4.1 Lynne's idea splash.

Spring makes me happy because I can hurry outside on my driveway and play basketball, my favorite sport. I love the sound of the ball when it swooshes as it drops through the net. My arms grow tired and more tired as I dribble harder and faster. Then I shoot. The ball rolls around and around the rim like a moon orbiting a planet, almost in and then . . .

Philip (grade 3)

The line inched forward again. I had a don't-make-me-do-this look on my face. I squeezed my dad's hand (harder than I ever did before.) I held back small tears. We were next. The cars moved up. We got on the middle car. I squeezed the handle bar. It took off faster and faster. Then, suddenly it stopped. "Oh, no!" I thought. The hill. It went higher and higher. I stuttered to Dad, "I'm really scared." He remarked, "Don't worry." The roller coaster came to the top. I held my breath (longer than I thought I could). Then, it burst forward. I came three inches off of the seat! The next hill, the next one . . . one after the other. CREEEEEEEEK! It came to a stop.

The bar lifted and released us from this torture trap of a roller coaster. I stood up, stuttering and shaky-legged. Surprisingly, I had a do-it-again look smacked onto my face. I heard myself saying in a shaky voice, "That was fun."

Kelley (grade 5)

After the students have created several small-moment entries in their writer's notebooks, Lynne asks them to choose one and create a narrative with a beginning, a middle, and an end. The most important thing here is to be sure to include a small moment that has been placed under a magnifying lens so the reader can linger there with you. *The Yellow Ball* is a second grader's attempt to play with time. See Figures 4.2a–4.2d.

After reading *Up North at the Cabin*, Frank, a fifth-grade student, knew exactly what he wanted to write about in his writer's notebook that day. Author Marsha Wilson Chall describes the special moments at the cabin one by one with such precision that you feel as if you know the place. She has you convinced that you are there.

> *Up north at the cabin, I am a smart angler. Grandpa tries pink spinners, leeches, and dragonflies—but I know what fish like. I bait my hook with peanut-butter-and-worm sandwiches, then jig my line and wait.*

Perhaps Frank was imitating Chall, and we believe that imitating the experts (the authors themselves) is exactly why we need to use mentor texts and revisit them often. At the very least, the picture book brought back a flood of memories and gave Frank a topic to write about in his notebook. The words seemed to spill out of him with an urgency of waters racing toward the falls—effortlessly, hungrily, and powerfully. This kind of first-draft writing happens for young writers only when they write about what they know, what they love, and what is important to them. Frank wrote about one event, not an entire day or even an entire afternoon. Consider his small moment about fishing with his uncle. Notice his appeal to the senses, use of a sprinkle of dialogue, thoughtshot, exact nouns (even a proper noun!), and vivid verbs.

> I am wearing my gold and blueberry-blue Scooby Doo life jacket. "Hold on!" my uncle says as we leave the spring-boarded dock. As we start to pull away, the old gas motor smells like a

Mentor Texts: Teaching Writing Through Children's Literature, K–6

My mom and I were in the soothing, blue water playing with my most favorite yellow ball. We were having so much fun that we didn't even notice an enormous wave in back of us. When I turned around to get my ball I saw it the enormous wave. I called my mom over. All we could say was AAAAAhh! It felt like my heart stopped beating. My face must have looked as white as my white bed sheets. The next moment it

FIGURE 4.2a Billy's story "The Yellow Ball."

turned ripe apple red from holding my breath. I was so scared I couldn't even move. When it started to tip, I started to fall! In my mind I was saying, "Good-bye, Ball." My mom and I were tumbling over each other.

FIGURE 4.2b Billy's story "The Yellow Ball."

I thought I was going to die before it was over! I came out of the ocean, and I must have taken a million breaths. I will be much more alert next time. And my favorite ball? The ocean still has it!

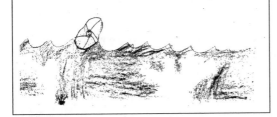

FIGURE 4.2c Billy's story "The Yellow Ball."

FIGURE 4.2d Billy's story "The Yellow Ball."

thunderstorm that has just finished. I throw my grass-green and Crayola-purple jig into the water. All of a sudden . . . PLOP! My rod dips into the water like an Oreo when you dunk it into cotton-white milk. After battling hard, I win the battle that takes me a long five minutes. "Fifteen-and-a-half-inch flounder," I yell. So *close*, I think, but I'm proud about my first flounder that looks sunflower-yellow and dirt brown and smells like a skunk's spray. "Half an inch and he is almost a keeper!" my uncle yells back.

Revision and Reflection

Revision can be used to get at the "inside" story, to change tense, to change person (first to third or vice versa), or to find the place in your piece that is begging for a moment in time to be expanded. Writing in the present tense is a great strategy to help young writers "be in the moment" to remember all the juicy details. The teacher can model how to write about something that has already happened as if it is happening right now. Teach students about revision by asking them to take a piece they've written in past tense and revise to write it in the present tense. *Shiloh* by Phyllis Reynolds Naylor makes a great read-aloud for intermediate elementary and middle school students who need to hear it for themselves. Haiku is also written in the present and often describes an action or event as if it were continuing, even as we finish reading it.

In Frank's case, he has several choices. He can leave the entry forever in his notebook as part of his history, his past. He can turn it into a poem—haiku, perhaps. Or he can write around this moment in time to produce a longer personal narrative by engaging in some self-reflection.

- What is my point, or "so what"?
- What is my purpose for writing this piece?
- Who is my audience?
- If I have already written about the most important event in my story, where should I begin without getting too far away from this event?
- How can I write a satisfying ending? What do my readers (target audience) need to know and feel in order to be satisfied?

Mentor Texts: Teaching Writing Through Children's Literature, K–6

Since reflection is built into the Your Turn lessons, our students are used to thinking about their writing and how what they have attempted to do helps them become better writers. This self-reflection is one of the most important steps in helping writers of any age continue to move forward.

As we share our writing with our students, we always begin with our thinking. That's what prewriting is—thinking before you write. With Frank, was it Lynne's example of a prewriting scaffold that helped him find his small moment in time? To begin that lesson, Lynne showed the students a notebook entry where she had made a two-column chart of important people in her life and some activities and events she connects with those people.

Grandpa and Me	Mom and Me
Long walks in the Poconos	Coloring pictures at card table in the living room when I was sick and had to stay home from school
Swimming at Sailor's Lake and learning how to float	Walking to the library on Wadsworth Avenue
On the Ferris wheel at Dorney Park	Buying clothes for college at the Cameo Shop and Gimbels
Driving around and looking at horses	Eating cheeseburgers and milk shakes at Barson's restaurant as a special treat
Ice-skating on the "pond" Grandpa created for me on the lawn in Coopersburg	"Teaching" me how to drive

Then she shared a notebook entry that came directly from her thinking on the chart. The following notebook entry is titled "On Driving with Mom" and may have influenced Frank's thinking. Lynne thinks Chall's book certainly provided the model she needed. In turn, her model may have helped Frank. It's a chain reaction. The combination of children's authors and writing teachers as authors is very powerful. After Lynne modeled, her students discussed her piece (as they often do) and her use of proper nouns, color words, use of present tense, and dialogue in this example:

I slide behind the wheel of the big, sea-green Impala and my mom slides into the passenger seat. She glances at me as I insert the key and turn on the ignition. "Hold on one minute," she says. "Don't be in such a hurry." After a (what seems like forever) review of the brake, gas pedal, and mirrors we are ready.

I pull away from the curb smoothly and drive down Durham Street between parked cars on either side. No problem. We stop at Thouron, and I put on my right blinker and look both ways, pulling out onto the main road. Same thing on Mt. Pleasant, and again on Woolston Avenue.

Finally, we are back on Durham. I pull up beside my father's new, midnight-blue Rambler, and back into the empty spot in front of my house. "There!" I say. My mother is open-mouthed. When the words finally come she demands a little too sharply, "Have you ever done this before?"

"Of course not, Mom!" I answer.

We try to model these notebook entries—small units of time that can be expanded into an entire narrative during a writing workshop period—as often as we can. First, we firmly believe that we need to be trusted members of our students' writing community, not just someone who assigns writing as a spectator but never a participant. Second, we need to demonstrate that writers write about what they know. They don't need Disney World vacations or white-water rafting trips to be able to write well. They can write about catching fireflies in their backyards on a warm June night with their friends as Julie Brinckloe describes in *Fireflies!* If they include the juicy details, we can imagine it, too, making connections about our own backyards and warm summer evenings.

Sometimes we share before we ask the students to write in their notebooks. Other times, we share with a student during a writing conference. Additionally, we share bits and pieces of our writing when we join a peer response group on a particular day. It is important to show students that writing is much more interesting when we develop a few high-quality ideas rather than write in list fashion. We are careful to model with events that our students can relate to and enjoy. We want them to find everyday moments that can be expanded by details, dialogue, appeal to the senses, thoughtshots, and anecdotes. We want them to understand the importance of writing for a target audience. Most important of all, we want our students to learn how to slow down and write small in order to write big. By slowing down the writing, they will be able to add the content that develops their ideas. It will make their writing as big as life.

In *Pictures of Hollis Woods*, Patricia Reilly Giff plays with moments of time by alternating her chapters about her main character, traveling from the past to the present. Each chapter about Hollis's past is written as an expanded moment that helps the reader visualize that moment—to feel as if Giff has magically transported us there. It is as if she is giving us the chance to be eyewitnesses to these important events that play in her main character's memory. She even calls these chapters written about past events "pictures." Consider how Giff has "exploded" this small moment in time:

> *Like a miracle I caught my first fish that afternoon. Hooked it and watched the silver curve as it broke the surface of the water. It was a huge fish, and Steven said, "Bet you a buck you can't hold on to it."*
>
> *He was right there with the net, though, wanting me to get it, as I slipped on the rocks, feeling the water on my legs and then my back as I slid. I tried to get my balance with one hand, my feet going out from under me, not sure how deep the river was, wondering if my head would go under.*
>
> *Steven's arm was on my elbow then, holding me up, and the Old Man called, "You're alright, Hollis."*
>
> *My feet anchored into the sand then. I edged myself back, pulling on the rod, and then the fish was mine.*

That is what writers do. They take moments in time and put them under a magnifying lens, examining every small detail for its worth, its importance to the whole. Each time we "explode a moment," we write small in order to write big. We write with the specificity we need to keep our audience's attention. We write with anecdotes, sensory details, thoughtshots, and dialogue. We write with rich description. We want our readers to continue reading. We want our words and pictures to linger on their minds long after they have finished reading. Teach your students how to look at people, places, objects, and events with a magnifying lens.

Adding Details Through Questioning

Hook: Kevin Henkes's books provide excellent models of the importance of adding details to writing, especially for young writers. The hook used in this lesson is *Lilly's Purple Plastic Purse*. In order for this lesson to be effective, this book should be a very familiar read-aloud. Return to it and read the first few pages, but leave out all the details.

> *Lilly loved school.*
> *And, most of all, she loved her teacher, Mr. Slinger.*
> *At home Lilly pretended to be Mr. Slinger.*
> *One morning Lilly came to school especially happy.*
> *"Look, everyone. Look what I've got!"*

By this time, students should be noticing that the book does not go like that. Acknowledge that they are indeed correct, that when you read it you left out all the details. Reread the first sentence: *Lilly loved school.* Ask students what questions they have when they hear that sentence. What do they want to know right away? Ideally, they will say that they want to know what she loved about school. Then read the three sentences that follow and directly answer the question. Continue with the other sentences.

Purpose: *Writing without details leaves too many unanswered questions and makes writing fuzzy. Today I will show you how to ask questions as you write. Asking questions will help you think of the details to add to your writing so that it is clear to the reader.*

Brainstorm: Ask students to think about some things they recently did, things they like to do, or perhaps places they recently went. For example: played soccer, went to art class, went to a friend's house. Ask students to jot down these ideas in their notebooks, or have them share orally and record some ideas on the board.

Model: Share some of your ideas about things you recently did or places you recently went, pick one, and record the idea in one sentence on a chart or overhead. Here is Rose's example:

Writers, today I'd like to tell you about the walk I took with my dog Casey last night. So I'll write here: Last evening I took Casey for a walk.

Ask students what questions they have. In this example, they asked what kind of dog it was, where she and Rose went, and what they saw. As each question is asked, answer it orally and also add it to your writing. Tell students that by answering the questions they have, you are adding details to the story to make it clearer and more interesting. The story started above might end up something like this:

Last evening I took my yellow Labrador retriever, Casey, for a walk. We strolled all around the neighborhood, past houses and parked cars, for almost an hour. We saw children playing street hockey and riding bikes. Casey wanted to run after a squirrel she saw scamper by, but I held her tightly so she wouldn't run away.

Shared/Guided Writing: Ask students to choose something from their brainstormed list and write it in one sentence in their notebooks as you first modeled. Invite one or two students to the front of the room for a guided conversation. Ask them to share their sentence; then share the questions you have. As the questions are answered, do some oral writing, demonstrating how these details, generated from the questions asked, could be added to the writing to make it clearer. Ask students to turn to a partner, share their sentence, and then ask their partner to share the questions they have. Have students return to their seats and add the details to the piece they began with the one sentence they wrote in their notebook. The details should be based on the questions asked by their partner.

Independent Writing: Students can return to a draft or published piece and look for places where they have questions. They can mark the places with a small colored dot or simply a checkmark. Students add more details by answering their own questions. Older students can work with a partner to mark each other's drafts and ask questions. The goal here is to create writers who can ask their own questions as they write, adding details their readers want to know that would help make their writing clearer. Encourage them to ask more questions themselves, until their writing becomes as clear as possible. They can then share again with their partner and receive feedback.

Reflection: Ask writers to reflect on how the strategy worked for them. As a group, discuss how the writing became clearer as questions were answered. Ask them to think about how they could use this strategy when they share with a partner or in a small response group. Make sure students understand that when questions arise, more details are probably needed. Ask them to think about how they could use this strategy in writing a research piece or a persuasive essay.

2

Building Content Through Show, Not Tell (Using Illustrations)

Hook: Choose some mentor texts that use pictures to show characters' emotions, adding to the content of the text and layering meaning. One of our favorites to use is the last page in *Widget* by Lyn Rossiter McFarland. You could also use pictures from *The Painter* or *Dad & Me* by Peter Catalanotto, *Yo! Yes?* by Chris Raschka, or *Chrysanthemum* by Kevin Henkes. Find a picture and ask students to describe the feelings they get from the picture.

Purpose: *Writing by telling alone is boring. Authors try to balance telling with showing. One of the easiest things that authors can show is emotions. Today we will use the emotions that illustrators reveal through their pictures to help us describe them in words so we are showing, not telling.*

Brainstorm: Return to the picture you chose in the hook. Ask students how the illustrator helped to convey the feelings they get when they look at the picture. List the responses on a chart or the board. In the example from *Widget*, Jim McFarland surrounds Widget with the six cats. Students' responses might sound like this:

> *The cats are rubbing against Widget.*
> *They are probably purring.*
> *They are looking at him with love in their eyes.*
> *It looks like they are smiling.*

Model: Take the responses from the students and show them how you would use them to create the text or add to the preexisting text for the page. For *Widget*, you might write the following:

> *The girls gathered around Widget. They pressed against him, rubbing and arching their backs. Soft purring rhythms filled the air. The cats almost smiled, gazing at their hero with love in their eyes.*

Shared/Guided Writing: Choose another picture from the same text or a different text. In a whole-class shared writing experience, decide on the feeling that has been created by the illustration, chart responses that describe the picture in a show-not-tell fashion, and write the text to go with it.

Independent Writing: Ask the students to return to a previous story where they made use of illustrations as well. Ask them to add details to their picture to add show, not tell to create a sense of feeling, time of day, or season of the year. Then ask them to add the words to their writing that would show, not tell. Students could also be given calendar pictures and describe the emotions, time of year, or time of day through words that show, not tell.

Reflection: Have students think how illustrations help them find the words they need to show feelings when they write. How does this help to build content and develop ideas presented in the text?

3

Building Content Through Show, Not Tell

Hook: Choose some mentor texts that show characters' emotions. One good choice is Roald Dahl's *The Witches* where he shows the fear of the main character as he discovers that the nice ladies on the other side of the screen are really witches. Reread the chapter "The Meeting" and chart all the words that Dahl uses to show fear such as "My blood turned to ice. I began to shake all over."

Options: *Dad & Me* by Peter Catalanotto, *I Remember Papa* by Helen Ketterman, *The Memory String* by Eve Bunting, *Lilly's Purple Plastic Purse* by Kevin Henkes, and *Crab Moon* by Ruth Horowitz.

Purpose: *Writing by telling alone is boring. Authors try to balance telling with showing. One of the easiest things that authors can show is emotions. Today we will find ways that reveal the emotions of our character through showing instead of telling just like Roald Dahl did.*

Brainstorm: Have students brainstorm a list of emotions that they could show, not tell. This list could include excitement, disappointment, anger, sadness, happiness, anxiety, frustration, surprise, loneliness, and joy, to name a few. Ask them to think about how nonverbal cues or actions could show these emotions in a piece of writing.

Model: Ask the students to imagine other ways Roald Dahl could have shown fear in the scene from *The Witches*. This list could include such things as hands shaking, an inability to speak, dry mouth, turning pale, goose bumps popping out, cold shivers, being rooted to the spot, knees knocking together, whimpering, crying. Then choose another emotion and write a scene around it. Let the students guess what the emotion is. Then have them come to the board and underline the words or phrases that helped show that emotion. Here is an example from Lynne's notebook that shows nervousness:

Ryan <u>fumbled</u> with his shoelaces. He couldn't seem to tie them with his <u>shaking hands</u>. A <u>sickening feeling in his stomach</u> was creeping up into his throat. The big game today would decide who would be champions—state champions. Playing goalie wasn't ever easy. He knew if he wasn't at his best today, the team would probably lose. As he grabbed his jacket, he <u>shook his head to clear his mind</u>. His <u>legs felt like spaghetti noodles</u> as he <u>trudged down the steps while holding on to the banister</u>. "Bye, Mom," he <u>called out weakly</u>. "I'll see you later at the game." He <u>swallowed hard</u> and walked to the bus stop.

Shared/Guided Writing: Choose another emotion and have the class brainstorm a list of nonverbal cues or actions for it, then create a scene around the emotion in a shared writing experience. It is best to choose something that centers around school so that the students can all join in. Stage the scenario in the cafeteria, nurse's office, classroom, or somewhere similar. Students could also work in pairs if you think they are ready.

Independent Writing: Ask the students to return to a previous story in their writing folder or an entry in their writer's notebook and revise the content to show instead of tell to reveal an emotion. They could also start a new piece and try out the show, not tell strategy to build content.

Reflection: Ask students to reflect on how this strategy worked for them.

How did adding details to show an emotion rather than just tell it make your writing better?

What kinds of words help you show an emotion? (For instance, strong verbs can be used to show actions that indicate anger.)

When is this strategy best used? Is it sometimes better to tell?

Ask students to find other examples as they read independently where authors have used the show, not tell strategy and copy them into their notebooks.

CHAPTER 5

Creating Powerful Beginnings and Satisfying Endings

As a community of learners, we discovered how
thick and tight the story line must be from its beginning all
the way to its end.

–Pamela Murphy

Have you ever read the first page of a book to decide whether or not you want to keep reading? Are you one of those people who peeks at the ending to have a sense of what emotions you might be left with as you finish your reading? E. B. White used a provocative question written as dialogue to begin *Charlotte's Web*. "'Where's Papa going with that ax?' said Fern to her mother as they were setting the table for breakfast." What reader wouldn't want to continue? The ending of this well-known book leaves the reader with the warm feeling of friendship. "It is not often that someone comes along who is a true friend and a good writer. Charlotte was both."

Beginnings and endings are important parts of story writing and are tied together with threads woven throughout the middle in the same way that introductions of informational pieces are tied to their conclusions. Before students can begin to work on the beginnings and endings of their pieces, they must have internalized the scaffold of the narrative—the typical format of beginning, middle, and end.

Understanding and Controlling Narrative Time

Our students often struggle with writing stories because they don't know how to control time. They often don't know the best place to begin a story in order to get to the most important event that is going to happen in that story and do it justice. For example, students often begin their stories springing out of bed to the sound of an alarm clock ringing; or they use the ever-popular "One Saturday morning . . ." lead, even when their story is about something that happened later that afternoon or evening. By the time they get to the true focus of their story, they have lost stamina—they start writing lists or even omit chunks of important details. If students have the schema for a story structure and truly understand the focus of the story they want to tell, then they can start making decisions about when and where it should begin. The importance of setting becomes clear as an integral element of the beginning. Because our students are often reading chapter books, they lose sight of the simple truth that in writing workshop they do not have the luxury of a year or more to write a "book." Besides, they lack the writing stamina to write an entire book. But we can teach them how to write a good story, one that has an enticing beginning, an interesting middle, and a satisfying ending. Picture books will show students the way. In only thirty-two pages they tell a good story.

To help our students internalize the narrative scaffold and the literary elements of story—character, setting, problem/goal, plot, solution/resolution—we can provide a variety of mentor texts that clearly illustrate this concept. Books we continue to use over and over across grade levels include *Crab Moon* by Ruth Horowitz, *Fireflies!* by Julie Brinckloe, *Widget* by Lyn Rossiter McFarland, and *Shortcut* by Donald Crews.

In *Shortcut* Donald Crews manages to tell a good story that takes place in a matter of minutes. The characters in this book are on their way home and decide to take a shortcut because it is getting dark. Unfortunately, the shortcut is on the train tracks, and a freight train is approaching. Crews makes use of effective repetition in his lead to set the reader up for the problem and how the story is going to unfold.

As he begins the middle of his text, he uses a brief description of the setting followed by quick, short sentences written in noun-verb fashion leading up to the most important moment—the moment when the children realize that a train is approaching. He uses effective repetition again for the ending of the story to help the reader understand the magnitude of the children's feelings. Crews ends the story with a decision that was reached based on the poor choice made at the beginning: "We decided to take the shortcut home. [Beginning] . . . we didn't take the shortcut again. [End]" *Shortcut* helps students understand that one small moment of time can be captured and told with excitement and strong emotion. Sometimes that's enough.

Julie Brinckloe's story *Fireflies!* spans an entire evening from dusk to bedtime. Brinckloe's main character is sitting at the dinner table looking out the window when he sees the fireflies beginning to flicker. He quickly joins his friends and catches many fireflies in a jar. In the end he comes to the realization that to save them he must set them free. This story is a great mentor text because it helps students understand the importance of writing a beginning that is not too far away in time from the most important event of the story. Students can easily see the logic of writing a story about catching fireflies when it is beginning to get dark outside. They clearly understand that starting this story at daybreak with the character springing from his bed would not be a good choice.

Ruth Horowitz's book *Crab Moon* tells the story of one boy's adventure with saving a stranded horseshoe crab. The book is a great mentor text to show students how they can span a larger period of time, transitioning from one essential moment to the next and skipping everything in between. The beginning of this story describes the setting—the when and the where—and ends with the promise that Daniel's mother will wake him in the middle of the night to see the horseshoe crabs. Turn the page, and Horowitz's words help the reader take the leap in time: "That night, the fat, round face of the full moon wavered on the surface of the water." Horowitz doesn't tell us what Daniel did all afternoon and evening because it's not important to the story she wants to tell. Horowitz needs to make yet another jump in time to get to the most important moment in her story. To do this, she uses another time-order transition phrase: "In the morning, Daniel raced back to the beach." Now she can slow the action down to linger here as she describes in detail how Daniel rescues the lone horseshoe crab that is stranded on the beach.

When we talk to students about how the authors of our mentor texts have told their stories, we can help them better understand where to begin their own stories and how to make good decisions about what to include and what to leave out. A good beginning leads to a more satisfying ending, and ultimately to a better story.

When young students begin to write, their pieces are usually quite short—one or two sentences about something from their lives. For example, "I went to a birthday party," or "I helped my mom plant flowers." With lots of modeling, guided conversations, and supported peer talk we can help young writers envision a structure to their life stories. We can help them see that the stories they share have a beginning, middle, and end, just like the stories they hear in the classroom.

Rose works collaboratively with the teachers in the kindergarten classes in her school during journal writing, a loosely structured writing workshop time. After the modeled lesson, Rose always invites students to come to the front of the room and talk about the idea they have for writing that day. Through guided conversation, she helps them add the important details that make their stories come alive. In the beginning of the year, the students typically use one sheet of paper in their journals during each writing time. Although many of the details that are unearthed during the conversation end up in the illustration, they aren't always included in the text. But as these young writers progress in their ability to form letters, stretch out the sounds in words, and become more confident in their ability to express themselves in writing, they are eager to add more details or to continue their stories over several days. To facilitate this development, the journals gradually give way to small books—three journal pages stapled together where students can record the moments of their lives with more elaboration. *Bunny Cakes* by Rosemary Wells is a true mentor text for the kindergartners Rose works with, helping them understand the different ways we write and the reasons we write, showing them the importance of details and word choice, and providing examples of word spacing and end marks. This book is also an excellent model for helping young writers understand how they can write a story with a beginning, middle, and end.

On one particular morning, Rose placed three blank journal pages on the whiteboard, then asked the students to gather on the rug. "Writers, let's think for a minute about the story of Max and Ruby in *Bunny Cakes*. What happened in the beginning of this story?" she asked them. As the children retold the beginning of the story, she pointed to the first blank journal page. She then asked them to tell the middle. As they came up with responses, she repeated their suggestions while pointing to the middle page. Finally, as she pointed to the last page, she asked them to tell how the story ended. Then she told them, "Today I'm going to show you how you can write a beginning, middle, and end just like Rosemary Wells did in *Bunny Cakes*." The lesson proceeded as Rose modeled a beginning, middle, and end with a story of her own.

> 66 *Writers, one spring I planted beautiful daffodils in my backyard under an oak tree. The next spring the leaves came up, but there were no flowers. This happened again the next spring. I thought there might be something wrong with the bulbs, so I dug them up. I threw them away behind the shed where we throw grass clippings and weeds. Guess what? The next spring the daffodils bloomed—right in the place where I threw them!* 99

This time, after telling the story while pointing to each blank page on the board, she also recorded it on the page.

| One spring the daffodils under the oak tree did not bloom. | I dug them up. I threw them behind the shed. | The next spring my daffodils bloomed right where I threw them. What a great surprise I had that day! |

She asked the students to think about their topic for writing that day, then invited Cassidy to come to the front of the room to tell her story about the time her friend got stuck in a tree. They first engaged in a guided conversation so Rose could be sure Cassidy included all the details. When it seemed like Cassidy was stopping, Rose encouraged her to tell more by asking her, "Then what happened?" When they finished the conversation, Rose gave Cassidy one of the three-page books and helped her tell the story again as she put her hand on each page. As some writers do, Cassidy put her finger on the page, then moved her finger along as she said each word. Rose then asked the class what they saw Cassidy do. She wanted them to understand that the story doesn't just stop after the first sentence—there is more to tell. (See Figures 5.1a–5.1c) Before the students returned to their tables to write, they turned to their partners and shared their ideas for the day's writing. Rose encouraged the students to use the phrase "Then what happened?" to encourage their partners to tell more.

As students become more proficient at putting words to paper, they tend to write the infamous bed-to-bed stories. This kind of writing usually occurs at the end of first grade or the beginning of second grade. Students write everything that happens from sunup to sundown and sometimes continue into the next day. Now is the time to make use of the mentor text *Widget* by Lyn Rossiter McFarland. Widget is a stray dog that desperately needs a home. He finds a home with Mrs. Diggs, but she already has six cats. The strength of this story is that it has a clear beginning, middle, and end and is the perfect story map. Because it is written in simple language, young writers can imitate the structure. Traditionally, when a story is mapped, the beginning includes the characters,

FIGURE 5.1a Page 1 of Cassidy's story: "My friend and I were climbing my tree in my backyard."

FIGURE 5.1b Page 2 of Cassidy's story: "She tried to get down. I put something underneath of her but when she turned to get down she scraped"

FIGURE 5.1c Page 3 of Cassidy's story: "her knee getting out of the tree. My mom and her mom put a special bandage on her."

the setting, and the problem or goal. The middle describes how the character(s) attempts to solve the problem or reach the goal. Usually there is a series of events that contain both fast and slow action. We tell students they need to keep the reader waiting and not solve the problem too quickly. Otherwise, the story is over before it gets started and there is no excitement or adventure. The middle of the story builds to the most important event where the goal is reached or the problem is solved. The ending ties everything together in a way that satisfies the reader and lets us know what the main character is thinking and/or feeling.

The hardest thing for elementary school students to learn how to do is to write a satisfying ending. Very young students will often omit the ending of a story entirely, satisfied with writing "The End." They simply stop because they are tired of writing and don't know where their story is going or what they need to do to successfully end their piece. In *Widget*, McFarland has created a satisfying ending. She also has a page that is ideal for stopping and pretending that the book is over. "Everyone came. Mrs. Diggs was saved!" Sound like an ending? It certainly sounds that way to the students until you ask them to think about story maps.

"What was the problem the book presented?" Lynne asked her third graders.

Carly's hand shot up. "Widget was a stray and he needed a home."

Steven added, "And he couldn't stay because he was a dog and the cats didn't like dogs."

"I see," Lynne said. "So what is the most important thing the reader needs to know at the end of the story?"

Isabel replied, "Oh, I get it! If the story ended here, we don't know if Widget gets to stay."

Lynne continued, "That's right. That's why Lyn Rossiter McFarland didn't end her story here." When Lynne finished reading the book, a discussion followed about how the author uses dialogue to reveal what the main characters are thinking and feeling at the end of the story. Lynne talked about how the ending satisfies the reader because it relates back to the beginning of the story and the problem of the main character.

Patches Lost and Found by Steven Kroll is another excellent mentor text that easily lends itself to story mapping and clearly illustrates how the ending must satisfy the reader. In this book Jenny, who would much rather draw than write, is having difficulty coming up with a topic for her writing assignment. A second problem occurs when she arrives home and discovers that her guinea pig, Patches, is missing. Jenny makes several attempts to find Patches, all the while drawing pictures of where she thinks he might be or what might have happened to him. Eventually, Jenny's neighbor returns Patches. We can lead students to the understanding that if the story ended with finding Patches, they would still wonder if Jenny ever thought of a topic for her writing assignment. In the end, Jenny engages in a final action: she uses all the pictures she drew of what she thought might have happened to Patches to write an imagined story. *Patches Lost and Found* is also an excellent example for students of how they can use pictures to plan out a story.

Once students begin to internalize the flow of a story—a beginning that introduces the characters and setting and perhaps describes the problem or goal of the main character, a middle where attempts are made to reach the goal, solve the problem, or describe the experience, and an ending that leaves the reader satisfied—then they can begin to think about the many different ways that authors choose to begin and end the stories they write.

Beginnings

For all writers, the lead—the first sentence, the first paragraph, or the first several paragraphs that begin the story—is absolutely crucial. E. B. White wrote more than a dozen leads for *Charlotte's Web* before he settled on a question written in dialogue form. His entire first chapter captivates the reader as Fern engages in a mental battle—a heated debate with her father—to save the runt, Wilbur, one of the story's main characters. The common ingredients of a good beginning include creating the mood by establishing the setting; information about the main character that reveals his hopes, thoughts, and feelings; and at least a hint of the problem, goal, or direction of the story. It's like receiving an invitation to a party where you expect to have a wonderful time. Revisiting mentor texts can provide students with examples of well-crafted beginnings that they can try out with their own stories.

Linda Oatman High's beginning for *The Girl on the High-Diving Horse* makes us feel like we are there in Atlantic City, in 1936, with the main characters, seeing it for the first time. She does this by including a rich description of setting that uses proper nouns and appeals to the senses. We know immediately how Ivy (the main character) is feeling.

Other books that begin by painting a picture of setting in the reader's mind are *Angels in the Dust* by Margot Theis Raven, *Wingwalker* by Rosemary Wells, and *Owl Moon* by Jane Yolen. Another favorite of ours is *Tulip Sees America* by Cynthia Rylant because the entire book is basically a series of rich descriptions of setting.

The beginning is also a writer's chance to create a mood through the description of the setting. Consider these two beginnings that create a feeling of loneliness:

> *Alejandro's small adobe house stood beside a lonely desert road. Beside the house stood a well, and a windmill to pump water from the well. Water for Alejandro and his only companion, a burro. It was a lonely place, and Alejandro welcomed any who stopped by to refresh themselves at the well. But visitors were few, and after they left, Alejandro felt lonelier than before.*

(from *Alejandro's Gift* by Richard E. Albert)

> *Amber lived on a mountain so high, it poked through the clouds like a needle stuck in down. Trees bristled on it like porcupine quills. And the air made you giddy—it was that clear. Still, for all that soaring beauty, Amber was lonesome. For mountain people lived scattered far from one another.*

(from *Amber on the Mountain* by Tony Johnston)

Students can imitate these beginnings—first, in their writer's notebooks—or they can simply try them out. Lynne often begins by asking her students to make a list of settings. Then she asks them to choose a setting and try to describe it through their senses, keeping in mind the mood they wish to create. Often she returns to *Amber on the Mountain* because it is a mentor text and the children are familiar with it. Sometimes it is easier for students to start with Tony Johnston's beginning, placing Amber in a different setting, rather than composing one from scratch. Jessica, a fourth grader, chose to put Amber on an island:

> Amber lived on an island so small it stood in the deep-dark sea like a lost whale. Palm trees tangled on it like monkey tails. And the coconuts made you giddy—they were that delightful. Still, for all the spectacular sights, one thing put Amber in her darkest mood. There were few hut-like houses near hers—less friends, more tears.

Some students will return to a previously written piece and revise their beginnings to add a description of setting that also creates mood. This strategy of using the author's syntax is described in detail in Your Turn Lesson 1 at the end of Chapter 9.

Often authors begin a book with a description of the main character. Sometimes, they include a physical description as Judith Schachner does in *The Grannyman*:

> *Simon was a very old cat. With the exception of his nose, most of his parts had stopped working long ago. He was blind and deaf, and his bones creaked as he climbed up and down the stairs.*

Sometimes they talk about the characters' likes, dislikes, or traits. In *Amazing Grace*, Mary Hoffman opens with a description of what her main character loves:

> *Grace was a girl who loved stories. She didn't mind if they were read to her or told to her or made up in her own head. She didn't care if they were in books or movies or out of Nana's long memory. Grace just loved stories.*

In *The Recess Queen* by Alexis O'Neill, the main character is described through a trait:

> *Mean Jean was Recess Queen and nobody said any different. Nobody swung until Mean Jean swung. Nobody kicked until Mean Jean kicked. Nobody bounced until Mean Jean bounced.*

Sometimes an author even begins with what other people say about the characters as Jerry Spinelli does in *Maniac Magee*:

> *They say Maniac Magee was born in a dump. They say his stomach was a cereal box and his heart a sofa spring.*
>
> *They say he kept an eight-inch cockroach on a leash and that rats stood guard over him while he slept. They say if you knew he was coming and you sprinkled salt on the ground and he ran over it, within two or three blocks he would be as slow as everybody else.*
>
> *They say.*

Introducing Characters Through Settings

Many times the character description is woven into a description of setting. One good example for primary students can be found in *Widget*:

> *Widget was a little stray dog. He had no home. He had no friends. He was sad and lonely. He was cold and hungry, too. He saw a house at the end of the road. There was a door just his size. He peeked inside. He saw six cats, six warm beds, and six bowls of hot food.*

Pat Mora combines a description of setting with a description of how her main character is feeling in *Tomás and the Library Lady*:

> *It was midnight. The light of the full moon followed the tired old car. Tomás was tired too. Hot and tired. He missed his own bed, in his own house in Texas.*

In a third-grade classroom, Lynne spoke to the students about doing just that—creating a good beginning for an informational piece or a narrative by placing the main character in a familiar setting. Lynne returned to *Widget* and *Tomás and the Library Lady* to open her discussion with the students on how they might combine a description of character and setting. The students examined other books they had used that year such as Cynthia Rylant's *The Great Gracie Chase* and *Little Whistle's Dinner Party, Mr. George Baker* by Amy Hest, and Margaree King Mitchell's *Granddaddy's Gift*. The students shared their discoveries in whole group, then Lynne modeled for the students by first placing the people she knew the best in a setting where she could clearly see them. "I would place my dad," she explained, "in the yard pushing the lawn mower or planting bushes and trees. I can see him now in his Bermuda shorts and sneakers, his long skinny legs with his calf muscles bulging. If I close my eyes, I see my grandma in her kitchen with her fingers deep in a doughy mixture. She's dressed just like Mrs. Cleaver in *Leave It to Beaver*—a string of pearls around her neck, a tailored dress, and a pair of low heels. But my mom—I see her sitting somewhere else." She asked the students to try to visualize the setting and the description of her mother as she wrote:

> Long, slender fingers with perfectly manicured ruby-red nails rest on the ivory keys. They press down gently and the beautiful

music, "Lara's Theme" from *Dr. Zhivago*, spills out into the air. I smile at her, and her blue eyes twinkle as she tosses her golden brown hair from her face. I snuggle next to her on the bench, trying to understand the language of the black notes on the page. She smells squeaky clean like Ivory soap. She sighs and stands up, her red-checkered apron still wrapped around her middle. She squeezes me and I squeeze back. She's perfectly perfect. She's my mom.

The students' responses when Lynne finished clearly indicated that they could see her with her mother at the piano. Together, they discussed how Lynne had used words to effectively help them visualize the scene. Lynne also told them that she had written the scene in the present tense because this strategy often helps her be there in the moment. She gave them the option of writing in past or present tense but told them to make sure they chose a character that they knew almost as well as they knew themselves—mother, father, grandfather, grandmother, or caregiver. Together they listed some possible settings for their special person such as the garden, a golf course, at the computer, shopping at the mall, the kitchen, the living room, the bedroom, and the supermarket. Many of the children decided to use their mom. As you can see from Figures 5.2 and 5.3, Lynne's modeling served as an integral part of the lesson.

Probably the best way to help students develop a beginning when they are having trouble getting started is by describing the weather. They hear people talking about the weather all the time. A description of weather will use strong verbs and striking adjectives. It's easy to make a leap and create a simile or metaphor or even use personification. Besides, it helps students show, not tell, the time of day or season. Additionally, use of vivid color words and appeal to the senses help build a strong beginning. Consider these examples from mentor texts we use with our students:

> *Snow drifted through the streets and now that it was dusk, Christmas trees glittered in the windows.*
>
> (from *Too Many Tamales* by Gary Soto)

> *Early morning is the best time to climb a tree because the sun has not yet had time to bake the earth until it is hot and steamy like a roasted plantain. If you wait until afternoon, rain will make the trees too slippery to climb.*
>
> (from *Cocoa Ice* by Diana Applebaum)

We dive through the shining blue-green water as she puts on sunblock and takes off her sandals. We splash her, and she dives in to get us back. She hides under the blue-green water, and finally we see her blond hair swishing in the water like a waving hand. I wave back at it. She tags me. I'm it! I stare into her pickle-green eyes and ask if I can have a dolphin ride. She smiles and nods slowly at me. I hold onto her back as we dive in. She's extraordinarily extraordinary, and she's my mommy

by Alexis

FIGURE 5.2 Alex's beginning paragraph for a piece about her mom.

Long, skinny arms go back and forth spreading dirt over bunny-ear plants and yellow roses... not caring if she gets dirt on her old white shirt and jeans. Her short brown hair dangles in front of her. She pushes it back with her sparkling hazel eyes spreading a dazzling smile as the sun shines on her perfect face. I run in the gate to give her a hug. She's wonderfully wonderful and she's my mom.

by Katie

FIGURE 5.3 Katie's beginning paragraph for a piece about her mom.

In the month of the Maple Sugar Moon, the snow's too wet for angel making, icicles rain from Grandpa's porch roof, and something is stirring in the woods. It's sugarbush spring.

(from *Sugarbush Spring* by Marsha Wilson Chall)

The wind rattled the front door of Poppa's cabin. Marie shivered. Winter was arriving on the lake.

(from *From Poppa* by Anne Carter)

The snowflakes were resting after their twisting twirling dance through the crisp night air. Every twig in the forest wore a new coat of glimmering white.

(from *Stranger in the Woods* by Carl R. Sams II and Jean Stoick)

After studying a handful of weather beginnings, students are ready to try it out. We have found that starting with a shared experience and working through several different seasons helps students hold on to the strategy so they can use it when they work independently. We ask the students to choose a season and an activity they might be doing as the main character in a narrative. We remind the students to show, not tell, whenever possible. It's usually feasible to ask students to show, not tell the season and the character's feelings. Older students can also add what the character is thinking or feeling to create a good beginning. The following three examples were written as shared writing experiences in second-, fourth-, and fifth-grade classes:

A soft, cool wind blew through my hair as I pushed my new, shiny, royal-blue bike outside into the bright sunlight. Rust-colored leaves crunched under the tar black wheels as I slowly walked my bike to the corner. My knees were knocking together, and a large lump rose in my throat. I swallowed hard. "I sure hope I don't fall off again on the hard cement," I thought. It was the sixth time my dad was trying to teach me how to ride my two-wheeler bike that I had received on my birthday. That was two weeks ago, and I still couldn't do it.

Soft, puffy marshmallow clouds were piled high against a robin's-egg blue sky. A balmy breeze tickled the leaves that were already beginning to turn shades of scarlet and gold. Earlier that morning, a light, cold drizzle had threatened to change my mother's mind about driving me to the stables. Now (thank goodness!) the sun was brightly shining on this warmer-than-usual Saturday afternoon. I bounded to the car and promptly rolled down the windows. "Wow!" I thought. "What a great day for my first riding lesson!" I leaned way out the window and yelled, "Hey, Mom, hurry up! I don't want to be late!"

Frosty puffs of breath hung in the air as I sighed deeply. I glanced up at the silvery mountain that was already filled with children and adults zigzagging down the slopes with ease. Following several steps behind my sister through the deep, dry, white snow I silently wished I was back home on the couch with a good book. We sat down on the hard, cold bench, and my sister removed her heavy gloves to strap my boots into the skis. I shivered even though I was wearing long underwear, heavy socks, a sweater, and a warm sea-green parka. "I will never learn to do this," I thought to myself.

Choosing the Right Lead

The important thing about beginnings is that students have choice. There are so many ways to craft a good beginning for narratives and informational pieces. Many of the strategies apply to all the modes of writing. Lynne often models with a narrative she has written that takes place in an amusement park. Her main characters are Billy and Lyddie. The problem is that Billy, who is usually brave, is afraid to ride the roller coaster but does not want to admit his fear to his sister and her friends. She returns to the story to demonstrate how she could craft many different leads for the same text. Revising the lead, or beginning of a piece, can be a powerful revision strategy. Students can make better sense of the different kinds of leads when each is written in the context of one setting. The following examples show the possibilities for Lynne's story:

Onomatopoeia: Clickety, clickety, clickety, clickety. The roller coaster slowly pulled along up the steep hill.

Snapshot Setting: It was hard to walk through the throngs of people—women pushing carriages, kids running and bumping into each other, older couples strolling along arm-in-arm—as bits of notes floated in between from the merry-go-round, my favorite ride.

Snapshot Character: Billy was not a coward. He just didn't like the twisty, turny rides, especially the ones that turned you upside down. For an eight-year-old, he usually was pretty bold. He even didn't mind sleeping in his own bedroom without a nightlight.

Foreshadowing: If only Billy had known that he was tall enough to ride the Rolling Thunder. Why did he always talk before he thought things out?

Simile: The roller-coaster track twisted and turned like an enormous boa constrictor wrapped around the limb of an ancient tree of the rain forest.

Short, Choppy Statement: No. No. I'll never do that again!

Question: Is there any better way to spend a beautiful Saturday than at Great Adventure Amusement Park with your best friends?

Name Statement: I, Lyddie Jones, will never, ever take my younger brother to an amusement park with my best friends.

Action (Suspense): Higher and higher it climbed, until it almost disappeared into the billowing clouds, and all we could hear was the screaming.

Thoughtshot: "Why am I afraid to tell my sister how I feel?" Billy thought to himself.

Dialogue: "Come on, Billy! Hurry! If we run, we can ride in the front car!" Lyddie squealed with excitement.

Exclamation: "Look at how steep that hill in the roller-coaster track is . . . Why, it looks like it stretches to the sun!"

Metaphor: It was a beautiful day, but windy enough to send wispy cloudships sailing through the blue-ocean sky.

Personification: The old cars moaned and groaned as they were pulled up the wooden track by invisible hands.

Appeal to the Senses (other than sound): The sickeningly sweet scent of fear drifted to my nose as I stared at what seemed like miles of roller-coaster tracks. I glanced around me to see if anyone else caught a whiff. Salty beads of sweat had formed on my brow. I wiped them away with clammy hands.

Creepy Statement: The track rose up like a dark spirit across the blue sky, turning my insides to mush.

Weather: A soft rain spattered against the car windows as we drove down the New Jersey Turnpike. But there was a ray of hope, poking between dark clouds with golden spokes.

Quote (what people say): My mother always said that Lyddie should have been born the boy, Lyddie, who was always daring, courageous, and full of life.

Controversial Statement: Amusement parks! They should really be called torture chambers!

Taking a Reader Back into the Past: When Billy was only two, his grandpa swung him upside down and round and round. At first he giggled and laughed, but when he started sputtering and gagging and spitting up everywhere, he ran for his grandmother, burying his head in the folds of her skirt and crying his eyes out. Yes, that's when my brother must have started hating roller coasters.

A list such as this could be kept on a chart in the writing center or distributed as a handout for students' binders or stapled into the back of a writer's notebook. As students explore mentor texts, they can label beginnings, add the examples to a chart such as the one above, and try to imitate them. Students should remember that descriptive language in a beginning acts as a hook to reel in the reader. It is worth spending time working and reworking the beginning of a text. Just as E. B. White did in *Charlotte's Web*, students should be given the opportunity to try out many leads to discover which one fits best.

Endings

As with beginnings, there are many ways authors choose to end a story. Sometimes, as in the ending of *Widget*, *Lilly's Purple Plastic Purse*, *Fireflies!*, or *Night Tree*, we learn what the character is thinking and feeling. As in *Patches Lost and Found* or *Crab Moon*, sometimes there is a final action. Sometimes the characters learn a lesson as Stellaluna and her friends Pip, Flitter, and Flap do in *Stellaluna* by Janell Cannon, or linger on a memory as the young girl in Chall's *Up North at the Cabin* or the homeless boy in Eve Bunting's *Fly Away Home* do. The important thing is not only that the ending be connected to the story in some way and leave the reader satisfied, but that it be interesting and memorable. As Ralph Fletcher (1993) says, "It is the ending, after all, that will resonate in the ear of the reader when the piece of writing has been finished. If the ending fails, the work fails in its entirety"(92).

To move students beyond thinking that a story ends when they write "The End," we must show them the possibilities that exist for creating satisfying endings. In our classes we usually begin by returning to the books the students are already familiar with—the mentor texts we have used as read-alouds, whose words and images have found their way into the hearts and minds of our students. We begin by examining them together as a group, then making a chart of types of endings and the books that are examples of each type. (See Figure 5.4.) Students are quick to find books (such as the ones mentioned before) where the author ends with a memory, a thought or feeling, a final action, or a lesson learned.

Depending on the books examined, students also may come up with many other interesting categories to add to the chart. In a second-grade class Rose was working with, one child offered a different category. "Look, Mrs. Cappelli," Timmy said, "in this book [*The Kissing Hand* by Audrey Penn] Chester's kiss is saying, 'I love you' to his mother. Could that be a different kind of ending—where something speaks?"

"I suppose it could be," Rose answered. "Let's see if we can find that type of ending in any other books." Other students joined Timmy on the search for this unusual ending, and before long they had added *The Whales' Song* by Dyan Sheldon and *Someday a Tree* by Eve Bunting to the category they added to their chart labeled "Something Speaks." Sometimes the categories that students create are simple ones such as "Happy Endings," or "Funny Endings," or "Surprise Endings." Students should be encouraged to add their thinking to the chart as new discoveries are made. Charts do not have to be completed in one session. They are ongoing in the unit of study—in this case, the study of endings.

As students continue to explore endings, they will soon discover that the books may fit into more than one category. Often, the endings to books don't fit neatly into one definite type of ending but are actually combinations of endings. For example, while Daniel engages in a final action in *Crab Moon*, he also expresses a wish for something in the future:

> *Slowly and grandly, the crab pulled herself forward. Stepping and pausing, Daniel's feet felt their way into the bay. He followed until she disappeared. Then he gave the water one last, long look and whispered to his horseshoe crab, "See you next summer."*

Memory That Lingers

Up North at the Cabin
 by Marsha Wilson Chall
Fly Away Home
 by Eve Bunting
Miss Opal's Auction
 by Susan Vizurraga
I Remember Papa
 by Helen Ketterman
Betty Doll
 by Patricia Polacco

Final Action

Crab Moon
 by Ruth Horowitz
Tomás and the Library Lady
 by Pat Mora
Patches Lost and Found
 by Stephen Kroll
Something from Nothing
 by Phoebe Gilman

Hope, Wish, Dream

Best Little Wingman
 by Janet Allen
Jeremiah Learns to Read
 by Jo Ellen Bogart
Lilly's Purple Plastic Purse
 by Kevin Henkes

Lesson Learned/Decision Reached

Shortcut
 by Donald Crews
Stellaluna
 by Janell Cannon
Tulip Sees America
 by Cynthia Rylant
Alejandro's Gift
 by Richard E. Albert

Thoughts or Feelings

The Divide
 by Michael Bedard
Fireflies!
 by Julie Brinckloe
Night Tree
 by Eve Bunting
Widget
 by Lyn Rossiter McFarland

Bookends

Jessica
 by Kevin Henkes
The Sunsets of Miss Olivia Wiggins
 by Lester Laminack
One Tiny Turtle
 by Nicola Davies
Miz Berlin Walks
 by Jane Yolen

Accomplishments/Discovery

Something Beautiful
 by Sharon Dennis Wyeth
When I Was Five
 by Arthur Howard
The Other Dog
 by Madeleine L'Engle
The Girl on the High-Diving Horse
 by Linda Oatman High
The Memory String
 by Eve Bunting
Amazing Grace
 by Mary Hoffman

Starts All Over Again

Chester's Way
 by Kevin Henkes
Imogene's Antlers
 by David Small
The Relatives Came
 by Cynthia Rylant

Fireflies! also combines a final action with the emotions of the main character:

> *I flung off the covers.*
> *I went to the window, opened the jar, and aimed*
> *it at the stars . . .*
> *The moonlight and the fireflies swam in my tears,*
> *but I could feel myself smiling.*

In *Muncha! Muncha! Muncha!* by Candace Fleming, Mr. McGreely is so happy to have finally outsmarted the bunnies that he picks the vegetables and places them in his basket (final action), only to discover that the bunnies were hiding inside. G. Brian Karas's final illustration shows Mr. McGreely munching the carrots with the bunnies—he has made a decision to share his vegetables. This same technique of using an illustration as part of an ending can also be found in *Click, Clack, Moo: Cows That Type* by Doreen Cronin (pictures by Betsy Lewin), and *An Angel for Solomon Singer* by Cynthia Rylant (pictures by Peter Catalanotto). Both of these books combine a decision with a final action.

For older students, this categorizing can be expanded to their individual notebooks. Students may actually copy several lines, label the type(s) of endings involved, and give the source (title, author, and page number when appropriate). When students have the opportunity to revisit charts and notebooks, their learning becomes more powerful because it is ongoing. Learning about endings is not a finite process; it continues to develop as the writer develops.

Although we certainly can introduce books that illustrate a variety of types of endings that we think our writers can imitate, it is important to let students explore and discover endings on their own. Using books from library, home, and classroom collections, students can work individually or in pairs to explore endings, adding to class charts or lists in their writer's notebooks. This process of self-discovery will open their minds to the possibilities of creating meaningful and satisfying endings.

We return once again to several favorite mentor texts when our students are ready to craft their own satisfying endings. An easy ending for students to compose is one that reveals the main character's feelings through thoughts or dialogue. In fact, almost all narratives seem to end by revealing the main character's emotions. Although this type of ending can stand by itself, it is also often used in combination with one or more types of endings.

We begin by asking students to retell the stories they have heard many times before. This helps them remember what they were feeling as the stories' endings resonated in their hearts and minds. By doing this, students realize the importance of an ending. The next step is to have students return to a previously written story and revisit the ending. We often ask them to see if there is a place for dialogue or the character's thoughts to help the reader know and understand what the character is feeling. Sometimes we might suggest that the students try to show the character's emotion with a physical description—a wide grin, teary eyes, or arms raised in triumph. Here is an opportunity to make reading and writing connections. Students understand that the most common response a reader makes to a text is a personal connection. It is in the ending that the reader gets the full impact of what has transpired in the story and how it has affected the character. Therefore, it is up to the writer not to lose writing stamina and quit before he delivers a satisfying ending.

After revisions are made, students share their endings in small response groups. We encourage the students to act as a writing community and continue to praise and polish. In whole group, the students reflect on how it worked for them—how their endings improved and why they think they did so.

Maggie, a second grader, is just beginning to understand the importance of endings. In the ending of the following piece about a trip to the zoo with her family, she combines her feelings with a wish for the future.

> The sun was shining. It was a wonderful day to go to the zoo. I ran downstairs and said, "Dad, let's go to the zoo!" Dad said OK. We went with Aunt Madeline, Libby, and Max. When we got to the zoo we first went in the monkey house. I smelled a rotten egg smell. I heard crazy ha-has. I felt like I was on a safari. When we got out of the monkey house we saw the penguins. They were black with sharp beaks. I heard them yap and yap as they waddled along then splashed in the water. When it was time to go we walked back to the car. I was TIRED! When I got home I laid on the couch and fell asleep. I can't wait to go back—maybe on the next sunny day.

Kyle, a third grader, effectively added dialogue to a final action to end his story about snowboarding. The explanation attached to the dialogue shows us that Kyle is happy.

One snowy day when it was icy-cold outside, I put my winter clothes on and made a tunnel to my friend's house with my snowboard. We ran like graceful deer through the snowy grass to Cold Spring Elementary School. It had the best sledding hill ever!

We built a ramp out of snow, packing it down with my snowboard. I tried out the ramp first. I did a 360! Then my friend Brandon used my board and wiped out. My snowboard flew into a tree. CRASH! So we made snowballs and threw them at the snowboard to try to get it loose, but it wouldn't budge.

"We can't throw high enough," I said. Slowly, I tried to climb the ten-foot tree. It did not work. CRASH! I was covered in snow, lying on my back and looking up at the tree that still clutched my snowboard in its arms. But I did not want to give up. "I have a plan!" I shouted.

We dashed home to get basketballs, and to our surprise, when we got back to Cold Spring's hill, the snowboard was on the ground! "How did that happen?" I asked. I picked up my snowboard and looked at the tall spruce tree. "Thanks," I said with a grin. Then I jumped on my snowboard and rocketed off the ramp.

Once students understand the importance of the ending, they can begin to experiment with other types, possibly using them in combination with the thoughts and feelings of the main character(s). It is not enough just to show students a type of ending and assign them to use it. Students need to be able to choose from a variety of endings so that they are sure to use the kind that fits best with the story they are writing. They can learn to recognize that the ending of the story is tied very closely to its beginning.

Writers often plant a seed of their ending in the beginning of their story. We see an example of this in *Shortcut* by Donald Crews. Twice in the opening pages of the book, the narrator tells the reader, "We should have taken the road." The second time he says it, the reader is starting to wonder why that is so. By the end of the story we realize an important lesson was learned: they should always take the road. In *Alejandro's Gift* by Richard E. Albert, the loneliness of the main character is evident from the first page. The reader understands that the resolution will need to deal with the character's emotions. In the end Alejandro discovers that the gift he has given to the animals is an even greater gift to himself because he will never be lonely again. In Anne Carter's book *From Poppa*, people describe the wooden duck decoys that Marie's grandfather carves as being so lifelike that they could almost fly away. In the end, the special decoy he has carved for Marie disappears from view and we are left wondering if it actually did fly away.

Students can return to their stories to see if they have planted the seed of their ending in their beginning and share with a partner or small response group. They should be encouraged to find more examples of stories that clearly connect the beginning to the end and record them in their notebooks. Sometimes students can add one telling detail that will create this effect in their story. In Maggie's original piece about the trip to the zoo with her family, she ended by simply saying, "I can't wait to go back." After a class discussion about endings relating to beginnings and conferencing with her teacher, Maggie decided to add the last part— "maybe on the next sunny day" to relate it to her beginning.

In Kelly's piece, "The Wave," the beginning clearly contains the seed of the ending. Kelly's story is about plucking up her courage to jump the ocean waves. Kelly's ending is filled with self-discovery and a sense of accomplishment.

> Beginning:
>
> On a cool, crisp summer day, I had to face my biggest fear of all. I gulped as I walked with my dad to the dreaded ocean I feared most. I felt that feeling you get when you know something is very wrong, but mine was a much worse feeling. I put my bare foot on the damp sand and the cool tidewater raced across it. I looked out at the never-ending ocean. I was ready (unless I didn't jump the wave).
>
> Ending:
>
> As soon as I jumped, all the butterflies burst out of my stomach. There I was floating in the freezing water with so much joy and happiness. I knew I could do it if I put my mind to it! I had finally conquered my biggest fear.

Sometimes authors plant the seed of the ending in the title of their story. The reader doesn't realize the significance of the title until the very end. Judy Schachner does this in her book *The Grannyman*: "So it was with the greatest respect that they gave their dear old cat a brand-new name. They called him the Grannyman."

In *A Taste of Blackberries* by Doris Buchanan Smith, we learn the significance of the title in the very last chapter: "'Do you remember,' I asked Jamie in my mind, 'the taste of blackberries?'"

Lynne uses her own example from her story "One Quarter Too Many" when working with her students. Originally, Lynne had titled the story "Darren's Lost Tooth." She wasn't happy with the title and asked her students for revision help. "Sometimes an interesting title is enough to make a reader read on, and sometimes a boring title makes a reader decide not to read the story at all." Her fourth graders read the story and came up with some new titles. When Curtis suggested "One Quarter Too Many," the entire class knew it was the right one. Lynne decided to insert the phrase into her final paragraph. That one revision made the ending more satisfying and provided the link she needed between the beginning and the ending of the story. Several students tried it out right away. In Ashley's story she describes taking care of her uncle's cat, Meowlie, who is furious at having been left in her care. Her title "Gaining Her Trust" plants the seed of what will eventually transpire:

> A jolt of surprise filled me suddenly, and I couldn't believe what I was hearing . . . purring! Her small throat rumbled with pleasure, and I was shocked to find that happen. Stroking her, I was happy—so happy that I felt like dancing and singing. She finally had let me pet her. I had gained her trust. It was an incredibly warm feeling that spread inside me and filled my heart. Meowlie and I were friends.

In Sarah's piece, "Sunday Surprise," about finding a litter of kittens in her garage, we find the title in the very last words. Sarah had been struggling to find a way to close her piece in a meaningful way. When she finally found the right title, she remembered *A Taste of Blackberries* and decided to use the title in the ending. As soon as she made that decision, the words spilled out of her.

> That night we called the S.P.C.A. "What happened Mommy? What happened?" I asked in excitement. Mom explained that the kittens were nursing from a cat that loved them. My mom was wearing a grin. I felt a grin spread across my face, too. I closed my eyes and almost cried with joy. My family had worked together to save the two little angelic kittens we had found in our garage, our Sunday surprise.

The Importance of a Road Map

Mentor texts provide road maps for students to follow. It is important that students almost have the text in its entirety in their heads to be able to imitate it. They don't need every detail, but they do need a story map. Noting powerful beginnings and satisfying endings through read-alouds, literature circle discussions, and conference time will help students internalize the strategies authors use to create a text worth reading. Francisco, an English language learner, wrote the following story as a fifth grader. It was his first year in the United States. The influence of the mentor texts *Fireflies!* and *Crab Moon* is evident. Francisco also tried several different leads before he settled on using a name statement. But as you can see, it is quickly followed by a description of setting and character.

A Bird Called Pipo

By Francisco

It was afternoon and I, Francisco Goncalves, was studying my Portuguese vocabulary. I was in my house, a yellow building with a gigantic palm-tree rounded by rocks on its front, with my grandma Beatriz. She has grey hair and green eyes and is not a very tall person. I already towered above her by almost a head.

It was hot and I was sweaty, so I decided to take a shower to cool off. After I took my shower, I was surprised to see something falling from the window—something black and small. I ran to the door.

"A bird!" I exclaimed. "Surely he broke his wing if he fell from the palm tree. It is like diving to the death!" The palm tree towered over everything else—even the house. It was gigantic. I gently picked him up. The bird seemed to know I was trying to help. "He needs a name if I'm going to keep him. Aaaa . . . Pipo! Yah! Great name! Hi, Pipo!"

When I brought him home, I explained to everybody what had happened. After that, I put a bandage on Pipo's wing. Later that evening, I grabbed a box and make some holes on it so that Pipo could breathe. I put a one-inch cup of water and a cup with food (bread and grains) so that Pipo could eat and drink.

"Dinner!" Mom yelled.

After dinner, I brushed my teeth and went to bed. It was hard to get to sleep because I kept wanting to check on my new feathered friend. Finally, I could not keep my eyes open.

"Good night, Pipo," I whispered softly. Pipo whistled. He seemed to understand.

When I woke up, Mom and I had a talk about Pipo's presence at home. "He's mine!" I yelled. "I gave him a name . . . a home!"

"Son, you have to understand that nature is his home, not here, and he is already cured," Mom replied.

I thought, and thought and finally arrived to a conclusion . . . she was right. I hated her at this moment . . . but she was right. This was not his place. I grabbed the box and now that we were outside, I opened the box and freed him.

With a jump he flew and flew until he disappeared. "Good-bye, Pipo. Good luck!" I called after him. I waved my hand and grinned even though my eyes were filled with salty tears.

Creating a Physical Description of Character Using Roald Dahl

Hook: Read excerpts of Roald Dahl's *Matilda*, using the physical description from the chapter titled "The Trunchbull." Place the description on a visualizer or chart paper and read it several times. Continue to share descriptions of character from other Dahl books such as *James and the Giant Peach* or *The BFG*. See the examples included here.

> The giant took off his black cloak and hung it against the wall. Sophie saw that under the cloak he was wearing a sort of collarless shirt and a dirty old leather waistcoat that didn't seem to have any buttons. His trousers were faded green and were far too short for his legs. On his bare feet he was wearing a pair of ridiculous sandals that for some reason had holes cut along each side, with a large hole at the end where his toes stuck out.

> *The BFG* by Roald Dahl

> That face of hers was the most frightful and frightening thing I have ever seen. Just looking at it gave me the shakes all over. It was so crumpled and wizened, so shrunken and shriveled, it looked as though it had been pickled in vinegar. It was a fearsome and ghastly sight. There was something terribly wrong with it, something foul and putrid and decayed. It seemed quite literally to be rotting away at the edges, and in the middle of the face around the mouth and cheeks, I could see the skin all cankered and worm-eaten, as though maggots were working away in there.

> *The Witches* by Roald Dahl

Dahl's character descriptions are wonderful models of how an author brings readers into a book by helping them visualize the character and experience the mood created by the description. Often, snapshots of character are sprinkled throughout a book, but many books begin with a snapshot of setting or character, and many times, it is a combination of both. A snapshot is a photograph in words. It is useful in informational and persuasive modes of writing as well as narrative. After sharing many of Dahl's books as read-alouds, explore other favorites to find snapshots of character.

Options: *Charlotte's Web* by E. B. White, *Stone Fox* by John Reynolds Gardiner, *That Magnetic Dog* by Bruce Whatley, *Wingwalker* by Rosemary Wells, *Olivia Saves the Circus* by Ian Falconer, and *A Taste of Blackberries* by Doris Buchanan Smith. (These books are listed in Chapter 10, "A Treasure Chest of Books," under Chapter 4.)

Purpose: *One important strategy to build a beginning is to create descriptions for the characters and settings. As you can see, Roald Dahl chooses to create a vivid painting in our minds of each of his characters. He describes what they look like, even telling us what they are wearing, and they become very real to us. Today we are going to write some snapshots of people who may have appeared or who will appear in our personal narratives and memoirs. We can use this strategy when we create essays about famous people or as a way to open a research report around a historical event by using a snapshot of one or more key players in that event.*

Brainstorm: Ask students to turn and talk with a partner or small group about characters they are familiar with in real-world experiences or ones they can vividly recall from books. Have them jot down ideas for characters in their notebooks and in whole group, share some of their thinking.

Model: The paragraph below is intended as a model for upper elementary and middle school children.

> *I am going to use Roald Dahl's descriptions to write my own lead paragraph about my riding instructor. It is important to choose a character who is familiar to me. As I write, I am going to think about the feelings that I associate with that person and the specific times or events that I remember. It will help me when I decide to create an entire draft during writing workshop.*

> *His long nose unevenly divided a face that was strong, noble, and weather-beaten. The china blue eyes spelled mischief as well as cynicism, and the long (much too long) gray-blond locks lazily curled this way and that. On the right side, he often tucked them behind his one good earlobe. The other lobe, half-removed after a mishap with the Jeep and a telephone pole on a whiskey-soaked summer evening, would not hold back the wealth of hair, so he often raised a large hand to brush away the hair from his face. He towered above all of us, his enormous frame filling the doorway. We were crazy about him, thrilled by his British accent and willing to obey every command if he so much as smiled in our direction.*

Shared/Guided Writing: Ask students to choose something from the class list of characters or something else they think of and write a lead paragraph that describes their main character. Make sure that all the students have examples from various books or samples from Roald Dahl's books. Display the sample model on the board, chart paper, or visualizer. Leave your model on a chart stand or blackboard or a transparency on the overhead projector. Students can share their drafts with a partner and talk about what they have revealed about their character through their description. Share a few in whole group on an overhead or visualizer. For struggling or younger writers, ask them to first orally write by talking about their ideas with a partner. The teacher can model this technique with another student. Another helpful strategy is to get the students to draw a picture of their character before they begin to write.

Independent Writing: Ask students to revisit a draft or a finished portfolio piece. Revise the lead paragraph to include a vivid snapshot of a character. If they are ready, students can begin a new draft for a narrative. Furthermore, students can use this strategy to begin an informational essay or research piece with a snapshot of a character where it is applicable. For example, informational reports about the Civil War could begin with a description of Robert E. Lee or Ulysses S. Grant or both (in a comparison format). It is always a good idea to have young writers share their writing with a partner, with a small response group, or in the general sharing session of writing workshop.

Reflection: Students can turn and talk with a partner about their lead paragraphs.

> *How did the description of character help your readers (peer response group/teacher) to visualize him or her?*
>
> *How did your snapshot of the character help create a certain mood for the story or essay?*
>
> *What strategies did you use to create a strong, clear description of the character?*
>
> *How can you use "show, not tell" strategy here?*
>
> *Where would you use this strategy—a snapshot of a character in the lead paragraph or scattered throughout your draft—again?*

Crafting a Lead Sentence

Many young writers are still developing their understanding of more complex language structures. Sometimes we can assist in this development by borrowing the syntax of the authors of our mentor texts. Students can then play around with word substitutions as they internalize the structure and make it part of their schema.

Hook: The first sentence of *Too Many Tamales* by Gary Soto provides an excellent model of a beginning that describes the setting. Options for other books with openings that work well with this type of activity are *Owl Moon* by Jane Yolen and *Cocoa Ice* by Diana Applebaum.

Purpose: *Writers, today I'm going to show you how you can borrow an author's sentence structure to help you write an opening sentence. We've talked about the different ways that authors begin their stories. Today we're going to practice writing an opening sentence that helps the reader visualize the setting.*

Brainstorm: Write the first line of *Too Many Tamales* on the board or overhead with three important words underlined:

> *Snow drifted through the streets and now that it was dusk, Christmas trees glittered in the windows.*

Ask students to brainstorm other nouns that could be used in place of *snow*. These could be weather related or seasonal. Begin a new column and list verbs that might be used with some of the nouns listed (they don't have to be lined up next to the noun they will be used with). Make a third column of words that could be used in place of *dusk*. These would relate to time. For example, a list might include the following:

rain	poured	morning
sunshine	pelted	dawn
hail	drizzled	twilight
wind	shone	evening
clouds	filtered	night
leaves	pounded	afternoon
flowers	blew	fall
pumpkins	scattered	autumn

Model: Use some of the words from the list to replace the underlined words in the original sentence. Revise the rest of the sentence as needed. Here are two examples:

> *Leaves scattered through the streets and now that it was autumn, jack-o'-lanterns glowed in the windows.*

> *Flowers bloomed in the garden and now that it was summer, butterflies flew from bloom to bloom.*

Shared/Guided Writing: Invite students to try creating new sentences just like you did. You may want to start with a shared experience, then invite students to work in pairs or individually.

Independent Writing: Ask students to return to a notebook entry or a piece they already wrote that could be revised to begin with a sentence that describes the setting. The use of this structure does not necessarily have to be the opening sentence, but generally would be part of the beginning. Students could also be given the option of using a sentence they created to begin a new piece of their own.

Reflection: After students share their revisions or new beginnings, ask them to reflect on what they did.

> *How did using this sentence structure help you begin?*

> *How did your piece improve by beginning with a description of setting?*

> *How did the words you used help the reader visualize the setting?*

> *Is the setting important to what you are writing about?*

> *When could you use this again? Would you change anything?*

Option: Students can post the sentences they composed in a writing center. Other students can borrow them as leads for new pieces.

3

Adding a Satisfying Ending

There are many ways in which authors end their stories. As we discussed in this chapter, the most satisfying endings relate to the story in some way. For young writers, understanding that endings often include what the main character is thinking or feeling, a final action or decision, a wish for the future, or a lesson learned provides enough choice for them to begin to craft their own endings.

Hook: Choose some of the mentor texts you have been using in the classroom and examine the endings closely with the students. Look for books that have the types of endings you think your students can imitate in their own stories such as thoughts and feelings, final actions, wishes for the future, lessons learned, or discoveries made. Many of the books listed in the Treasure Chest of Books for this chapter are good resources. If you write the endings out on chart paper, they can be posted in the classroom. You might try underlining the words that describe the feelings, final actions, or future wishes.

Lilly <u>ran and skipped and hopped and flew</u> all the way home, she was so happy.

(final action)

And <u>she really did want to be a teacher when she grew up</u>.

(future wish)

Purpose: *As we have been discussing, endings are very important to any piece of writing. Since the ending is the last thing you will leave your reader with, it must be memorable and satisfying. A story without a good ending is like eating cake without the icing—there is something missing. Today I will show you how you can write that kind of ending—one that satisfies the reader—in your own stories.*

Brainstorm: In this case *brainstorming* is closely tied to the use of literature in the *hook*. As students examine books and discover different types of endings, they are actually engaging in a type of brainstorming.

Model: Either read a previous notebook entry of your own or compose a new entry in front of the students. Stop before the ending and think aloud about how you would include the parts of a satisfying ending as you compose it. If it is a personal narrative, be sure to include your thoughts and feelings as the main character and perhaps combine it with a final action, a future wish, a lesson learned, or perhaps a memory.

Shared/Guided Writing: Ask students to return to a previous notebook entry or piece of writing and consider how the ending could be revised. Invite some students to offer their pieces for group revision, or hold a guided conversation in front of the group. For example, Angela, a second grader, wrote a short narrative about how she and her brothers had built a snowman. It ended with the sentence *And this is how we made the snowman.* Through guided conversation, Rose learned that it was the first time the children had finished a snowman complete with accessories (eyes, nose, scarf, hat), all of which was part of the description of the event. With a little more questioning and some help from the class, the ending was revised as follows:

> My brothers and I were all exhausted by the time we finished! We sipped hot chocolate and thought about how working together made it happen. We hoped our snowman would last for a very long time.

Rose guided the students to realize that this ending matched the story of Angela and her brothers working together to create the snowman.

Independent Writing: Ask students to continue revisions of previous pieces. Students may also wish to start new pieces and concentrate on a satisfying ending.

Reflection: After students have the opportunity to revise or write, ask them to share in whole group or small group. The following questions can help guide their thinking:

> *How did your ending change?*
>
> *How is it satisfying?*
>
> *Does the ending you wrote fit the story?*
>
> *Would a different ending be better?*
>
> *What kinds of things should you think about as you write an ending to a piece?*

CHAPTER 6

Using Scaffolds
to Organize Texts

How to make a text work together in interesting, efficient ways
is a challenge all writers face . . . We try to oversimplify this aspect of writing,
teaching students to write everything either as a story with a
chronological beginning, middle, and end, or as an essay with three to five
paragraphs . . . but I believe that for students to write well, they need
a repertoire of structural understandings that go beyond
these two basic forms.

–Katie Wood Ray, *Wondrous Words*

When Rose's daughter, Ann, was quite young, they went into Philadelphia to see a performance of *The Nutcracker.* As they were walking to the theater, they passed a construction site. Being a weekend, there were no workers about, but you could clearly see a building emerging behind the elaborate scaffolds that were assembled. Ann inquired about the reason for the boards and platforms, and Rose explained that it was a scaffold—a framework to support the workmen and their materials while they built the structure. "Look beyond the boards," she explained, "and try to envision what will soon be finished. Without the framework, the workers could not do their job."

So it is with young writers. They need a scaffold, a framework, to help them do their job. As with buildings, sometimes the scaffolds are temporary, providing the words necessary to help developing writers organize their thinking. These framing words can stay and become part of the structure, or they can be taken away, allowing the writing to stand on its own. Sometimes the scaffold is more permanent, providing an internal structure to help writers organize ideas. Almost always, the scaffold becomes part of a writer's schema. It gets in the head and finds its place in the context of what a writer knows about writing. Katie Wood Ray (1999) tells us that by studying the work of well-loved authors we can help our young writers envision possibilities for ways to structure words and texts.

Organizational Scaffolds in Children's Literature

Children's literature provides our students with endless possibilities for imitating scaffolds that authors use to help organize their texts in interesting and meaningful ways. Sometimes the scaffolds are in the form of words. For example, Sarah Thomson uses a simple phrase to scaffold her creative thinking about the paintings of Rob Gonsalves in two picture books: *Imagine a Day* and *Imagine a Night.*

> *imagine a day . . .*
> *. . . when everything you build*
> *touches the sky.*
>
> (from *Imagine a Day*)

imagine a night . . .
. . . when candlelight rises
on butterfly wings
to greet the lonely stars.

(from *Imagine a Night*)

Every page in both books begins with the phrase *imagine a day* or *imagine a night.*

Sometimes authors use one internal structure to organize the entire book. *Did You Hear Wind Sing Your Name? An Oneida Song of Spring* by Sandra De Coteau Orie is an example of such a book. Written entirely in questions, it captures the celebration of spring by the Oneida people.

Did you see
Sun's face in the Buttercup?
And did you see Sky's blue in the wildwood Violets?

(from *Did You Hear Wind Sing Your Name?*)

Other times authors use both words and an overall text structure to help organize their writing. Cynthia Rylant uses this technique in *Tulip Sees America.* This book uses snapshots of setting (the overall structure) as the main character travels across the United States from Ohio to Oregon. In addition, Rylant frames each snapshot by telling what is exceptional about that place and finishes by using a repeated phrase to tell the reader that they won't find that exceptionality anywhere else.

By introducing our young writers to the organizational scaffolds authors use, we can help them envision new possibilities for their writing. One way to accomplish this is to engage our students in writing text innovations, a technique in which teachers and students collaborate to compose parallel versions of books using the author's scaffold, but changing the topic or subject and perhaps sometimes varying the structure itself. *Brown Bear, Brown Bear, What Do You See?* by Bill Martin, Jr., *I Went Walking* by Sue Williams, and *When I Was Little* by Jamie Lee Curtis provide easy scaffolds for shared writing lessons. Shared writing provides a context in which writers can try out a particular writing strategy or, in this case, experiment with a specific structure, by collaborating with their teacher and peers to compose text. A shared writing experience offers the model and practice necessary to writers who may not yet be ready to try something on their own. By helping to construct the text and participating in reading and rereading it, developing writers are better able to internalize the structure and will be more likely to use it independently. The following is a compare/contrast scaffold from *When I Was Little* by Jamie Lee Curtis:

> *When I was little, I . . .*
> *Now I'm . . .*

It could easily be changed or adapted for writers to talk about ages, grade levels, or even seasons:

> When it was winter . . .
> Now that it's spring . . .

Sometimes the scaffold can become an innovation in itself. Margaret Wise Brown uses a basic scaffold that bookends her text on each page of *The Important Book*. However, she varies the sentence structures within the scaffold to maintain a fresh, unique quality for each page.

When we point out to students how authors sometimes vary their own structures, we allow them to come up with unique text innovations that fit their particular needs and their writing voices. Here is one class's shared writing experience that borrows the bookend scaffold from *The Important Book* but varies the structure within:

> The important thing about school is that it has books.
> It is true that its halls are silent in summer,
> But they are filled with voices from September to June.
> It is a place to make new friends.
> It has kind teachers.
> But the important thing about school is that it is filled with books.

After a shared writing experience using the scaffold, students are ready to write their own pieces. William, a third-grade English language learner, wrote:

> The important thing about shoes is that you wear them.
> Shoes protect your feet from the hard sidewalk.
> They come in different sizes.
> You can buy them in all the colors of the rainbow.
> They can help you run faster.
> There is a multitude of different types of shoes.
> Shoes are fun to wear because you can do a lot of stuff with them.
> But the important thing about shoes is that you wear them.

The paragraph structure in *The Important Book* can be modified to create a more sophisticated scaffold for older students. It also can be adapted for use in writing informational or persuasive pieces. In a third-grade class, Lynne took the opportunity to use the scaffold from *The Important Book* to synthesize information the students had learned about the *Mayflower*. She wanted the students to understand the value of oral writing to help them organize their thinking before composing independent drafts. Oral writing is a prewriting experience where students can get their ideas flowing without experiencing the intimidation of putting pencil to paper. Like shared writing, oral writing is a particularly useful strategy for reluctant writers or at-risk writers as well as ESL students, but everyone can benefit. After reading and discussing many texts that described the *Mayflower* and its voyage across the Atlantic, Lynne asked the students to share with a partner some of the interesting and important facts they remembered without returning to the books. By relying on their memories only, the students were offering the ideas that really stuck in their heads, the ones that were important to them. The books could be revisited at a later time for clarification, if needed. In whole group, Lynne recorded their responses on the whiteboard. Using this information, she modeled how to orally write a paragraph using the scaffold that she had created. The students immediately recognized the similarity to *The Important Book*. Lynne scanned the board for each idea that she thought could be meaningfully placed in each sentence, with the following result:

> The important thing about the *Mayflower* is that it carried the Pilgrims to the New World. It had several sails that filled with wind to move it across the water. Another interesting fact is that it had a poop deck. I also learned that it was really a cargo ship that mainly carried barrels of wine. Something that surprised me was that the *Mayflower* was a good-smelling ship for its day. Most of the ships smelled like rotten garbage. But the important thing about the *Mayflower* is that it carried the Pilgrims to the New World.

Together, Lynne and the class used oral writing to create a new paragraph, still using facts from the board. Some of the information was repeated or moved to a new place (they loved talking about the poop deck!). Next, the students were invited to create oral paragraphs with a partner. Finally, they independently wrote their own paragraphs about the *Mayflower*. It is important to note that many students returned to this scaffold on their own later in the year to write about people, places, or events they had researched. Oral writing and shared writing are powerful teaching tools, used alone or together, to help broaden the boundaries of organization within a writer's schema. When we help students recognize the scaffolds that authors use to organize their ideas, they are freed from the limitations of using a structure such as "first, next, then, finally" over and over. Although this structure seems to work well if you are giving directions on how to bake a cake or build a snowman, it doesn't fit every writing scenario. Different genres and modes of writing require different thought processes and different formats. When we make our students aware of the many structures authors use, they have a better understanding of how to organize their writing in a logical and meaningful way.

The Seesaw Scaffold

One of the easiest scaffolds for young writers to discover and imitate is the seesaw scaffold. Books such as *Fortunately* by Remy Charlip, *That's Good! That's Bad!* by Margery Cuyler, and *My Mom Travels a Lot* by Caroline Feller Bauer bring the up-and-down motion of a seesaw to the back-and-forth structure of words.

While Rose was in a second-grade classroom assisting with writing conferences one day, she had the opportunity to suggest this scaffold to a budding writer. Rose pulled her chair next to Amanda, who was obviously proud of the piece she had written about her new puppy. "Tell me about your work today, Amanda," Rose began.

"Oh! We just got this new puppy and he's so funny and does all these crazy and sometimes bad things, but he's really good, too, and well . . . just listen," Amanda gushed.

Rose realized that Amanda wrote much like she talked, in a random-thought way that just spilled out onto the page. Her piece lacked organization, and Rose immediately thought of the seesaw structure as a way to help her. She gave Amanda the book *My Mom Travels a Lot* and suggested that she think about how the author, Caroline Feller Bauer, had organized her thoughts. Rose helped Amanda identify the seesaw scaffold and then guided her into thinking about how her piece might look if it were written in this way. Together they separated all the good, cute, and lovable things the puppy did from the naughty and mischievous things. Amanda then decided which things went together best. She talked it out, first using oral writing—trying it on for size, so to speak. Katie Wood Ray (1999) reminds us that it doesn't help writers just to read and think about how authors structure their pieces; they must also envision it for themselves. Then they are more likely to internalize it and add it to their schema for organization.

Sometimes the seesaw scaffold is not found within the entire book, but in certain short passages when an author wants to emphasize a specific point. In *Widget* by Lyn Rossiter McFarland we are introduced to a little dog that is looking for a home. He finds a comfortable place in the house of Mrs. Diggs, but in order to stay, her six cats must accept him. When Widget and the cats first meet, we read,

> *The girls puffed up.*
> *Widget puffed up.*
> *The girls hissed and spit.*
> *Widget hissed and spit.*

A similar structure is found throughout *Tough Boris* by Mem Fox:

> *He was tough.*
> *All pirates are tough.*
> *He was massive.*
> *All pirates are massive.*

Students can imitate a partial seesaw scaffold for nonfiction writing as Martin Jenkins does in *Chameleons Are Cool*:

> *Some lizards eat bananas—chameleons don't.*
> *Some lizards walk upside down on the ceiling—chameleons can't.*
> *There's even a lizard that glides from tree to tree—a chameleon certainly wouldn't do that!*

Knots on a Counting Rope by Bill Martin, Jr., and John Archambault offers a variation of the seesaw scaffold. The book is a conversation between a Native American boy and his grandfather about the story of the boy's birth. The words of each character are positioned in a way that allow the reader to easily identify the speaker and follow the back-and-forth rhythm of the conversation. Young writers could use this technique as they begin to experiment with conversation, before they are skillful with the use of quotation marks. This book came to the rescue one summer when Rose was working in a program for young writers sponsored by the Pennsylvania Writing and Literature Project. The class comprised students who had just completed first grade, so the range of skill level was wide. Although all the students were interested in writing and viewed themselves as writers, not all of them had the ability to express their thoughts in a way that made sense to the reader. One student, Alex, had a particular interest in Scotland and the Loch Ness monster. That interest was often reflected in the writing he did. One afternoon Rose had a particularly difficult time understanding the story Alex was so confidently and earnestly working on. As she talked with him, it became clearer that the opening was actually the dialogue of a ship's captain interspersed with the sound effects from an underwater beast. But there was no punctuation to guide the reader, no character identification, no clue as to how this little scene might be connected to a larger piece. Because it was the work of a first grader who was about to be a second grader, Rose understood that some of this might still be beyond Alex's skill level. Still, she tried to help.

"Alex, you have an exciting scene here, but it is difficult to understand," she said. "Authors don't write down dialogue without identifying the speaker and using quotation marks to let us know the words that were spoken. Since this might be hard for you to do, why don't you just describe the action," she suggested. Alex tried to comply, but describing the scene was not what he had intended, and Rose could tell that the confidence he was demonstrating in himself as a writer was being compromised. That evening, she thought a lot about what had happened, knowing she needed to do something to help move Alex's writing forward in a way he was ready to handle. Finally, a title surfaced in her memory, and the next day she returned to Alex with a copy of *Knots on a Counting Rope*.

"Alex, I think I found a book that can help you organize your piece about the beast," she said. "The whole book is a dialogue between a young boy and his grandfather. The authors, Bill Martin, Jr., and John Archambault, let us know who is talking by the way the lines are arranged on the page." Together, Rose and Alex examined the structure of the book, then Alex used what they had discovered to reorganize his work. He placed the words of the captain on one side of the page and the sound effects from the beast on the other side. This line placement was similar to a poem for two voices, and provided enough structure to make sense of the scene he had created.

Global Structures vs. Substructures

Sometimes a piece of writing has a global or overall structure and one or more substructures within the piece. In *Outside, Inside* by Carolyn Crimi, the global structure is the seesaw: outside one thing is happening while inside something else is going on.

> *Outside, puddles bubble and churn with the falling rain.*
> *Inside, maple syrup slides down a pancake mountain.*

The substructure within the text shows the passing of time. The author's outside story describes her observations of a storm that is about to begin, and then the rain comes, until finally at the end the sunshine breaks through. Crimi simultaneously tells the inside story of her main character, Molly, who gets out of bed in the morning and fills her day with various activities until she can finally go outside.

Another text that includes a global structure as well as substructures is the nonfiction book *Arctic Lights, Arctic Nights* by Debbie S. Miller. The overall structure in this book is the passing of time in Alaska from one summer solstice to another. The substructures include a snapshot of setting and characters (wildlife) on each page. These snapshots describe what is happening on one particular day each month. Each snapshot includes an onomatopoeia lead. This book could perhaps provide an interesting way for a student to organize a science report about the changes that occur in a particular place or to a particular animal throughout the seasons.

In *Everglades*, Jean Craighead George provides a unique organizational format by telling a story within a story. She uses italics to separate the conversation between the storyteller and the children who are listening to him from the actual story he tells about the Everglades. Lois Lowry uses a similar technique in *Gooney Bird Greene*. Gooney Bird's stories are printed in a larger size to separate them from the narration of the book. Books such as these can help students better understand how to incorporate anecdotes into any mode of writing. It is important to show students that anecdotes can even be used within a narrative. When students understand and are able to recognize that within any mode of writing authors often use more than one structure, they are free to do the same in their own writing.

In Chapter 2, "*Digging for Treasure*," we discuss how some books that are organized around objects, such as *Aunt Flossie's Hats* by

Elizabeth Fitzgerald Howard or *Wilfrid Gordon McDonald Partridge* by Mem Fox, can be used to help students find writing topics. After the connection is made, after writers realize that they also have stories to tell just like Mem Fox and Elizabeth Fitzgerald Howard, they can begin to see other possibilities with these books. Students can examine the books with new eyes, turning their attention to *how* the author made the book instead of just *what* the author wrote. Sometimes the book revolves around one object as in *Betty Doll* by Patricia Polacco or *Hairs/Pelitos* (written in both Spanish and English) by Sandra Cisneros. An author could use a series of anecdotes or small stories that revolve around one place, as in I*n My Momma's Kitchen* by Jerdine Nolan, *Up North at the Cabin* by Marsha Wilson Chall, *In Our Backyard Garden* by Eileen Spinelli, or *All the Places to Love* by Patricia MacLachlan. Students can examine their writer's notebooks for evidence of stories that revolve around an object, a place, or perhaps a person. For instance, they might have lots of entries describing the details of their Saturday morning soccer games, or the adventures they share with their best friend, or special times at their grandparents' cottage. When it comes time to work on a larger project, we can help students realize the structural possibilities within their notebook entries by revisiting the books that have become part of the classroom community. Sharing books that are written around people, objects, places, or events can show students that they, too, might find common threads running through their notebooks that can be woven into a single extended text.

Structures That Complete a Circle

Books written in a circular structure end where they began. Laura Numeroff has written several such books, beginning with the popular *If You Give a Mouse a Cookie*. Sometimes students call this the "start all over again" structure. It can be very obvious, such as in the Numeroff books, or more subtle, as in Cynthia Rylant's *The Relatives Came. Two Bad Ants* by Chris Van Allsburg and *Where the Wild Things Are* by Maurice Sendak provide variations of the circular structure. In these books the main characters are at home as the story begins, they set out on an adventure, and finally they find their way home again. Books with these structures can be particularly helpful scaffolds to students who are beginning to move away from personal narratives to simple fictional stories.

A variation of the circular structure can be found in books where the entire first line is repeated at the end, as in Libba Moore Gray's *My Mama Had a Dancing Heart* or Lester Laminack's *The Sunsets of Miss Olivia Wiggins*. These repeated lines act as bookends to the story told between them and are easy for young writers to identify, although they may or may not notice it on their own. However, once we make students aware of a particular structure, they will look for it in other books or pieces of writing. Through reflection and discussion that may be part of a Your Turn lesson, young writers can be led to the realization of why the author chose a particular structure, or why it worked in that particular piece of writing. Our teaching should always be purposeful, helping our students understand the "why" behind the "what." It is not enough to engage students in a writing activity simply because it is fun. Writers must understand how a particular strategy or technique can help them move forward in their own writing.

In some books a line is not repeated just at the beginning and the end, but rather throughout the text. Sometimes, these repeated words act as a scaffold to provide rhythm to the writing, sometimes writers purposefully repeat a word or phrase to emphasize an important idea, and sometimes the words do both. Cynthia Rylant uses this structure in many of her books such as *In November* and *When I Was Young in the Mountains*. The repeated phrases in each book, which are also the book titles, are used to set off small vignettes while providing a rhythm to the writing. Another book that uses a repeated phrase is *Up North at the Cabin* by Marcia Wilson Chall. Chall uses the title as the repeated phrase for her book as well. Each time she begins a page with "Up north at the cabin . . . ," she shares a tiny memory of the time she spent there. One memory captures the loons landing on the lake at sunset while the little girl sits with her grandparents on the same side of the table so they can all watch "the loons dance down the sun." By studying books with repeated refrains, young writers can perhaps envision a new way to organize a piece about a particular place, or perhaps a particular time of the year. In one fifth-grade classroom, Lynne returned to *In November* to create a shared writing experience imitating Rylant's organizational structure.

In December snow lazily floats on the crisp, cold air while flickering fires fill our fireplaces, lighting up rooms with a rosy, warm glow. We nestle among plush pillows and comfy cushions to sip foamy hot chocolate and share our sledding stories.

In December Santa comes to town, and adults are swarming to malls that are as busy as beehives. Houses are filled with the sweet scent of pine wreaths and trees. Parents hide presents away and grandmas bake those wonderful butter cookies in the shapes of bells, angels, and reindeer. We dream about Christmas morning when we will awake and leap from our beds without the help of a single alarm clock or a parent's wake-up call.

In December it's a time for thinking about those hard-to-keep resolutions. It's a time for wishes, hopes, and dreams. It's a time for families to come together and celebrate the end of one year and the beginning of a brand new year. It's a time for making memories that last. It's December.

Your Turn Lesson 2 at the end of this chapter offers another option for using this type of organizational structure.

Borrowing scaffolds is not just limited to the work of student authors. We can find many familiar scaffolds in the work of published authors. Pamela Duncan Edwards used the cumulative text structure from the nursery rhyme "The House That Jack Built" to create two nonfiction texts *Boston Tea Party* and *The Wright Brothers*. Cumulative texts are no strangers to students. They have listened to stories and sung songs that have this type of structure since they were young. A cumulative text takes the first sentence and builds on it, repeating all the phrases or sentences that went before. The following excerpt from *Boston Tea Party* illustrates this structure:

> *These are the leaves that grew on a bush in a far-off land and became part of the Boston Tea Party.*
> *This is the tea that was made from the leaves that grew on a bush in a far-off land and became part of the Boston Tea Party.*

The Napping House by Audrey Wood also uses a cumulative text structure:

> *This is the house,*
> *a napping house,*
> *where everyone is sleeping.*
> *And in that house*
> *there is a bed,*
> *a cozy bed*
> *in a napping house,*
> *where everyone is sleeping.*

Students can borrow the cumulative text structure for narrative or informational writing. When used for report writing this structure helps students know their topic thoroughly, understand a sequence of events, and be able to write about it in a unique way. Structures such as these can actually serve to motivate students to work longer and harder on a project that requires writing.

Reader's Theater as a Scaffold

Composing reader's theater scripts from children's literature teaches students how to use the play format to scaffold text. Play format is a wonderful scaffold for elementary students. It's useful for a variety of reasons. First, it allows students to write conversation before they are able to use the necessary conventions to make it easy to read and understand. When they are ready to write conversation that uses punctuation correctly, they can go back to the play format as a starting place. In addition, it gives the students a chance to "fill in" the "telling" part of the story through the narrator. But best of all, plays can be performed as full productions, mini-skits, and reader's theater. These performances provide a real-world audience for student writing.

Reader's theater can be performed with any text. It helps students make reading-writing connections by giving them the opportunity to create their own personal interpretation of a piece of literature. Usually, the students render text exactly as it has been written. They read directly from the book and try to read the words the way they believe the author would have read them. It is an activity that can involve the entire class and is actually fun and nonthreatening. Most of the time, reader's theater involves reading, not memorizing lines. However, it is easy enough to evolve into a storytelling theater where students also write in actions and create props to use. Here, it is important for the teacher to model improvisation. Lines can be changed slightly so long as they do not affect the logical sequence of events or omit important information the audience will need. Reader's theater can also be a wonderful extension to your writing program. It can stimulate your students' imaginations and bring magic into your classroom.

The way Lynne uses reader's theater makes use of all the communication areas: reading, writing, speaking, and listening. Lynne worked with third graders as they studied African folktales as a genre study. They read widely, starting with *Bringing the Rain to Kapiti Plain* retold by Verna Aardema. They chose *Anansi and the Moss-Covered Rock* by Eric Kimmel to experiment with as a reader's theater with some actions (such as Anansi falling down when he said the words *moss-covered rock*). After building some enthusiasm for a performance, Lynne suggested that they choose a book to rewrite in play format and take their "show" on the road to kindergarten and first-grade classes. Lynne worked with the class to write the skit collaboratively. She recorded their statements, telling them not to worry about saying everything and not to always use the exact words of the author. They did decide that echoic words, or words that create onomatopoeia, should be included because these words are a characteristic of the genre. The class also used the repeated phrases because effective repetition is another visible characteristic.

For the first draft, Lynne took everything the students suggested. Next, the whole class revised the skit to eliminate some words or entire sentences that were not needed and sometimes to change a word to make it more their own. Lynne pointed out the use of the colon and the bold print for the names of the characters. The group talked about how the organizational format of an African folktale helps the reader remember the story because things are repeated many times. Lynne told them that many stories are passed on orally, so the form of the folktale helps people tell the story to each new generation.

Three groups were formed, and the students decided for themselves who would play what part. They practiced, thought about their entrances and ways to introduce the actors, designed posters to advertise the production, and sent out invitations. The students even used paper plates to create masks for their characters. Finally, they performed for younger classes and their parents. Here is a piece of the revised script the class wrote and performed:

Narrator: *Today we are here to present* Why Mosquitoes Buzz in People's Ears, *retold by Verna Aardema. Our class is performing their version of the story as readers' theater for Round Meadow students. The characters are wearing masks, so they will now introduce themselves . . .*

    This tale is from West Africa. When the story begins, Iguana is drinking from a waterhole and Mosquito comes along. Mosquito starts to brag.

Mosquito: *Today I saw a farmer digging yams as big as I am!*

Iguana:	*I would rather be deaf than listen to your stories!*
Narrator:	*Iguana decided to put sticks in his ears so he couldn't hear Mosquito.*
Python:	*Sssssssssssss. Good morning, Iguana!*
Narrator:	*Iguana couldn't hear Python.*
Python:	*Why don't you sssssssssssspeak to me? Iguana must be angry with me. I'm afraid he isssssssssssss going to do some missssssssssssschief.*
Narrator:	*So Python went into Rabbit's hole to hide . . . wasawusu, wasawusu.*
Rabbit:	*Help! Python is after me!*
Crow:	*Kaa! Kaa! Kaa! Run for your life! Danger!*
Monkey:	*I must warn the other animals. Crow is sounding the alarm.*
Narrator:	*Then Monkey stepped on a dead limb, and it cracked and fell, killing one of the owlets. Mother Owl was out hunting. But when she came home . . .*
Mother Owl:	*Oh! One of my babies has been killed. Who would have such a cruel heart? I am so sad, so sad, so sad.*

After the performance, the students wrote their reflections about the experience. One student wrote, "I loved readers' theater because we got to do something with our writing. It was so much fun to go back to my first-grade teacher and do this skit for her class. I liked being the python because I got to speak in a deep voice and I hissed a lot, too! That was the part I got to write into our skit, and luckily I got to play the part of Python, too!"

I Am the Dog, I Am the Cat by Donald Hall and *Hey, Little Ant* by Phillip and Hannah Hoose are already written in play format and can serve as great models for students. They are also very useful for teaching point of view as part of a unit of study centering on the persuasive mode. Besides African folktales, *Boston Tea Party* and *The Wright Brothers*, both by Pamela Duncan Edwards, make great choices for readers' theater performances. Older students can use the organizational scaffold that Edwards used, "The House That Jack Built," and write their own readers' theater performances around other historical events. One of Lynne's favorites is *The Great Kapok Tree* by Lynne Cherry. The book naturally lends itself to a rewrite in play format. Of course, fairy tales are great rewrites for plays, either retold as traditional tales or revised as a modern fairy tale or told from another point of view. *The True Story of the 3 Little Pigs!* by Jon Scieszka, *Sleeping Ugly* by Jane Yolen, or *Help Yourself, Little Red Hen!* by Dr. Alvin Granowsky are examples of fairy tales retold through the eyes of another character.

Organizing Around the Alphabet and Numbers

Two other common scaffolds that can be used as models for student writing are books that are organized around the alphabet and numbers. Students of all ages can use the alphabet structure as well as a number structure to organize their thinking. Alphabet and counting books range from the very simple, such as *Matthew A.B.C.* and *Daisy 1, 2, 3* by Peter Catalanotto that have one statement per page and are used to entertain, to the more complex, such as *Capital! Washington D.C. from A to Z* by Laura Krauss Melmed. This book has elaborate text as well as nonfiction features such as captions, time lines, and labels used to inform the reader. *Soccer Counts!* by Barbara Barbieri McGrath and Peter Alderman is an example of a more complex counting book. In this book a rhyming couplet introduces the number. Italicized text gives the reader a more complete explanation. These structures can be studied as a genre, especially for older students, who can examine a wide range of alphabet book formats to choose an appropriate model for a piece of writing they are about to begin. In Lynne's fourth-grade class, the students chose an ABC format to reconstruct their research about Alaska and display it as a quilt. (See Figure 6.1.) Each student chose a letter and explored a host of possible topics for it, often consulting with peers or the librarian, as well as the teacher, to ensure that they made the most appropriate contribution to the total accumulated knowledge about Alaska. The students decided to display the final product as a quilt hung in the hall, instead of a book, so that it could be shared with more people. Once they had tried out the ABC format, some students chose to use it again for a book report on "The ABCs of Maniac Magee" or as an alphabet book about dinosaurs written for a first-grade audience. Once students become comfortable with this structure, the possibilities are endless. One third-grade class decided to surprise Lynne with a writing ABC that captured the spirit of the writing workshop time they shared together.

The A, B, C of Writing

Adjectives and adverbs don't take the place of strong nouns and verbs!

Begin your piece with an exciting lead.

Capitalization of proper nouns is checked during the edit.

Dig deep to find memories and stories that are important to you.

Every sentence should not begin the same way!

Find places to add rich details.

Give your writing your full attention by reading and rereading your words.

Happy, sad, angry, embarrassed—just appeal to the emotions.

Intelligent readers want you to show, not tell!

Just write it down in your writer's notebook before your ideas escape.

Kindness is okay when you confer, but honesty is important if you're going to help.

Let your voice be heard! You are unique!

Metaphors are great to use when they are appropriate.

Never be afraid to take a risk and try something new.

Open up your heart when you write and be passionate about the language!

Poetry is for everyone—free verse, haiku, limericks, tanka, acrostics, ballads.

Quit your whining when you write to persuade or no one will listen!

Revise, revise, revise, revise, revise, revise, revise, revise, revise. . .

Similes can be tired if you are always as slow as a snail or as fast as a cheetah.

Take time to appeal to the senses with sounds, smells, and tastes.

Unusual ways of seeing everyday things—that's what a writer does!

Vivid word choice and voice make up your very own style.

When you have time, use the thesaurus and dictionary to help you.

Xtra, extra . . . read all about it: writing workshop is extra special because we have a voice.

Your character is revealed through actions, thoughts, talk, and physical descriptions.

Zany and crazy are allowed. It's okay to be different in writing workshop.

FIGURE 6.1 This Alaska ABC quilt was created by a fourth-grade class.

Getting Inside a Character's Head: Letters, Journals, and Scrapbooks

Letters and journals are real-world structures that appeal to writers of all ages. Sometimes they have a serious tone, such as *Dear Levi— Letters from the Overland Trail* by Elvira Woodruff or *One Day in the Tropical Rain Forest* by Jean Craighead George. Sometimes they are more humorous, such as *Diary of a Worm* by Doreen Cronin or *First Year Letters* by Julie Danneberg. This structure allows students to organize information about people, places, and events in a familiar format while allowing them to practice the conventions of letter or journal writing. When Lynne was a fourth-grade teacher, her class was studying Harriet Tubman and the Underground Railroad. Together they examined books with journal entries to understand what a journal format looked like as well as the type of information it contained. Lynne's students then created journals and wrote in the voice of Harriet Tubman to record memories—descriptions, thoughts, and feelings—that they thought she would have written in a journal if she had been literate.

Perhaps students could write about a place or region in the world using a scrapbook format as Loretta Krupinski did in her book *A New England Scrapbook: A Journey Through Poetry, Prose, and Pictures*. She uses the repeated refrain scaffold "New England Is . . ." as the title for each page and completes it with a characteristic of New England. For example, "New England Is Maple Syrup," or "New England Is Barns." On each page she offers a paragraph to elaborate on the idea offered, as well as a poem from another author. Students can enhance their scrapbooks with original poems, drawings, or photographs. This scaffold offers an alternative to the traditional report format for presenting research or firsthand accounts.

Writing in the voice of another person, animal, or thing is an organizational structure all its own. We can find many examples, including *My Light* by Molly Bang, *Atlantic* by G. Brian Karas, *Sierra* by Diane Siebert, and *Look to the North: A Wolf Pup Diary* by Jean Craighead George. This structure helps students write from a point of view other than their own. This is the necessary practice they need to get better at persuasive writing. By using this scaffold, they have the opportunity to think from another's perspective—to walk around in someone else's skin—and to understand what it feels like, looks like, or sounds like. In other words, it prepares students to view the world not only through their eyes but also through the eyes of another individual or group. This scaffold helps them think outside the box. It promotes writing as thinking in a creative way.

By helping students see structures in literature that they might not see themselves—to walk alongside them and point things out—is the job of both teacher and mentor text. Students need to read a variety of texts and internalize the structures they present. Once they understand how those representations help readers make sense of text, they can use them as scaffolds for their own writing. Teaching students to use a variety of scaffolds adds another layer to helping them become more strategic writers.

Using a Seesaw Structure to Organize Writing

Hook: Return to familiar books that are written in a seesaw structure. These might include *My Mom Travels a Lot* by Caroline Feller Bauer or *Fortunately* by Remy Charlip. With your students, identify the scaffold and its characteristics. For instance, the same words are used back and forth, over and over (Fortunately . . . Unfortunately . . . The good thing is . . . The bad thing is . . .); the books begin and end with a positive statement. Option: *That's Good! That's Bad!* by Margery Cuyler or *Tough Boris* by Mem Fox.

Purpose: *Writers, sometimes authors organize their ideas by using a seesaw structure. Today, I will show you how to do that and you will have a chance to try it out in your own writing.*

Brainstorm: Ask students to think of situations they have experienced that might have a good side and a bad side. Some possibilities are playing a sport, having a little brother or sister, having a pet, or rain on the day of a picnic. You might want to get the class started by sharing a few ideas of your own. Search your memory or look through your notebook for things that might fit, such as hiring a babysitter for an evening out, taking a long plane ride, or snow in April. Record the ideas on the board or on chart paper.

Model: Using one of your own ideas, relate the story or experience and write it up using the scaffold from one of the books previously presented. Here's an example:

> *I was looking through my notebook, and I noticed an entry where I wrote about it snowing in the beginning of April when the trees were already blossoming. There are good things and bad things about snow in April, so if I borrowed Caroline Feller Bauer's scaffold, I could write the following:*
> *It's spring and the trees are beginning to blossom.*
> *The good thing is, the birds are returning to build their nests.*
> *The bad thing is, a light snow has started to fall.*
> *The good thing is, the trees look beautiful.*
> *The bad thing is, the snow is hiding the branches and berries.*

Shared/Guided Writing: Return to the list of brainstormed ideas. Pick a few and discuss some of the good things and bad things about each. Invite students to try out the scaffold by choosing one of the ideas and writing a few lines. This lesson also works well as a collaborative effort. If students are not ready to work on their own, consider constructing a text through whole-class shared writing. Students can also work in partnerships to begin a short piece.

Independent Writing: Ask students to return to their notebooks and search for some ideas or previous entries that might work well using the seesaw scaffold. If they have difficulty identifying something from their notebooks, they can choose one of the brainstormed ideas or continue the piece started during guided writing.

Reflection: After sharing some pieces, ask students to reflect on how this scaffold worked.

> *How did the scaffold help you organize your thoughts?*

> *When could the seesaw structure be effectively used?*

For students who rewrote an existing notebook entry:

> *Did the use of the scaffold improve the writing? Would the writing work better in a different format?*

This is also a good time to explain to students that the words of the scaffold (the good thing, the bad thing, and so on) don't always have to be included. The idea is to use the comparing and contrasting of ideas as an organizational strategy. Through discussion, help students come to identify additional situations where the structure could be effective, such as comparing or contrasting two characters.

Using a Repeated Refrain as a Scaffold to Create Paragraphs

Hook: *In November* by Cynthia Rylant gives students a chance to see how an author uses a repeated phrase to organize the information presented in the text. The book is a collection of small descriptions that help the reader visualize and remember November. Each description begins with the words *In November . . .* and is organized around a different topic. Reread the book and chart with the students the topics and details Rylant uses to develop her ideas. Other books with this same type of scaffold are *Up North at the Cabin* by Marsha Wilson Chall, *If You're Not from the Prairie . . .* by David Bouchard, and *When I Was Young in the Mountains* by Cynthia Rylant.

Purpose: *Writers, today we are going to use the same structure Cynthia Rylant used, a repeated refrain, to organize information in paragraphs about your favorite months. Like Rylant, we will have to make a decision about the big ideas we want to develop. (Refer to the chart you created listing topics and details about them.) For example, see how Rylant talks about the trees, the birds, the food, and the special holiday that takes place in November. Each time she talks about a new idea, she starts with the phrase "In November . . ." I'm going to show you how you can do the same thing.*

Brainstorm: With your students, choose a month they might like to try out together. Brainstorm big ideas that relate to that month. For example, if you chose October, your list might include football, Halloween, leaves changing color, and weather. Develop ideas under these big categories as well. For instance, under Halloween you might have pumpkins, jack-o'-lanterns, trick-or-treating, costumes, haunted houses, or scarecrows. Brainstorm lots of ideas so you have lots to choose from. It's always a good idea to have more than you will actually use.

Model: Using the ideas listed, write one or two paragraphs around each topic. Think aloud as you write, demonstrating how you are building a paragraph around one central idea. For example, you might write the following:

> *In October, fat, heavy pumpkins dot the farmers' fields. A scarecrow stuffed with bright oat straw stands nearby, watching parents and children scurry to find the perfect one to take home. After scooping out the guts, parents help carve a scary face and place a candle inside. The golden light flickers as the jack-o'-lantern flashes a toothy smile at the trick-or-treaters on Halloween night.*

Shared/Guided Writing: Ask the students to work with a partner or a group of three to choose another month and brainstorm the big or main ideas they have about this month. Working together, they come up with details to support each main idea. As you circulate, encourage the students to think about holidays, sports, and weather and add appeal to the senses as part of the detail work. Next, have each pair or group report their thinking. Students in other groups can offer suggestions either aloud or on sticky notes (for older students). This greatly enriches the possibilities for everyone's success. Now they can begin to draft a paragraph or two beginning with the refrain "In [month] . . ." Students should think about how they are going to place their details in a meaningful way. Younger students can write their ideas on sentence strips so that they can more easily manipulate the order. Students can volunteer to share first-draft writing.

Independent Writing: Before students try this out on their own, brainstorm things other than months that they could write about using a similar organizational scaffold such as seasons, holidays, or days of the week ("On Monday . . ."). They could also do this with a place in mind ("In Grandma's garden . . ."). Remind them to plan or prewrite first, getting their big ideas and details sketched in their notebooks before trying to write the paragraph.

Reflection: Ask students to think about how the repeated phrase helped them scaffold and focus their thinking as they created their paragraphs.

> *When could you use this again?*

> *Are there drafts in your notebook that could be organized in this way?*

> *Could it work for informational or persuasive writing?*

> *How could it be used to create an advertisement, a song, or a poem?*

Option: If all the students are writing about a different holiday, month, or state, you could create a quilt around that particular theme.

Writing in the Persona of Another

This type of writing ties in easily with science or social studies topics. It is a different way for students to demonstrate what they have learned and is a fresh alternative to report writing. For example, after you have studied a particular topic such as the rain forest, ask students to take on the persona of an animal, plant, or the biome itself to write about the things they learned. For younger students, this can be done as a shared project. In some first-grade classrooms, teachers have incubators and hatch baby chicks. Students could write their daily observations in the persona of a baby chick.

Hook: *Atlantic* by G. Brian Karas is a book written in the persona of the Atlantic Ocean. Return to this text and ask students to think about how the author used the voice of the ocean, writing in the first person, to give us information about it. Other books that use persona writing are *My Light* by Molly Bang, *Sierra* by Diane Siebert, and *I Am the Mummy: Heb-Nefert* by Eve Bunting.

Purpose: *When authors write in the first person as if they are something else—an animal, an object, a place, or even another person—it is called persona writing. Today I'm going to show you how you can organize information by using the voice of someone or something else just like G. Brian Karas did.*

Brainstorm: Choose a place that is familiar to students, such as a backyard or the school playground, and brainstorm a list of things they might be comfortable writing about. One class chose their backyards and created a list that included the following: sandbox, patio, trees, robin's nest, squirrels, rabbits, groundhogs, rosebush, mosquitoes, hammock, picnic table, sprinkler, garden hose, and barbecue grill. Record the ideas on a chart or board.

Model: Choose one and show students how to create a chart to organize and stretch their thinking. Think aloud as you write. The example below charts the thinking about a crab-apple tree. The categories could be different, depending on your purposes. For example, you might use a category for actions (G. Brian

Karas describes many actions of the ocean), or you could use a category for changes (if you are taking on the persona of a caterpillar or a tadpole).

Description	Feelings/Thoughts	Observations
Tall	Eager for spring rain	Squirrels are leaping from limb to limb.
Standing in center of yard	Waiting for the boy to come and climb me	Robins yank worms out of the lawn.
Milk chocolate bark	Thrilled by the little girl's laughter as she pulls through the air to move the tire swing	Sparrows are starting to build their nests again.
Arms reaching into nearby maples		Today my blossoms fall like pink rain.
Rough and sturdy	Feeling rather pretty with all my new leaves sprouting	People are reading poetry about me.
Bend under weight of snow		The little girl holds Shel Silverstein's *The Giving Tree* in her lap.
Yield to strong north wind	Ouch! That pesky woodpecker just keeps hammering away.	
Tiny pink blossoms		
Limbs pointing in every direction that a compass points		

Using the model, create a beginning, perhaps starting with a snapshot using the ideas under description.

> *I am standing, tall and sturdy, in the very center of a large backyard. The winter snows have melted and my milk chocolate bark no longer wears a coat of white. I stretch toward the sun, warming my numb limbs that have felt cold all winter long. Now, my new green leaves are sprouting everywhere. I am becoming beautiful once more.*

Shared/Guided Writing: Have students work with a partner or small group to develop a chart of ideas about an object from the brainstormed list. Encourage the students to draw sketches if they need to. These can be placed around the chart like a border and could also contain some labeling. As you circulate around the classroom, don't be afraid to jump-start their thinking by offering a few ideas or asking some questions to help them visualize themselves in that persona. Share their thinking in whole group so that others can offer suggestions or layer the thinking. When enough ideas have been gathered, have them try to write a few paragraphs. In the above example, the feelings and thoughts column could lend itself to several paragraphs—the boy coming to climb, the girl coming to swing, and the woodpecker coming to find a tasty meal. The observations column could lend itself to individual paragraphs. You may want to model this over several days to give students lots of options.

Independent Writing: Students could return to the shared chart and try out one of the ideas they didn't use in partnership. After writing, encourage them to have an ear conference with a partner to make sure they are writing in the first person, staying in the persona of what they are writing about. (An ear conference focuses on revision, not editing.)

Reflection: Have students reflect on how this strategy worked. The following questions can help guide their thinking (choose according to what you think is appropriate to your grade level):

> *How did this work for you?*
>
> *Was it enjoyable?*
>
> *Was it easy or difficult?*
>
> *How did it help you organize your thinking?*
>
> *When could you use this again?*
>
> *Could you suggest a different prewriting strategy to help organize your thinking?*
>
> *How does writing in the first person affect point of view and the tone of the text?*

Option: Students can rewrite their piece using a friendly or business letter format while still maintaining the first-person voice.

CHAPTER 7

Poetry: Everybody Can Be a Writer

Poetry happens when people begin to look at the world differently.
It is a way of uncovering the ordinary world: suddenly, in the
hands of the poet, commonplace events take on new life and importance.

–Donald Graves, *A Fresh Look at Writing*

Chances are you shy away from reading, much less writing, poetry. Memories of high school and college come floating back to you and you shudder. You remember reading the poetry of Donne, Yeats, and Tennyson and recall how the secret meanings of the poems they wrote seemed to remain a mystery to you. Only the poets themselves (and your esteemed English professors) understood what the poem was expressing. So why would you try to write poetry yourself or have your students write poems? Jean Little's character Kate in *Hey World, Here I Am!* talks about how Robert Frost's "Stopping By Woods on a Snowy Evening" had become an unpleasant experience for her:

> *But today, the teacher told us what everything stood for.*
> *The woods, the horse, the miles to go, the sleep—*
> *They all have "hidden meanings."*
>
> *It's grown so complicated now that,*
> *Next time I drive by,*
> *I don't think I'll bother to stop.*

Peter Elbow (1981) tells us that many people feel like they could be poets—that they could even write a good poem. He goes on to explain that they might not even have a topic, image, or feeling that they want to write about. And yet, they still feel poetic. Unfortunately, he laments, we learn to put those feelings away and instead search for something to write a poem about. So poetry becomes too hard and complex a task and we abandon it. Like Kate, we no longer bother to stop, and in our writing workshops, poetry does not get the attention it deserves.

Many times we'll choose to read the poetry of Shel Silverstein and Jack Prelutsky because our students delight in the rhythm and humor. We may also have our students write poetry, but we build poetry writing only around special holidays, like creating cards for Mother's Day or Father's Day. The poetry might sound something like this:

> Roses are red,
> Violets are blue.
> Chocolate is sweet,
> And so are you.

This poetry sounds more like a greeting card—there is a general (mothers) rather than a specific (my mother) target audience, and it doesn't express the feelings of the writer. Although there is nothing wrong with creating poetry for special occasions, those poems should sing with emotion. Poems should express the unique thoughts and feelings of the writer. But poetry writing does not have to be reserved for special occasions. We can weave poetry into the writing workshop throughout the year and across genres. We can use poetry to introduce ourselves and build community in a classroom, compose a lead for an informational text, or playfully respond to a persuasive argument. Poetry creates pathways to songs, jingles, or entries in our writer's notebooks. Poetry offers a unique response to literature and makes the greatest gift of writing to those we love and care about when we express our true feelings.

We fill our classrooms with poetry that is fun to read and hear but that may not always provide the best models for writing. When writing poetry, students should be allowed to concentrate on the feelings and images they wish to create through precise language rather than concentrating on rhyming patterns. You've probably received a poem like this from one of your students:

> I went outside to play.
> It was a sunny day.
> Ships sailed on the bay.
> I have nothing more to say.

This poem is an example of forced rhyme. The child, instead of concentrating on meaning, was concentrating on finding rhyming words, and the poem ends up not saying anything at all. This kind of wordplay is important in teaching phonological awareness to emergent readers and may help students develop an interest in language, but in writing workshop, the word choice must be more purposeful. This is not to say that students should be discouraged from using rhyme if they wish to do so, but it is to say that by filling our classrooms with mentor texts that provide many different models of poems that do not use rhyme, we can provide students with many more choices. We need to teach our students to look at poetry for specific word choice, economy of expression, voice, effective repetition, rhythm, use of an organizational scaffold, line breaks, and appeal to the senses as well as our emotions. An excellent resource for teachers is *A Kick in the Head: An Everyday Guide to Poetic Forms*. Paul Janeczko does a great job of introducing twenty-nine poetic forms, including a few that you may not have heard of such as the triolet, the roundel, and the villanelle. In *R Is for Rhyme: A Poetry*

Alphabet Judy Young provides many examples of literary devices, and poetic techniques and forms. *Baseball, Snakes, and Summer Squash: Poems About Growing Up* by Donald Graves is a wonderful book of unrhymed poetry. Students will make connections with these poems because they are filled with childhood experiences, laughter and tears, and wonderful words.

Seeing Poetry Everywhere

Children love poetry, and they can be successful poets if they have a host of mentors, a useful scaffold, and a lot of practice. The first step is to find poetry everywhere and to help students recognize that the best prose sounds like poetry. Powerful sentences often make use of the literary devices we so often find in a poem—alliteration, onomatopoeia, hyperbole, metaphor, simile, and personification. When Isaac Bashevis Singer began his book *The Fearsome Inn* with "It was as if the snow treasures of heaven had been opened," he could have just told readers that it was snowing really hard, but our ears and our hearts are not thrilled with those words. When children read books and find sentences that make them want to reread them and linger there, they have probably found prose that sounds like poetry. Consider the following examples from mentor texts:

> *The trees stood still*
> *as giant statues.*
> *And the moon was so bright*
> *the sky seemed to shine.*
>
> Owl Moon by Jane Yolen

> *The prairie is stitched together*
> *in brown and yellow patches,*
> *like Grandma's quilt spread over the hills.*
>
> Prairie Train by Marsha Wilson Chall

> *In her dreams she saw them, as large as*
> *mountains and bluer than*
> *the sky. In her dreams she heard them singing, their*
> *voices like the wind.*
>
> The Whales' Song by Dyan Sheldon

Blinking on, blinking off,
dipping low, soaring high above my head,
making circles around the moon,
like stars dancing.

Fireflies! by Julie Brinckloe

Sometimes you're lucky enough to stumble across a picture book that sounds like poetry from beginning to end and is appropriate for any grade level or level of readers. Ron Hirschi's books on the seasons are filled with beautiful prose created through use of exact nouns, powerful verbs, simile, alliteration, personification, and specific color words. In *Spring*, he writes:

Waking like mother bear and her cub from a long winter nap . . .
the wildflowers march up the mountainside. As the snow melts
away, weasels change from winter white to golden brown.

When books such as these fill our classrooms, students begin to understand what beautiful language sounds like long before they can label it as a literary device such as simile or metaphor, or talk about the verb use in a particular context as unexpected or surprising.

Found Poetry

A natural segue into writing poetry is the use of found poetry. To create found poetry it's best to start with a short text with which you (the teacher) are very familiar and whose language you have already played around with. Begin by reading the piece silently and aloud. Poetry is meant to be read aloud, and often our ears will tell us what sounds like poetry. Start to make a list of words and phrases from the text. Place them on a page, line by line, in the form of a poem. After you are finished, you can do several things. You can read the poem just the way you wrote it down and leave it like that, or you can rearrange the lines, even deciding to use one or several lines as a repeating pattern, as effective repetition. You can decide where you need white space—for example, between couplets or quatrains—or that you don't need it at all. You can revise for word choice to create an alliterative phrase, add a color word, or substitute a more powerful verb. You can combine some thoughts or take something and find your own unique way to say it. In Lynne's classrooms, she asks the students to try to remain true to the content— in other words, not to change the content of the text or the feelings the original writer was trying to create—but often asks them to make the poem their own through revision efforts. When her students are finished and want to publish, Lynne asks that they include their source (author, title, publisher, and copyright) since their found poem started with someone else's words. Even the most reluctant writers will write found poetry since the words they start with are already written. No one suffers from writer's block.

Lynne's mentor text for introducing found poetry is Russell Freedman's nonfiction book *They Lived with the Dinosaurs.* She models with a short found poem about starfish, using information from Freedman's text. The students read the page about starfish with her, both silently and aloud. She shows them how she chooses the phrases, sharing her thinking as she places the words on the board.

> Brightly colored starfish
> Creeping along the ocean floor
> Feeding on shellfish
> Dancing along the ocean floor.

The students always ask her where the last line of her poem comes from, since it is not directly stated in the text. "From the photograph on the opposite page," Lynne tells them. "And by using the second line in my found poem and changing it a little—by thinking of a verb that would sound like poetry."

Although the reader can find poetic language throughout Freedman's text, Lynne likes to use the information about horseshoe crabs for the shared writing because her students often vacation at the seashore and are familiar with them. The original text is as follows:

> *Horseshoe crabs were crawling up on ancient beaches 400 million years ago. They looked the same then as they do now. They still swim through shallow water near shore, hunting for worms, clams, and dead fish. They will eat almost anything that they can shovel into their small mouths. Their name comes from the horseshoe shape of their tough shells. As a horseshoe crab grows, it gets too big for its shell. Finally the shell splits open. The crab crawls out. It walks away with a new shell on its back, leaving the old one behind.*

Lynne starts with the first paragraph and asks the students to look for the action words. "What is the first thing that the horseshoe crabs were doing?" She queries. When they find it, she copies a phrase from the sentence, starting with the verb. They proceed through the paragraph, looking for the action words, and Lynne writes the phrases on the board. When they get to the last sentence of the paragraph, Lynne notes that two actions are described there. "Look for the most specific one, or combine the actions into one, but try to be specific," she instructs them. Then she repeats the same process for the last paragraph. When they are finished, they have something like this:

Crawling up on ancient beaches,
Swimming through shallow water,
Hunting for clams, worms, and dead fish,
Shoveling almost anything into their mouths.

Growing too big for its shell,
The shell splits open,
Walking away with a new shell,
Leaving the old one behind.

Next, Lynne adds a new twist to the found poem they have created. "Remember when we talked about the use of effective repetition?" she asks them. She reminds them of the use of this technique in Carl Sandburg's "Buffalo Dusk" and Julie Brinckloe's *Fireflies!* or *What Does the Rain Play?* by Nancy White Carlstrom. Then Lynne adds two lines to the end of the first verse of poetry and repeats them again at the end of the second verse of poetry. Through discussion the students engage in whole-group revision. Because they have had the opportunity to try out many excellent writing strategies through the Your Turn lessons, they bring their expertise to each new writing experience. When these fourth graders are finished collaborating, the poem looks like this:

Crawling up on lonely beaches,
Swimming through shallow sapphire seas,
Hunting for clams, worms, and dead fish,
Shoveling almost anything into its mouth . . .
This ancient creature,
This horseshoe crab.

Growing too big for its house,
The shell splits open,

Walking away with a new home,
Leaving the old one behind . . .
This ancient creature,
This horseshoe crab.

There are many picture books, like *Owl Moon* and other books previously mentioned, that serve as wonderful sources for found poetry. *Twilight Comes Twice* by Ralph Fletcher, *Snow Comes to the Farm* by Nathaniel Tripp, and *Crab Moon* by Ruth Horowitz are also good choices. Working in a second-grade classroom, Rose used *Crab Moon* to teach the students how to work in small groups to create a found poem. After reading the book aloud, Rose copied just the text onto chart paper. She told the students she wanted to think like a poet and identify the words that sounded like music to her. She started to read aloud, sharing her thinking about the phrases she liked best and why she liked them. "'The weekend of the full moon,'" she read. "I get a very clear picture in my mind when I hear those words. I'm going to underline that phrase. 'Coming ashore for hundreds of millions of years,'" she continued. "I like the way the words work together to create a perfect rhythm. I think I'll underline that phrase." She continued reading through the book and modeling what she was thinking until she thought the students were ready to offer their own suggestions. Together they collaborated to identify phrases such as *under the sandy shuffle of the surf, little by little, barnacles and slipper shells—like jewels on a crown,* and *slowly and grandly.* Some students just liked the way the phrases felt in their mouths when they said them; some identified powerful images, or noticed the use of alliteration or simile. The next day Rose returned with the phrases listed on chart paper. She modeled how she could choose a few of her favorites, move them around, and then do some revising by adding, subtracting, or changing words. With some suggestions from the students, she created the following piece of found poetry from Ruth Horowitz's *Crab Moon*:

Horseshoe crabs
Under the sandy shuffle of the surf
Horseshoe crabs
Like restless cobblestones
Horseshoe crabs
Pausing and pulling their shells through the sand
Horseshoe crabs
Quiet as queens

Then it was the students' turn. Working in pairs or triads, they picked between four and six phrases they liked best and recorded them in their notebooks. She asked them to share their thinking with their partners about the sounds of the words and why they liked the particular phrase they chose. She wanted them to become more aware of how powerful the language of poetry can be. An alternative to writing the phrases in notebooks is to have the students write the phrases on sentence strips. This makes it easier to move the phrases around. Next, Rose instructed them to work together to create a found poem with the phrases chosen from *Crab Moon*. As in the modeling she had done, the students could move things around and revise as needed. She also allowed them to use one "wild card" phrase if they wanted to—an additional one from the list or an original thought.

Crab Moon
by Nissi and Ashley

On the night
of the full moon in June,
horseshoe crabs came ashore
under the sandy shuffle of the surf.
Slowly and grandly,
little by little,
horseshoe crabs
floated to shore.

Crab Moon
by Sean and Colin

Little by little,
The beam of the flashlight
shone on the crabs.
Crowding and pushing,
They looked like a cobblestone road.

Once you've modeled and created a found poem as a shared experience with a mentor text, and once the students have had a chance to try it on their own, you can urge them to use their independent reading books, newspapers, *Weekly Reader*s or *Time for Kids*, *Highlights for Children*, magazines written primarily for adult audiences such as *Country Living* or *Cooking Light*, catalogues, or other mentor texts to "find" poems. They can even use their own notebook entries. In the example below, Lynne used her own writer's notebook to model how found poetry can be created from one's own writing. She searched her notebook entries to find an appropriate source and read it to the class. Next she copied the entry onto chart paper and underlined the words and phrases she thought she could use to create her poem.

Birds come into the world singing. They sing when they're little chicks crowded in the nest. They sing at daybreak—almost as if they are welcoming the new day. I think they are so happy to see the sun rise in the eastern skies that they have to sing about it. It sounds like a church choir, singing in unison. The world is their cathedral. Every morning I look forward to that and eagerly await their morning hymn.

> Birds come into the world singing . . .
> Singing at daybreak,
> Welcoming the new day,
> Happy to see the sun rise.
> Singing in unison,
> Like a church choir,
> The world—their cathedral.
> Eagerly I await their morning hymn.
> Birds come into the world singing.

Found poetry is a wonderful tool to use across the curriculum with works of fiction and nonfiction. Students can even create a found poem from another poem. Found poetry uses the four communication areas—reading, writing, speaking, and listening—and helps provide new audiences for the students' writing. It helps students better understand the powerful images and rhythmic sounds created by the language of poetry. In "Frost in the Woods" from *A Writing Kind of Day: Poems for Young Poets* by Ralph Fletcher, the author describes a walk through the woods with his uncle, who stops to recite a short poem by Robert Frost that the experience has called to mind:

> *When he's done the words keep echoing*
> *in a quiet place that has opened inside me.*
> *I ask him: Did you write that poem?*
> *He says: I rented it from Robert Frost.*

Found poetry is an opportunity to let the words of the authors of our mentor texts echo inside the hearts and minds of our young writers. In a sense, they "rent" the words to create works of their own.

Using Scaffolds for Writing Poetry

Another way to get young writers to spill poetry from their hearts and minds onto the pages of their notebooks is to use the idea of a scaffold. Peter Elbow (1981) talks about using a rule to help writers get started. He cautions us not to begin with the most obvious rule for poetry, regular meter and a rhyme scheme, because it can limit our language choice and does not let us capture our true feelings. He suggests that other rules can be more effective, helping writers gather ideas. Elbow suggests beginning each line the same way, such as "I wish . . . ," "Now . . . ," or "Once . . ." He talks about using poems of address, beginning each line with the name of a person the writer cares deeply about. Then he talks about taking away the rule and listening to the way it sounds without the imposed rule or structure. We refer to these rules as scaffolds and have found them to be very effective in our work with writers of all ages, including adults. One example we use is a poem by Mary Ann Hoberman titled "Hello and Good-by." In this poem she goes back and forth in a seesaw manner, describing the things she sees from a swing. After reading this poem to students, you can suggest a variety of scaffolds we call "hello/good-bye" poems. Students can choose two topics to compare through a hello/good-bye structure. For example, you can start by comparing two seasons or seasonal activities—hello to spring and good-bye to winter, or hello to summer vacation and good-bye to school, or hello to baseball and good-bye to football. Lynne used the hello/good-bye scaffold in a shared writing format with a group of special education third, fourth, and fifth graders.

Hello to spring,
Good-bye to winter

Hello to cloudy skies full of rain,
Good-bye to cold, snowy days.

Hello to glorious, warm weather,
Good-bye to dark, snowy storms.

Hello to yellow tulips and daffodils,
Good-bye to icy streets and sidewalks.

Hello to shorts and shades,
Good-bye to heavy jackets and mittens.

Hello to riding lawn mowers,
Good-bye to snowplows and snow blowers.

Hello to soccer games and baseball,
Good-bye to NFL games and ice hockey.

Hello to short sleeves and sandals,
Good-bye to snow boots and winter hats.

Hello to swimming pools and beaches,
Good-bye to frozen lakes and rivers.

Hello to Mother's and Father's Day,
Good-bye to Halloween and Christmas.

Hello to spring,
Good-bye to winter.

Lynne used a couplet structure so that the students could form a relationship between the first and second lines by comparing things such as weather, clothes, sports, and holidays. You can vary this scaffold by beginning with the single line "Hello to _____" followed by the couplets, and ending with the single line "Good-bye to _____." You could also reverse the beginning and ending lines so that the poem starts with "Good-bye to _____" and ends with "Hello to _____." This scaffold, similar to the seesaw structure we discussed in Chapter 6, lends itself to use with a variety of topics, and writers of all ages can feel successful when they use it.

With a chance to try it out and reflection on how it can best be used, a scaffold can easily become part of your students' schema for poetry. As a matter of fact, students often carry around scaffolds they have tried out just like they carry around the multiplication tables in their heads. Once the scaffold has been practiced, it can be used again and again in many different contexts. After Lynne had used Charlotte Otten's poem "February" (see Your Turn Lesson 1 at the end of the chapter), several students chose to use the scaffold months later when they were composing rain poetry. They didn't ask permission, they didn't need a review, and they didn't need any direction from the teacher. They used the scaffold because it was as comfortable to use that structure as it is to walk around in a favorite pair of sneakers.

April
by Veronica

April turns everything drippy:
Drippy umbrellas, drippy cars, drippy roads.
Tiny birds get knocked to the ground,
smashing tiny ants in five drip-droppy raindrops.

Blue April
by Nichole

April turns everything blue:
blue raindrops, blue houses, blue streets.
Blue raindrops lock you inside
like a prisoner in a jail cell
drowning you in boredom.

Thunderstorms
by Sara

Thunderstorms turn everything loud:
loud skies, loud windows, loud sidewalks.
Loud rain thunders down onto rooftops
where children quietly stare
into the foggy loud darkness.

Poems of address are most effective when students write about someone they know very well. To stimulate your students' thinking before they begin writing, try reading books about grandmothers and grandfathers, mothers and dads, or brothers and sisters. *My Ol' Man* and *My Rotten Redheaded Older Brother* by Patricia Polacco, *Song and Dance Man* by Karen Ackerman, and *When Mama Comes Home Tonight* by Eileen Spinelli are good mentor texts for an activity such as this. Although not works of poetry, these books celebrate the unique qualities of these special people and can serve as models for our young writers of how they might think about the everyday words and actions of the person they are writing to. They can begin each line with the person's name and follow it by saying something to that person. For example:

Grandma, your arms wrap around me like a warm blanket
keeping me safe.
Grandma, your special blueberry pancakes are the best part
of Sunday mornings.

After writing four or more lines such as this, ask your students to reread the poem and decide if lines need to be moved, shortened, or omitted. Finally, have them read the poem without the scaffold—the name of the person—and see if they like it even better. Poems such as these make great gifts at any time of the year and have a specific, rather than general, target audience.

Following the scaffold of the Cree Indian naming poem "Quiet Until the Thaw" by Jacob Nibenegenasabe is another way that students can create poems about themselves or people they know and care about. They have great success here because again, they are writing about what they know. They are the experts. The poem has a simple scaffold that can easily be imitated. Rose models the use of this scaffold with a poem she wrote about her daughter.

"Does Not Taste Tomatoes"
Her name tells of how it is with her.
The truth is, she despises tomatoes.
Everyone learned not to give her a tomato,
or pasta with tomato sauce, or pizza, or ketchup,
once this was known about her.
As a child she would not wear red clothes, or write
with red pencils or pens.
She did not even like to ride in red cars.
But after a while she mellowed,
and would allow the occasional red ribbon in her hair.

You can use this scaffold in shared writing experiences with students by writing with them about their classroom teacher, principal, nurse, librarian, or gym teacher. Ask the students to first brainstorm a list of things that they think reveal a key interest, characteristic, or talent of the person. Together, choose one item from the list and use it as the focus of their collaborative poem. It is important to have this focus. Without it, students have no idea where to begin, what to include, and where to end. Once they choose a person for their poem, they begin with a similar process. When they have found their focus, they can brainstorm words and phrases that detail their ideas and help create images for their reader. Give students lots of opportunities to talk about their ideas and add to their thinking. The more planning they do, the better their first drafts will be. Remember, emotions are at the heart of poetry. If the writer is writing a poem and feeling nothing, then the reader will also feel nothing.

In the following example, Veronica, a fourth grader, focused on her dad as a sports fan. Through her words, we feel his intensity and enthusiasm for sports. By the end of the poem, with tongue in cheek, we understand how the rest of the family is feeling.

Fan

His name tells of how
it is with him. The truth is he has
March Madness all month long.
He never takes his eyes off the
screen,
hypnotized by the players,
screaming to the T.V.—
Go! Team! Go! Go!
Any sport . . . football, basketball, soccer,
lacrosse or skating . . .
He is on the list.
He buys tickets and goes screaming for his
team.
Coming for the weekend,
Can't get his attention
when the game is on.
Now it is April and
March is over, but . . .
BASEBALL SEASON is here.
Every year we have to suffer.
His name is Fan.
His name is Dad.

Whereas Veronica's voice is light and humorous, the following poem Monica wrote about her dad takes on a more tender and serious tone.

His Name

His name tells of how
it is with him.
The truth is
he loves music.
He has his own band
which takes a lot of his time.
But he always finds time to teach

me to play piano.
He doesn't get up and
leave when I make
a mistake;
instead he tells me what I did wrong.
He's always there at my recitals
with a smile on his face that seems to say . . .
"That's my daughter!" His name is Teacher.
His name is Dad.

Young writers can easily imitate the scaffold of Judith Viorst's "If I Were in Charge of the World." After reading the poem together in class, Lynne and her fifth-grade students discussed things such as humor, line breaks, use of punctuation, unexpected rhyme, and effective repetition. They read and reread the poem, getting a feel for the rhythm and the words created. In Sydney's example below, the poem follows Viorst's syntax more precisely. Taylor, on the other hand, chose to adapt the scaffold to suit her writing process.

If I Were in Charge of the World
by Sydney

If I were in charge of the world
There'd be five months of summer,
More time in the day,
And lots of fun places.

If I were in charge of the world
I'd cancel shots,
Shooting animals,
Boring dinners,
Cleaning your room,
And picture day.

If I were in charge of the world
You wouldn't have nervous,
You wouldn't have Brussels sprouts,
You wouldn't have to wear dresses,
Or "go do your homework" . . .
You wouldn't even have homework!

If I were in charge of the world
Tests would be a lot easier,
Vegetables would taste as good as fruits,
War would be over,
And a person who is sometimes in a rush,
And sometimes forgets to brush,
Could still be
In charge of the world!

If I Were in Charge of the World
by Taylor
If I were in charge of the world,
School would always be fun,
PSSA's wouldn't exist,
And no homework would come your way.

If I were in charge of the world,
Every boy on Earth would be on their best behavior ALL of the time,
Little brothers wouldn't bother you,
Or do anything you'd make them regret.

If I were in charge of the world,
Dads would let their 11-year-olds go to Fall Out Boy concerts,
No bad news would come your way,
No cavities would rot your teeth,
And a person who sometimes forgot to wake-up,
And sometimes forgot to shut-up,
Would still be allowed to be
In charge of the world.

Words as Scaffolds

Another way of thinking about an author's syntax is to study the way words are put together. One fall, as Rose was working in a first-grade class, she noticed Denise Fleming's book *Pumpkin Eye* on the read-aloud shelf. Because she knew the children had already met this book as readers, she wanted to reintroduce it to them as writers. Rose gathered the class together and asked them to listen as she read part of the book and to think about what they noticed about the words. She concentrated on the pages that used an adjective-noun structure:

swooping bats, hissing cats . . .
tattered rags, toothless hags, pointed tails, blood-red nails.

Although the young students could not quite use the proper terminology, they clearly communicated the "describing word-name of something" structure. They also noticed that the words rhymed. Rose led the class in brainstorming a list of nouns related to fall. She recorded these ideas on large chart paper, then had the class brainstorm some adjectives that might describe fall-related things. The list of adjectives was posted in front of the nouns:

spooky	pumpkins
chilly	jack-o'-lanterns
scary	bats
funny	ghosts
swirling	witches
flying	leaves
swooping	apples

She demonstrated how she could build phrases just like Denise Fleming did by using a word from each column. Although the original text used rhyming couplets, this was not a requirement for building the phrases. Rose just wanted the students to get the idea of how words could be linked to create the rhythm of a poem. She gave each student some small sentence strips and invited them to do the same. The session ended with a group share—the entire class stood in a circle and read their phrases in round-robin fashion. As expected, some phrases were repeated. Rose responded to the "Hey, that was my idea" complaint by returning to the book. She read it again and asked the students to listen for any repeated words. She was only about halfway through the book when Jacob's hand shot up. "I keep hearing some words over and over," he offered. "You know, like *trick-or-treat*." Indeed there was a repeated refrain:

Trick or treat—
pounding feet

So just like Denise Fleming did in her book, the students gave the class poem they were creating a repeated refrain. This was a powerful moment. The young writers in this class had not only created a class poem, but had also begun to internalize a way to structure words. Plus, they learned that using words over and over in a purposeful way can be effective. The strips were put in a pocket chart, and over the course of the next week were rearranged by the students in all sorts of combinations to create new poems.

Variations of word scaffolds such as this can be found in other books and used as mentor texts to teach young writers how to structure words. Karen Lotz uses a noun-verb/ing structure to create a poetic text in her book *Snowsong Whistling*:

> *Pumpkins plumping*
> *Bluegills jumping*
> *Apples thumping*
> *Sweet cider pumping*

Elizabeth Partridge also uses this structure in *Moon Glowing*:

> *Squirrel leaping,*
> *bat swooping,*
> *beaver gnawing.*
> *Bear, big bear, feasting well.*

This book follows the actions of a group of animals as they prepare for winter. When children borrow the syntax structures of authors, they begin to hear how words fit together to create images. They hear the sounds and rhythms that make writing come alive.

After studying a wide variety of scaffolds, students can begin to create their own. Lynne used "Come to the _____ . . . come!" to structure a poem about the Philippines and a poem about the stables. The first poem was written after doing a lot of reading; the second poem was created from personal experiences.

Islands of Beauty

Come to the Philippines . . . come!
Mountainous islands with volcanoes
Tops of coral reefs ringed by white beaches
Spectacular reefs meeting an azure sea
Come to the Philippines . . . come!
Rice terraces surrounding towns and villages
Beautiful, old Spanish churches
Tropical country with monsoon weather
Come to the Philippines . . . come!

Palms, rattan, vines, and ferns
Tiny striped clown fish flitting through the water
Dolphins, whales, sharks, and barracuda
Come to the Philippines . . . come!

My Special Place

Come to the stables . . . come!
Sweet-smelling alfalfa hay stacked in lofts
Crisp, pale wheat straw fluffed in box stalls
Oats, cracked corn, and sweet feed in bins.
Come to the stables . . . come!
Thoroughbreds snorting and pawing in pastures
Ponies rolling in warm, squishy mud
Riders going 'round and 'round the sandy rings
Come to the stables . . . come!
Bridles, saddles, halters, and lead shanks
Tack room smelling of Lexol and saddle soap
Tack trunks filled with brushes and blankets
Come to the stables . . . come!

After modeling with her poems, Lynne asked the students to list favorite places and events in their writer's notebooks. They shared these lists in small groups before making a big list on the board. As a class, they used shared writing to create a poem about the playground. Lynne took the opportunity to point out some of the craft techniques that were used, such as effective repetition and onomatopoeia. (See Figure 7.1.)

When the students were ready to write on their own, Lynne suggested they begin with the scaffold and repeat it as many times as they thought was necessary. She also pointed out certain lines of her models that were simply lists of things: plants, fish, objects found in tack rooms. She told them that listing could be effective if it was not overdone. Brandon asked if he was allowed to use rhyme. "Of course," Lynne replied, "so long as you concentrate on your ideas and feelings more than the rhyming." That was the information Brandon needed to make this scaffold work for him.

Come to the seashore . . . come!!
Come to the seashore where the ocean rises,
Come to the seashore where there are many cool surprises.
Come to the seashore . . . come!!

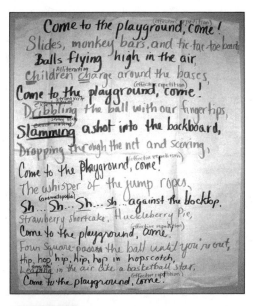

Come to the seashore where dolphins flip in the air,
Come to the seashore where I bet you will stare.
Come to the seashore . . . come!!
Come to the seashore where you can almost taste the briny air,
Come to the seashore where the wind will swipe your hair.
Come to the seashore . . . come!!
Come to the seashore where you say bye to the shore
And bye to the dolphins who flip in the air,
"See you next summer . . . Take care, take care."

Peter also wrote about the seashore. He didn't need Lynne's permission to change her scaffold, he just did it. The class loved hearing the unexpected rhythm and use of personification at the end of the poem. They also noticed that his poem showed the passing of time of a day at the beach.

Come to the beaches . . . come!
Endless views of water, restless and wild.
Waves come from far to flop on the beach.
Sand castles are built, containing crabs and shells.
Going into the water, shells brush against your feet.
Come to the beaches . . . come!
You feel the waves crashing over your head.

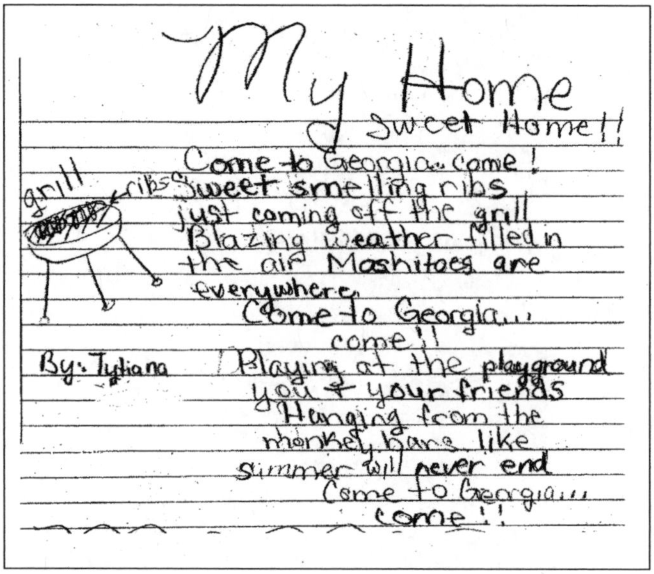

FIGURE 7.2 Tytiana's poem uses the "Come to the..." scaffold.

The water is cooling, so you lie and dry in the sun.
The sand is spanning everywhere.
Night crawls in.

Tytiana's poem provides us with tiny snapshots of the home she left behind. Her title "My Home Sweet Home" immediately tells the reader how she feels about Georgia. (See Figure 7.2.)

Building Scaffolds with Students

One fourth-grade class was immersed in a unit of study about poetry. They had been reading the works of Byrd Baylor to stimulate their thinking about nature. On a gray, rainy April morning, Lynne decided to read "April Rain Song" by Langston Hughes (from his book *The Dream Keeper and Other Poems*) to get students thinking about how they feel about the rain.

Lynne asked the students to write about rain in their writer's notebooks. "How do you feel about the rain? Can you explain what it is that makes you feel that way?" After a few minutes, she asked the students to talk about their feelings. Lynne returned to a mentor text, *What Does the Rain Play?* by Nancy White Carlstrom, to stimulate ideas for writing poems. The book follows the main character through a stormy day. Jon, who loves the rain, splashes in puddles, paints a picture of the rain falling down, and writes his name on the steamy window. Lynne had used this text in previous Your Turn lessons to talk about effective repetition and the use of hyphenated adjectives to describe a person, place, thing, or event in an unusual way. She decided to reread the text so she could create a mood for writing about the rain. She knew that the students' imaginations would be piqued if they could also linger on the beautiful paintings. Carlstrom uses the title of her book as a question that is repeated through-out the text and answers it with onomatopoeia to mimic the sounds of rain. The fourth graders, familiar with another book by Carlstrom, *What Does the Sky Say?*, started to talk about the different kinds of questions the rain might ask. Lynne recorded their words on chart paper:

What does the rain _____?

think	smell	sigh	write	sketch
do	taste	sing	dream	paint
spell	feel	speak	imagine	hiss
teach	cry	enjoy	build	love
share	learn	hoard	see	whisper
whine	save	play	celebrate	roar
hear	grow	say	hide	scream
chill	warm	wish	make	whimper
imagine	create	complain about	illuminate	steal
melt	ponder	spin	shelter	leave
save	cure	sing	protect	call
draw	plunk	hum	fear	pray
read	cause	eat	give	dance

Lynne reread the picture book one more time. "Today in writing workshop, you might consider writing about the rain. After listening to Carlstrom's words, what kind of scaffold could you use to create your poem?"

Chelsea offered her suggestion. "We could pick one verb from the chart and use it three or four times in the question. Then we could come up with different answers."

Lynne nodded. "That's effective repetition. Exactly what Carlstrom used to create her text. Are there any other ideas?" Jack thought he might choose a different verb to place in the question each time and then answer the questions. Michael thought he wanted to work on sounds of rain to answer questions about how the rain would speak— in a whimper, a whine, a shout, a hiss, and a cry. Shelby wanted to know if the poem could rhyme. "Of course," Lynne responded. "But don't let the rhyme control your poem. It's the feeling that you have about rain—that's what should come through. Rhyme is great if it doesn't get in the way of expressing your true feelings and thoughts." Jessica thought she wanted to create a book of questions about rain with watercolor illustrations like another book they had talked about, called *Did You Hear Wind Sing Your Name?* by Sandra De Coteau Orie. "These are all good ideas," Lynne said. Sometimes you need to draw a quick sketch and write down words and phrases that make you think of rain. Or you could start with your writer's notebook entry about rain. I've also brought some other books about rain for you to read. Let's write for the rest of the week and be ready to share our pieces on Friday. Remember, you can use scaffolds you've tried out for other poems, reports, or stories again here for your rain poetry. Change the scaffold in a way that makes it work for you. Or use the scaffold to create the poem, and then take it away. Sometimes the poem stands up by itself without the scaffold. Read your poems aloud many times and let your ear tell you which way it sounds best. Remember, poems are written to be read aloud."

One rainy Friday morning, the students were ready to share their drafts. They had used peer and self conferences to do some revising and editing. Although they weren't ready to publish, they were ready to share in whole group. They gathered on the rug and in comfy chairs. Lynne opened the windows and asked everyone to get very quiet. "Listen to the sound of the rain as I read this poem." She shared "Meditation in the Rain" by Federico Garcia Lorca from *Seasons*, a book of illustrations by Warabe Aska with poems selected by Alberto Manguel. "Who would like to share?" Lynne whispered, and a host of hands waved in the air. Chelsea shared her poem "What Does the Rain Sing?"

What does the rain sing?
The rain sings
a powerful song
that will shock you
like petrifying lightning.

What does the rain sing?
The rain sings
a steady song
that will guide you
through a pleasant day
with wonderful events.

What does the rain sing?
The rain sings
a soft, silent song
that will cradle you to sleep
like a sweet, sweet lullaby.
That's what the rain sings.

Madeline chose to use a question to frame her poem as well, but she added the onomatopoeia similar to the way Carlstrom used sounds of rain throughout her book. Her thinking was influenced by *Outside, Inside* by Carolyn Crimi and *Listen to the Rain* by Bill Martin, Jr., and John Archambault, two of the mentor texts Lynne made available to the students to explore.

What does the rain put away?

Tip-tap, drip-drop, pitter-patter.
That is the alarm for animals,
telling them it's going to rain.
What does the rain put away?
Dewy bunnies that hop across wet grass,
rain-dropped tips of blades

Clip-clap, clip-clap, clip-clap.
What does the rain put away?
Puffed squirrels with flattened tails
crawl up the soggy bark of tree
to get inside their home.

Patter-patter, pitter-pitter.
What does the rain put away?
The slippery-slick birds
glide through drip-down leaves
to get to their soft nests
hidden high in the branches.

Pitter-patter, drip-drop, tip-tap.
The rain has stopped
and the sun puts everything back
that the rain put away.

Sarah imitates the same mentor text but decides to frame her poem with three different questions. She finds a way to connect the questions in the conclusion of her poem:

"What Does the Rain . . . ?"

What does the rain grasp?
The rain grasps the little children,
pulls them outside and then . . .
SPLISH! SPLAT! Muddy children!
It's not the rain's fault.
What does the rain find?
The rain finds love.
Love that Earth needs to thrive forever?
What does the rain insist on?
Of course the rain insists on . . .
RAINING!
Everything would shrivel and die if it didn't.
So let the rain grasp the children,
Find the love,
And insist on raining!
It's for Earth . . .

Chelsea decided to take a second try at rain poetry. This time she let *Listen to the Rain* speak to her as a mentor text. You can see she used several strategies, including effective repetition, onomatopoeia, and the scaffold of the mentor text—the sequence of a rainstorm—to build her poem.

Listen

Drip-drop, drip-drop, drip-drop,
Listen . . .
the pitter patter of invisible dancers on our rooftops.
Listen . . .
the splash of mucky water as you hop into a puddle, then hop
back out like popcorn.
Listen . . .
the sad sky is crankily crying.
Listen . . .
the earth's delightful shower wipes away our fears.
Listen . . .
a watering can sprinkling the earth with a downpour of wetness.
Listen . . .
the precipitation slowly coming to an end.
Listen to the silence.
Listen to the rain.
Drip-drop, drip-drop.

Jacob created a completely different scaffold for his poem, but the influence of mentor texts is still apparent. In fact, he allowed the striking illustrations of Henri Sorensen in *What Does the Rain Play?* to help him create his images.

Split, splash, splish,
Rain's songs tuck the earth
with a silent splash.
Split, splash, splish.
Faster and faster
Then stops with a sudden halt.
All in yellow
a small boy comes trotting
like Paul Revere's horse
through murky, mucky mud.
In his mind he wonders,
"What will the rain sing next?"
No sooner does he ask
when the rain breaks out
in heavy metal rock.
Tip tip patter patter
tip tip patter patter
tip tip pat

tip tip patter patter
tip tip pat.
What does the rain sing?
What do these tips and taps
and pitters and patters mean?
Tip tip
        patter patter
               tip
                  tip
                    pat.
The mystery goes on . . .

Students can imitate the scaffolds they create and that you create as a teacher once they've had lots of practice. Lynne shared her poem about her grandfather's chair to demonstrate how she relied on a repeating line to get her thoughts down and organize them. She also showed them how she changed the structure to bring it to a close. (See Figure 7.3.)

Grandfather's Chair
   By Lynne R. Dorfman

Old, old chair
Mustard yellow cowhide
Sturdy and broad,
Arm rests worn burgundy
Where strong arms and hands
Once rested.
Cracked leather seat cushion
Gold metal tacks to hold the leather
Four strong, lion-clawed legs
To hold up its massive frame.

Old, old chair
Smelling of leather
Conjuring up faint whiffs of
Life Boy soap, Listerine
And Old Spice After Shave.
Warm, comfortable, and
Large enough to hold
A grandpa and his grandchild.

Old, old chair
Moved around a lot
Allentown to Emmaus
Emmaus to Coopersburg
Coopersburg to Quakertown
Then on to Telford
From Telford to Philadelphia
And finally to Dresher.

Old, old chair
A place to watch t.v. or read the paper
Snuggling in to listen to 45 records
Spinning out coal-mining songs
"I owe my soul to the company store…"
Or simple love songs -
"I give to you and you give to me,
True love, true love…"

Sometimes a lively polka
And then the chair would sit empty.
Grandpa would whirl/twirl us
Round and round and round
While we balanced on his stocking feet,
Laughing and throwing our heads back…
We didn't own a care in the world.

Old, old chair
A place to catch your breath
After the dancing's done
A place to sink down into comfort
Or nestle in a familiar lap
Seat cushion now cracked and split
Spilling stuffing outward
Great creases running like lifelines
Streaks of summer lightning

Lonely, old chair
Knows something's different
Something's missing
Even when it's filled
It's still empty
Poor, old chair
Everyone wrinkles a nose
Cries of "Throw it out!"
"Get rid of it!"
"Stop being so sentimental…
It's just a chair."

They call it junk
They call it trash
They call it an eyesore
They call it unattractive.
They don't see what I see…
A grand, old chair
Grandfather's chair
Mustard yellow cowhide
Sturdy and broad…

Comfortable
Familiar
Warmed with memories
Family treasure
Miss that old chair
Everyday

FIGURE 7.3 Lynne's sample poem "Grandfather's Chair."

Old, Old Baby Blanket
By Searra

Old, old baby blanket
Grassy green, mustard yellow silk
Soft and warm
Framed in snowflake white
Hat-wearing ducks
Swim across its mossy pond.

Old, old baby blanket
Smelling of childhood
Cuddly as a teddy bear
Makes me feel safe
Makes me feel loved
Covering my bed

Old, old baby blanket
Takes away bad dreams
Brings good dreams
Moved around a lot
Hospital to Detroit, Michigan
Detroit, Michigan to Reading
Reading to West Chester
West Chester to Hatboro
Finally on my bed

Old, old baby blanket
Something to keep me warm
Something to keep me occupied when I'm alone
Cozy
Familiar
Walked-all-over-the-world traveler
Love that old baby blanket every day.

FIGURE 7.4 Searra's poem "Old, Old Baby Blanket."

She was surprised when one of her fifth graders came to her with a poem modeled after Lynne's poem. Compare Lynne's poem "Grandfather's Chair" with Searra's poem "Old, Old Baby Blanket." (See Figure 7.4.)

Exploring Color Through the Senses

Mary O'Neill takes us into the world of color in her book of poems *Hailstones and Halibut Bones*. In this book she describes colors not only by the way they look but through all the other senses and feelings they bring to mind. Other books such as *My Many Colored Days* by Dr. Seuss, *Color Me a Rhyme* by Jane Yolen, and *My World of Color* by Margaret Wise Brown also stimulate connections to colors and can be used to support the writing of color poems. These mentor texts can help writers begin to think about colors in new ways. We can then provide them with a scaffold for creating color poems that involves all of the senses.

When we use *Hailstones and Halibut Bones* with our classes, we begin by telling the students that we might think about colors not only through what we see, but through the smells, sounds, tastes, and feelings we connect with them. We tell them that this is just what Mary O'Neill did in her book of color poems. As we prepare to read aloud, we divide the class into groups or sections. We instruct each section to listen for the connections to a particular sense as we read. For example, one section might listen for the way O'Neill describes the smells of the color, and another might listen for the feelings that the color brings to mind. Giving students a specific purpose for listening helps them focus their attention on the read-aloud. After several poems are read and the responses are shared orally, the next step is to brainstorm a list of colors. It is always interesting to note how even the youngest writers can think beyond the rainbow. They often come up with responses such as aquamarine, chartreuse, or turquoise. The list is recorded on the board or on chart paper and placed in front of a list of phrases that recalls each of the five senses:

> looks like . . .
> sounds like . . .
> smells like . . .
> tastes like . . .
> feels like . . .

Together, we choose a color and brainstorm specific things associated with it. For example, the color yellow might get responses such as the sun, honeysuckle, lemons, bumblebees, a dog's fur, canaries, or a school bus. We also encourage students to connect with feelings, so responses to yellow might also include warm or bright or cheery.

Next, we use a shared writing format to begin composing a class poem using the scaffold. The students are instructed to name the color, pick a sense, and complete the thought. Through questioning we assist students in extending their thinking to create a more complete image. In one first-grade class Danny volunteered the following response for yellow: "Yellow looks like a sunflower."

"Close your eyes and think about the sunflower," Rose said. "Where is it? What part is yellow?"

"We have giant sunflowers with big yellow petals in our garden at home," Danny answered. "They grow so big they almost touch the sky."

With a little more probing and some help from the class, the line became, "Yellow looks like the petals of giant sunflowers in my garden, reaching for the sky." In our classes, the shared experience continues as ideas are extended, recorded, and revised. Finally, students use the scaffold to compose individual poems in their notebooks. Madeline, a first grader, composed the following:

Pink

Pink feels like soft fur from a rabbit in the woods.
Pink looks like a tulip that blossoms in the spring
or the pink Valentine cards you get in the mail.
Pink sounds like quiet ballroom dancing.
Pink smells like beautiful flowers.

There are many variations to this scaffold. Students can be given the option of writing about one color with all of the senses as in the example, sticking with one color and one sense, or describing many colors with one sense. Older students may veer away from the scaffold and be less structured in their thinking of how colors relate to senses. Consider this collaborative poem from a group of third-grade students:

What Is Purple?

Purple is a violet singing a sweet, sleepy lullabye.
It is the taste of grape jelly spread on warm wheat toast.
The purple smell is the night sky on April Fool's Day.
Medicine trickling down your throat is a purple feeling.
Purple explodes in your mouth like Fourth of July
fireworks.
The full moon on a misty May night has a purple glow.
Purple is a forgetful two-year-old with a mind of his own.
It is the shy feeling that hides deep inside your heart.

With lots of input and options we have found that all students can be successful writing poems about color. By guiding them in reflecting about how they created the images and why they were so effective, writers begin to internalize the language of description that eventually spills over into all their writing. You will find a Your Turn lesson with an additional color poem scaffold at the end of this chapter.

A Place for Poetry in Every Classroom

We believe that all students can be successful with poetry—that poetry levels the playing field. Even your most reluctant or challenged writers can find their voice through their poems. Because poems are often much shorter than essays and narratives, they are perfect for concentrating on revision strategies, especially emphasizing the importance of word choice. They offer a wealth of scaffolds, ranging from the very simple to the more complex, and provide students with both choice and challenge. Poetry as a genre serves us well when we begin with a feeling—a strong emotion about a person, place, object, or event. Then we find the words that carry our emotions, creating vivid images to touch our readers' hearts.

In the summer of 2006, Gloria Gittelman, a graduate student in our Writing and Children's Literature course offered by the Pennsylvania Writing and Literature Project at West Chester University, found her voice through the scaffold of Gerald Stern's "I Could Live Like That":

> I could live like that,
>> showing samples of great writing
>> encouraging more focused revision
>> sharing golden tidbits of wondrous phrasing
>> helping students to grow.
>
> I could pull that one book out
>> and show the places where magic happens
>> and discover what makes it work
>> and grow alongside my students.
>
> I could love the world of writing
>> and fill my notebook with seeds of ideas
>> and play with words till they sound just right
>> and create memorable language for others to use—
>
>> a real writing teacher.

Creating a Color Poem

Hook: Read excerpts from *Hailstones and Halibut Bones* by Mary O'Neill to get students thinking about color in terms of the different senses. Dr. Seuss's *My Many Colored Days* can help students associate colors with feelings. Then return to *January Rides the Wind* by Charlotte F. Otten and read "February."

Purpose: Write the poem "February" on chart paper or have it on an overhead so that everyone can see it.

> *Writers, let's take a look at how Charlotte Otten uses color in her poem "February."* (Students should quickly realize that *gray* is repeated several times and is used to describe things that were, or appeared to be, that particular color.) *Now let's look at the way Charlotte Otten put the words together and see if we can find the scaffold.* (Lead students to identify the scaffold in the poem.)

> (thing, feeling, holiday, etc.) *turns everything to*   (color) *:*
> *Color word describes three things.*
> *Concluding sentence that begins with the color.*

> *Today I will show you how to use the scaffold from "February" to write your own poems.*

Brainstorm: Ask the class to brainstorm a list of colors. Pick some of the colors and have the class brainstorm things that could be that color. Encourage them to think about all the different senses as well as emotions. (See the books listed above for suggestions.) Examples:

> White—a blizzard, a pillow fight, a blinding light, a wedding, frosty air
> Black—a moonless night, Halloween cats, a bad mood, a loud boom
> Green—spring, St. Patrick's Day, an envious feeling, a grasshopper, April, a fresh breeze

Model: Return to the list of brainstormed ideas and use the scaffold to create a poem in front of your students. Think aloud as you compose so that students see how to go about choosing or changing words. Here is a poem from Rose's notebook:

> *A blizzard turns everything to white:*
> *white trees, white skies, white rooftops.*
> *White-tailed deer step gingerly,*
> *searching for a drink*
> *on white frozen lakes.*

Shared/Guided Writing: Create a poem as a whole-class shared activity, or invite students to work with partners to try out the scaffold. Take the opportunity to model the revision process as the class works together during shared writing.

Independent Writing: Invite students to continue to brainstorm ideas for other colors and to create their own poems using the scaffold.

Reflection: After sharing, ask students to reflect on how the scaffold helped them organize their thoughts. Here are some questions you might ask:

> *How did the scaffold help you use repetition effectively?*
>
> *Why was it effective?*
>
> *Could you envision using the structure of the first sentence from the scaffold as the lead in a piece of prose?*

2

Using the Endless Step Pantoum for Found Poetry

There are many ways poets choose to organize their words. Many times poems and song lyrics use effective repetition to create a sense of rhythm, to emphasize important words as an echo effect, and to place pictures firmly in the minds of the readers. Remember, a strategy is best modeled and practiced with a short text that is easily decodable for most or all of your students.

Hook: A picture book can be used. You may have already used *Owl Moon* (Yolen), *Snow Comes to the Farm* (Tripp), *The Whales' Song* (Sheldon), or *The Seashore Book* (Zolotow) for found poetry. Mentor texts work well here because students are already familiar with the content and probably can easily identify with the teacher's choice of powerful phrases and/or sentences and can understand the choice for a meaningful order.

Purpose: *As we have been discussing, found poetry is a wonderful way to create poems from books, newspapers, magazine articles, and even writer's notebook entries. One important strategy to help us organize our thoughts in poetry and create a rhythm without a particular rhyme scheme or meter is the use of effective repetition. Today we are going to write some poetry using a scaffold called "The Endless Step Pantoum." We can use this strategy when we create an introduction or summary about famous people or a historical event or as a way of describing a place or a person. So this scaffold is very helpful in writing nonfiction poetry. The scaffold is created by the way the lines are repeated, so it is not one that we can remove or "take out" after the poem has been written. The scaffold holds the piece together.*

Brainstorm: Ask students to turn and talk with a partner or small group about the found poetry they have written and their sources for the found poetry. Students should look through their writing folders or portfolios and their writer's notebooks. In whole group, share some of their thinking.

Model: The paragraph below is intended as a model for upper elementary and middle school children.

I am going to use They Lived With the Dinosaurs *by Russell Freedman and his selection about dragonflies to write a found poem using the endless step pantoum. I am giving each of you a copy of Freedman's book and the structure of the pantoum so you can follow my thinking as I write a poem. The first thing I need to do is read this section and pick out all the words and phrases that speak to me. I am going to list them on this chart paper.*

> giants with outstretched wings
> darting and swooping
> like a helicopter ready to land
> fast insects
> fragile beauties
> dining in midair
> surviving all these years
> expert fliers
> pausing in midair
> changing course quickly
> unable to fold their wings

Now I'm going to write the pantoum. Here is the scaffold for this kind of poem. (Distribute a handout that looks like the one included below and review with the students so they can see what lines will be repeated and where.) *I have to think about where I'm going to place the words so the poem makes sense and flows. I also see that the first line and third line are repeated at the end of the structure, so I should choose them carefully.* (Now write on the board or on chart paper. Try it out before you model in front of your students if that will help you feel more comfortable.)

Line 1 _____
Line 2 _____
Line 3 _____
Line 4 _____

Line 5 _____ (repeats Line 2)
Line 6 _____
Line 7 _____ (repeats Line 4)
Line 8 _____

Line 9 _____ (repeats Line 6)
Line 10 _____
Line 11 _____ (repeats Line 8)
Line 12 _____

Line 13 _____ (repeats Line 10)
Line 14 _____ (repeats Line 3 or 1)
Line 15 _____ (repeats Line 12)
Line 16 _____ (repeats Line 1 or 3)

Example:

> *Giants with outstretched wings.*
> *Fragile beauties,*
> *Surviving all these years.*
> *Expert fliers . . . dragonflies.*
>
> *Fragile beauties*
> *Changing course quickly*
> *Expert fliers . . . dragonflies,*
> *Darting and swooping.*
>
> *Changing course quickly,*
> *Pausing in midair.*
> *Darting and swooping,*
> *Helicopter insects.*
>
> *Pausing in midair,*
> *Giants with outstretched wings.*
> *Helicopter insects,*
> *Surviving all these years.*

As you can see, the phrases came from the chart where I did the brainstorming. Sometimes I just placed the phrases where I thought they would most logically go, and other times I tried to combine thoughts as I did with helicopter insects. *You can see that* fragile beauties *cannot be found in the running text, but the photograph helped me come up with that idea.*

Shared/Guided Writing: Now the students are ready to try it out. You can take down the chart papers and use the selection on dragonflies one more time, or you could ask the students to choose another creature from the Freedman book and start with reading silently and aloud, then finding meaningful words, phrases, and sentences that sound like poetry or are very descriptive. Encourage students to examine photos or illustrations as well and to combine thoughts in interesting ways. Try out certain lines, and let the students revise by moving, removing, adding, and substituting until they are satisfied with the results. Then try another shared experience or let them try it out on their own or with a partner. Students should be told to cite the source at the bottom of their drafts and include it in their final publication of pantoum poetry. Older children can use the pantoum to explore current events with newspapers and magazine articles.

Independent Writing: Students can certainly use another selection from Freedman's book. There are great descriptions of cockroaches, sharks, starfish, horseshoe crabs, crocodiles, and more. Or students can revisit a draft, a notebook entry, or a finished portfolio piece. Return to other mentor texts so students can comfortably begin here on their own. It is always a good idea to have young writers share their writing with a partner, a small response group, or in the general sharing session of writing workshop.

Reflection: Students can turn and talk with a partner about their poems.

What revision strategies did you use?

Where did you have to move lines? Why did you do that?

How did the brainstorming of key phrases, words, and sentences help you write?

Did you find a different way to begin?

How can you use "effective repetition" in other writing you do?

Where would you use this strategy, the endless step pantoum, to organize your thoughts again?

Creating Haiku With Personification

There are many ways in which authors use personification to make their writing come alive and add their voice or the voice of someone or something else. As we discuss in this chapter, sometimes poets use a particular form or scaffold to create a poem. For young writers, understanding haiku as a form of poetry may help them use personification to write about nature and their feelings; however, it is important to remember not to emphasize too many poems that require a specific form such as limerick, cinquain, tanka, sonnet, or ballad. Often, introducing one of them during the course of a year is enough! Haiku includes what the poet is thinking or feeling about an action, change, or event in nature—sometimes a question or a wish for the future. Haiku examines a very small moment and tries to capture an experience in a fresh, intuitive way. Nature's flora and fauna, its weather, its changing seasons, night and day all provide our writers with enough choice for them to begin to craft their own haiku.

Hook: Choose some of the mentor texts you have been using in the classroom and examine several haiku closely with the students. Look for books that have haiku with personification, if that is what you are going to teach, or books where haiku appeal to the senses. Share *One Leaf Rides the Wind* by Celeste Davidson Mannis. Copy one or two examples on chart paper and display them.

Options: *The Earth We Swing On* by Raymond Roseliep (does not rely on the five-seven-five syllable count). Another good source is *Cricket Never Does: A Collection of Haiku and Tanka* by Myra Cohn Livingston.

Purpose: *As we have been discussing, personification can be an important part of any piece of writing. As we can see from the poems we talked about from our read-aloud, haiku poets often use personification, sometimes talking to waves, birds, trees, and oceans as if they could talk back—as if they have feelings like we do. Today I will show you how you can write that kind of haiku, that takes ordinary things and talks about them in extraordinary ways. That's what writers do. Our poems will satisfy our readers by appealing to the senses and helping us see things that are not people behave, feel, and think like people.*

Brainstorm: Ask the students to use their writer's notebooks to brainstorm a list of things that have to do with nature. You might take them on a nature walk with their notebooks if it is appropriate. Remind them to think of the seasons, day and night times, and their own backyards and familiar parks. Have them turn and share with a partner or small group, then report in whole group. Record their thinking on chart paper or the blackboard. If your students are giving you nonspecific words such as *animals*, *birds*, and *flowers*, remind them to be specific and talk about deer, sparrows, and daisies instead.

Model: Take one idea from the board and compose a poem. Make use of the senses and personification, if that is the skill you want them to imitate and practice. Here are some of Lynne's examples that use her students' suggestions of wind, Mother Nature, and bluejays:

> Naughty Wind! You dare
> to turn umbrellas inside
> out and lift our skirts!

> Mother Nature sews
> shiny jewels into the
> midnight summer sky.

> Bluejay loudly scolds
> feasting squirrels that gather
> at his bird feeder.

Shared/Guided Writing: Ask students to choose a topic from the board. After a topic has been chosen, get the students to sketch a scene. Have them turn and talk with a partner. What is happening in their scenes? Call on some students to explain their ideas. Start to create the haiku line by line or as an entire thought. For the first draft, don't worry about the five-seven-five syllable count—worry about the content instead. Next, work on word choice. Replace general words with specific words. Have we personified an animal or inanimate object such as the moon? If not, how could we do this? Finally, play with the word choice and the number of words on each line until you achieve the syllable count. Don't sacrifice voice, word choice, and content for form. Repeat this process three or more times before releasing them to partner or small-group work. (Copy the haiku on chart paper and display it for future reference.) After students work with a partner or small group to create haiku, invite some groups of students to offer their pieces for group revision, or hold a guided conversation in front of the group.

Independent Writing: This part will probably take place the next day. Refer to the poems created during guided writing. First, ask students to continue revisions of their haiku from guided practice. Students may also wish to start new pieces and concentrate on using personification and appeal to the senses to create effective haiku.

Reflection: After students have the opportunity to revise or write, ask them to share in whole group or small group. The following questions can help guide their thinking:

How did your use of personification change the poem?

How is it satisfying to the reader?

Does your poem make us continue to wonder about something?

Would a different subject, season, or time of day work better?

What kinds of things should you think about as you write haiku?

When could you use haiku again?

When or where could you use personification again?

CHAPTER 8

Choice, Voice, and
All That Jazz

Writing teachers can do several things to help children revitalize
the language in their writing. First, we need to attune the
ears of young writers to magical language wherever they hear it—
in books, poems, the writing of their peers, talk.

–Ralph Fletcher, *What a Writer Needs*

For some people, listening to a melancholy aria from an opera can make their heart soar. For others, it's the toe-tapping, knee-slapping rhythms of a country song, or the soulful strains of a saxophone singing the blues. Others are drawn to an electric guitar screaming the sounds of chaotic melodies. That's what style is all about—it's the atmosphere that's created by the artist that makes you want more, that delights your senses and carries you to a new heightened awareness of everything around you. In music, style is expressed in the arrangement of the notes. In writing, it's in the words. Style is all about the words an author chooses to carry his ideas. It's about the way he chooses to combine them, repeat them, eliminate them, use them to establish a point of view or stance, or a certain tone or mood. Style is choice, voice, and all that jazz!

In our work with teachers of kindergarten and grade one students, the question of style always comes up. Can we teach our earliest writers what style is? Is this even appropriate while they are still learning about letters and sounds and aren't writing much more than a sentence or two, maybe even just a few words? Style is an integral part of writing, so it is hard not to keep the "whole" in mind as we work with our students, even our youngest students, on a specific writing trait such as content or conventions. Without style, writing is dull and lifeless. There is nothing to delight the senses or interest the reader. If we want our students to grow into confident and capable writers, we must teach all aspects of writing from the start. Because style is all about word choice, even the youngest writers can use their expanding vocabularies to write with specificity and interest. The attention to precise language helps them learn at an early age to make every word count. Through modeling and reflection we can show them that adding color words, or number words, or size words adds detail to their writing and makes it more interesting to the reader.

In a kindergarten class one spring morning, Rose returned to a mentor text, *Bunny Cakes* by Rosemary Wells, to demonstrate the importance of using specific words as adjectives or as proper nouns. After rereading the first few pages of the book, Rose pointed out to the students how the author didn't just say that Max and Ruby each made Grandma a birthday cake, but that one was an "earthworm" birthday cake, and the other was an "angel surprise" cake with "raspberry-fluff" icing. She also pointed out that Max didn't want just any kind of candy for his cake, but rather a specific kind of candy, Red-Hot Marshmallow Squirters. "How do those words help the writing?" Rose asked the students.

"They tell you exactly what it was," Jack answered.

"It helps you get a better picture in your head," Alexis added.

"Yes," Rose explained, "Rosemary Wells used specific words, sometimes names of things, to make her writing clear and more interesting. Today I will show you how you can do that with your writing, too."

Rose understood that word choice begins with an awareness of words—making them a part of writers' speaking and listening vocabularies so that they eventually spill over into their writing vocabulary. To heighten this awareness with the students, she asked them all to stand in a circle. "Max wanted Red-Hot Marshmallow Squirters for his cake," Rose explained. "Think about a different kind of candy you might want if you were making that cake. Then we'll all go around the circle and share our thinking. Remember to be specific." One by one the students shared such things as M&M's, Hershey Kisses, Twizzlers, and Lifesavers. Children who couldn't think of something were encouraged to listen to others' responses and borrow a suggestion, which ensured 100 percent student participation. Rose next conducted the same activity with other categories. The students were asked to share such things as specific kinds of dogs, names of stores, boys' names, and girls' names. After modeling with her own writing, Rose asked the students to add the name of something in the writing they did that day. Some of the students were able to apply the strategy immediately. For others, it came later as awareness of words became an integral part of the classroom experience—as students began pointing out names and other specific words in texts used for read-alouds and shared reading, as well as in their conversations. (See Figure 8.1.)

Making Use of Special Vocabularies

As an awareness of words grows, students develop special vocabularies that belong to topics in their writing territories. Many vocabularies revolve around sports such as basketball, football, and gymnastics. It is important that teachers help students become aware of the vocabularies that they possess, and that they let students know they don't necessarily need to know how to spell all the words in their vocabularies before using them in their writing. Students should never abandon a perfect word because they are afraid they will misspell it. (At the same time, we are often amazed at the words students can spell when those words help them write about their keen interests. Take, for example, the first grader who

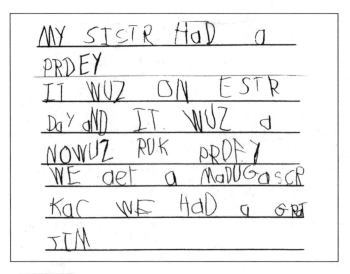

FIGURE 8.1 Jack, kindergarten: "My sister had a party. It was on Easter Day and it was a Noah's Ark party. We ate a Madagascar cake. We had a great time."

can spell *tyrannosaurus rex* because he is passionate about dinosaurs.)

We need to point out the special vocabulary that authors use to achieve specificity and help the reader form mental images. In *Up North at the Cabin*, Marsha Wilson Chall uses the vocabulary of a fisherman with words such as *angler, spinners, leeches, bait, hook,* and *jig.* She names the trees—birch and pine—and names places—Lake Mille Lacs and Live Deer Park. Mentor texts such as these show students that they should be using specific, rather than generic, words. Proper nouns particularly deliver a powerful punch.

After Lynne made the fifth graders she was working with aware of the importance of special vocabularies, the students intuitively used them in their writing. For example, in a piece about performing in a club, Amanda used the vocabulary of musicians, such as *microphones, guitar, gig, high-pitched vocals,* and *on-key voices.* Megan, a fifth grader who is crazy about horses, wrote a narrative called "A New Horse in the Stables." She used words of the equine world, including *double vertical gymnastic, oxer, stallion, dandy brush, trot, saddle, salt block, hooves,* and *muzzle.* She wrote for her audience, other horse lovers, including Lynne, her writing teacher. Word choice is closely linked with an awareness of the target audience. For example, this book is written with teachers as the target audience. It would sound completely different if we wrote it for parents.

One-of-a-Kind Word Choice

Sometimes you may notice a particular craft involving word choice in an adult book you are reading. It might be used so much that it jumps right out at you, and you realize that it must be the author's fingerprint. Such is the case with Nick Hornby. *How to Be Good* is filled with wonderful adjectives created by stringing together a group of words with hyphens. The effect in Hornby's book is often to make the reader smile or even laugh out loud. After reading several of Hornby's books, Lynne started to notice the use of hyphenated words everywhere, especially in books written for children. She pointed them out to the children in her class, noticing how they slowed the reader down and helped give a more vivid understanding of time and place, culture, or people. In *Talkin' About Bessie: The Story of Aviator Elizabeth Coleman*, author Nikki Grimes speaks in the voice of the schoolteacher and describes the school that Bessie attended as "the hot-in-summer, cold-in-winter, one-room Colored schoolhouse where I taught in Waxahachie." Another example can be found in *Granddaddy's Gift* by Margaree King Mitchell. A powerful feeling is created by her choice of "used-to-be friends." How many of us can make a connection right away and know exactly what she is talking about? Byrd Baylor uses hyphenated adjectives to create a rich description of setting in her lead sentence for *The Best Town in the World*: "All my life I've heard about a little, dirt-road, one-store, country town not far from a rocky canyon way back in the Texas hills." Sometimes the examples are more humorous, as in Don Graves's "no-thank-you helping" to describe the amount of summer squash his mother plops on his plate in *Baseball, Snakes, and Summer Squash*.

Lynne started to use hyphenated adjectives in her writer's notebook and noticed they began spilling into everything she wrote. Her students noticed it, too, and started finding examples in many other texts, such as *Twilight Comes Twice* by Ralph Fletcher and *The Divide* by Michael Bedard. Soon it appeared in their writing, too. Matthew had some fun in his story "That Day in the Sunshine State":

> I asked my dad for what had to be the umpteenth time on a hot and humid July 3rd, "How long will it take us to get to Florida?" He replied to me in a less-than-convincing tone. "We'll just be down there in the blink of an eye, and we'll get there before you know it." It appeared that I wasn't going to find out, so I just had

to wait. I had to wait an oh-my-gosh-how-long-is-it-going-to-take wait. I had to wait an are-we-there-yet wait. The objects going by as seen through the car window blurred like fruit in a blender . . . we were on the turnpike.

Later on in this piece he talked about a "wet-your-pants scared" as well as "a side-splitting-roll-over-and-beat-the-ground-with-your-fist laugh." Matt may have overused the technique, but he was trying it out, letting himself practice it. Eventually, he will hit his stride and be more selective. This time he was writing for an audience of fifth graders who loved it.

Some students began to try this strategy in their writer's notebooks. Connor wrote this sentence: "Taking an Altoid out of the tin box, Andrew popped it into his mouth and made a fish-pucker look with a hint of tears." Kyle had several notebook entries on hyphenated adjectives, including "I was on the diving board with an I-am-going-to-die look on my face." What reader couldn't imagine those faces? (A try-out-the-fun-for-yourself Your Turn lesson on hyphenated adjectives can be found at the end of this chapter.)

Colorful Words

One of the easiest ways to help students develop word choice is through color, and there are many books written about just that. In the chapter on poetry, we demonstrate how books such as Mary O'Neill's *Hailstones and Halibut Bones* and Jane Yolen's *Color Me a Rhyme* can be used as scaffolds for writing poems about color. However, students can be introduced to other books about color in different ways. For example, we use *My Many Colored Days* by Dr. Seuss to have students write about their feelings on any particular day in their writer's notebooks. Students must understand that there is never a "right" answer here—it's about what they are thinking and feeling. Seuss writes, "Then all of a sudden I'm a circus seal! On my Orange Days that's how I feel." This mentor text has many things to offer. Another way to write from it is to ask students to create their own books for their many colored days. Sometimes Lynne uses a question to get the students thinking and writing. "Where would you look if you were trying to find brown? What would you see? Smell? Hear? Taste? How does brown make you feel inside? Choose a color and write about it in your notebook." This exercise helps students use color in their writing to describe their thoughts and show their feelings with unique combinations of words.

We often point out how authors use color. Color is important to Cynthia Rylant's description about the farms of Iowa in *Tulip Sees America*: "They are pictures: White houses. Red roofs. Green, green rolling hills and black garden soil all around them." Margaret Wise Brown uses color in *The Days Before Now* to describe the places she remembers from growing up in New York City. She talks about "a flash and flicker of gold and candlelight and the mystery of the stained glass windows." Charlotte Zolotow uses color for her rich descriptions in *The Seashore Book*, describing oyster shells that are "crusty gray outside and smooth, pearly pink inside." Ron Hirschi calls winter "weasel white" in his book *Winter*. Libba Moore Gray uses hyphenated adjectives to describe the color of snowflakes as "paper-white delicate" and talks about the "red-orange morning" in *My Mama Had a Dancing Heart*.

Sandra and Myles Pinkney write wonderful books about color. Their books *Shades of Black: A Celebration of Our Children* and *A Rainbow All Around Me* are excellent choices to get students to think about using unusual color words as well as ways to describe color. For example, in *A Rainbow All Around Me*, Sandra Pinkney describes green this way:

> *Fresh*
> *Soft blades*
> *Ticklin' your TOES*
> *Barefoot in the park*

In *Shades of Black*, Pinkney celebrates the beauty of African American children with her rich descriptions of skin tones and hair textures. She talks about uniqueness. We can use this in our classrooms to celebrate uniqueness achieved by word choice, and one easy way to think about specificity here is through the choice of color words. In Pinkney's book, she talks about color in extraordinary ways:

> *I am the*
> **midnight blue**
> *in a licorice stick*
> *and the*
> **golden brown**

in sugar
I am the velvety orange
in a peach
and the
coppery brown
in a pretzel

Students and teachers are quick to imitate. Barbara Wright, a fifth-grade teacher in Lynne's school, writes in her journal about "Coconut brown leaves broken and tattered. Coffee-colored twigs ragged and lifeless." Lynne had modeled with her description of clothes flying on a clothesline as she talked about "buttercream skirts and tan trousers."

We often ask our students to think about where the authors of our mentor texts come up with their wonderful words. One place for color words might be a paint or fabric store. Making strips of paint samples available in your writer's workshop can help students add more precise words to their color vocabulary. Even our youngest writers can be made aware of the importance of color. Alex, a sometimes-reluctant kindergarten writer, is beginning to develop an understanding that color increases the appeal of her writing to the reader (see Figure 8.2). Color can add a dimension of description to almost anything.

Older students can explore the world of color by experimenting with hyphenated adjectives and words that are typically not color words. For example, in Jocelyn's story "A Dream Come True," she talks about the "firetruck-red kayak" and later on about "a sparkle of curiosity in her ocean eyes." Another fifth grader, Ashley, wrote "the splendid silver clouds rolled across the sky and confettied the earth with milk-white tears." Lydia wrote about a puppy named Sparky: "When I walked outside I saw nothing until, there it was . . . right in front of my face. It was a pearly-white wagging tail."

Applying Word Choice Strategies

Exploring word choice is exciting at any level. Writers fall in love with words, as do readers. In a third-grade classroom, Lynne's students were busily composing informational pieces to give the gift of writing for Mother's and Father's Day presents. Some students chose to write about a grandparent or godfather. One student wanted to write about his

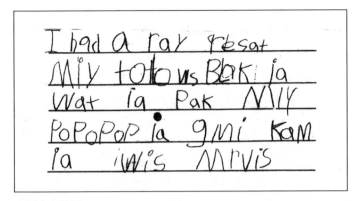

FIGURE 8.2 Alex's journal entry: "I had a real recital. My tutu was black and white and pink. My Pop Pop and Grammy came. It was marvelous."

favorite uncles, and another student wrote about a best friend. In writing workshop it is important to give options, even when the students are writing about the same thing, usually to practice a mode of writing, a genre, or a certain organizational form. Of course, there are some weeks in the year when students have complete control over what they want to write. As always, Lynne encouraged students to write about someone they know well. "You should write about people, places, events, and ideas where you consider yourself an expert. Remember to revisit your 'Expert List' in your writer's notebook and add to it throughout the year."

In a previous Your Turn lesson, Lynne had used Dar Hosta's *I Love the Night* to discuss the use of hyphenated words. She returned to this mentor text to note an unusual fingerprint. Lynne pointed out the author's technique of taking the adjective each creature names to describe why the night is particularly special for him, then emphasizing the word with an adverb that is created by using that same word and adding *-ly*. Here are some examples from the book:

> "It is so *beautifully beautiful* for finding just the right leaf for my dainty and delicate eggs." (luna moth)

> "It is so *gloriously glorious* for agile aerobatics." (whip-poor-will)

> "It is so *superbly superb* for getting some wind under the wings." (owl)

Lynne asked her students what they thought about the strategy. "Why do you think the author used it?" she asked. "Do you like it as a reader? Do you like it as a writer?" Here are some responses from the third graders:

"It makes you think about what each animal thinks is very important about the night. I started thinking that the night is important for us because it helps us grow." (as a reader)

"It is kind of different. But you start to look for it every time she (the author) talks about a new animal. That's what writers do. Like in *Suddenly* where something is gonna happen to the wolf so he won't get Preston Pig. You know 'cause the author says suddenly." (as a writer)

"I think the author used it because she wanted to do something that would make her book special so kids would remember it. I never read a book that does the *perfectly perfect* thing." (reflection)

As Lynne modeled by writing a piece about her mom, she used the phrase *perfectly perfect* in her introductory paragraph and again in the closing paragraph. Lynne encouraged the third graders to embed this technique in their own writing as well. As the students drafted, Lynne and their classroom teacher walked around the room, commenting on their vivid details, their use of strong verbs and exact nouns, and their use of Hosta's craft. Every once in a while, Lynne would ask the writers to stop and listen to a student's sentence that used the "perfectly perfect" craft.

When the students returned to their pieces to engage in revision, they first turned their attention to Lynne's piece of writing. Each student had a copy at his seat, and Lynne's copy was displayed on an overhead transparency. One student observed that Lynne did not really use the "borrowed" phrase exactly the way the author did. "You didn't tell what your mom was perfectly perfect for," Alexandra said. "Like the tree frogs say the night is fabulously fabulous for calling to their friends. That was my favorite page." Lynne asked the students if they thought she should do some revision work where she used the phrase *perfectly perfect*. It was unanimous! In front of the children, Lynne used a green transparency pen to draw a caret and added to her sentence "She's perfectly perfect" the words "for playing the piano and for making me feel loved." Then she looked at the closing paragraph and changed it to "She's perfectly perfect for the job of Mom." Again she revised: "She's perfectly perfect for making her daughter happy and for the hardest job in the entire world . . . being a mother."

The students reread Lynne's piece and were asked to reflect on the revision. Jamie liked the first change because she thought it sounded natural, like it belonged with the rest of the sentences. She also thought it sounded close to Dar Hosta's technique. "You gave me two good reasons, Jamie," Lynne said. "You always want your writing to come across to the reader as sincere and honest. It shouldn't be forced like trying to appeal to all five senses in a piece of writing when you don't really have a taste or a smell that works well in your description. It's the same thing."

Sam raised her hand. "I don't like the changes you made in the last paragraph." When Lynne asked her to be more specific, she answered that when she whisper-read the paragraph to herself, it sounded better the first way.

Lynne was thrilled. "Wow, Sammy, that's exactly what writers do. You know how we say that good revision comes from rereading your piece both silently and aloud? For me, my ear often tells me what isn't working in my piece."

Kevyn added his thoughts. "It sounds like you're trying too hard. Like when you hit a baseball—you can't hit anything when you get all stiff. You have to stay loose. Your writing sounds stiff there."

Lynne nodded in agreement. "Okay. I'm going to read the first paragraph aloud. Then we'll read it chorally. After we decide about my use of *perfectly perfect* in the introduction, we'll do the same thing for the closing paragraph and take a vote." The class was in full agreement with Jamie, Sam, and Kevyn. Lynne thanked her "response group" and reminded the third graders that as they held peer conferences, they should remember that suggestions can be used, adapted, or ignored. The writer has that right. She also reminded them that imitating an author's technique doesn't mean that a writer can't adapt it and make it his or her own. "The authors of our mentor texts help us learn how to be the best writers we can be by trying to imitate them and write like them. After some time, their fingerprints become your fingerprints. In fact, that's exactly what authors do. Authors are readers. They gather writing strategies as they read. Then they try it out in their writer's notebook—just like you. Maybe we'll find that Dar Hosta has actually borrowed this technique from another book she read. It's quite possible. Authors need mentor texts, too."

Two weeks later, Lisa Labow called Lynne into her classroom to share a chart filled with phrases the students had created to imitate the Dar Hosta technique. Spencer pulled a book out of his desk. "Look, this author uses the same technique. *Perfectly perfect* is everywhere!" he said. Margie Palatini in *Mooseltoe* uses the technique throughout her book. Labow noted that Spencer had immediately remembered the text at home and couldn't wait to go home to check it out. Later, we searched further and found that Palatini had used the phrase in a previously written book, *Moosetache*. So where did it all begin? The point is, real authors are readers and have mentors and mentor texts themselves.

Attending to Our Nouns and Verbs

The most important parts of speech are nouns and verbs. They are often neglected in favor of adjectives and adverbs to add style to a piece of writing. Although there is certainly a place for words that describe nouns and verbs, style can be vastly improved if students reread their drafts to revise for stronger verbs and precise nouns. A good place to begin looking at powerful and sometimes unexpected verbs is *Outside, Inside* by Carolyn Crimi. This book is filled with powerful verbs on almost every page. Look for words such as *sink, whisper, flap, darts, spills, slips, bubble, churn, scratches,* and *stomps.* Precise, vivid verbs such as these wake up one's writing. They appeal to the senses. Have your students note which ones make the reader feel, see, or taste. After working with some mentor texts, suggest that students read a few paragraphs from a piece they are currently working on, find the verbs, and try to replace vague verbs such as *do, make, put, get, go, have, run,* and *said* with more precise, vivid verbs.

When authors use personification, the verb is center stage. It is unexpected and surprising—it makes us want to linger there or even reread the sentence. In the beginning of *Journey*, a chapter book by Patricia MacLachlan, the main character is describing the time when his mother left, "before spring crashed onto our hillside with explosions of mountain laurel." Whoever thought that spring could "crash"! In *Through Grandpa's Eyes* MacLachlan writes, "My waterfall fingers flow down his clay head filling in the spaces beneath the eyes like little pools before they flow down over the cheeks." You can almost feel the clay sculpture, as if you are the one touching it. In *Fireflies!*, Julie Brinckloe writes, "And the fireflies poured out into the night." Often, it is not the fact that the verb is so unusual, but the context in which it is used that is unusual. Authors who write with style often use ordinary words in extraordinary ways. Ralph Fletcher's *Twilight Comes Twice* has many examples. For instance, he says that "Twice twilight slips through a crack." Fletcher also uses the verb *pours* and tells the reader, "Slowly dusk pours the syrup of darkness into the forest." His fireflies appear "swimming through the air." Strong verbs are everywhere—and they should be in your students' writing. Thesauruses may help, but students need to be on the lookout for precise and unexpected verbs when they read. They can keep track of them in their writer's notebooks or on charts hung in the room so that all students have access to them during writing workshop. Many writing gurus such as Lucy Calkins and Katie Wood Ray encourage teachers to make charts of their writerly discussions with children and post them to make the thinking visible and accessible.

During a writing conference with Kyle, a third grader, about a piece on snowboarding down Cold Spring's hill, he pointed to his best sentence: "I was covered in snow, lying on my back and looking up at the tree that still clutched my snowboard in its arms. But I did not want to give up." When Lynne asked Kyle why he chose that sentence, he knew right away. "It's my action word . . . you know, the verb. I changed it to *clutch* because it's a lot better than *held*. It's like when you really want something badly, and you're not going to give it up for anything." Lynne didn't even point out that Kyle had used *arms* to stand for the tree's branches. It wasn't important. This third grader was understanding how powerful verbs can be—how their specificity can lead to a deeper understanding and a clearer picture. Words are perhaps the writer's most important tool. When we engage students in the meaningful study of words, they become more aware of their power and the responsibility they have as writers to make good choices. Nicole, a fifth grader, expressed her fascination with words in this original pantoum:

Words

So smooth the sound
So enriched with culture
Never ending
Always magical

So enriched with culture
They never seem to end
Always magical
Like a spark in the air

They never seem to end
Words are never too large

Like a spark in the air
Waiting to fall

Words are never too large
Never ending
Waiting to fall
So smooth the sound

Identifying the Person in the Writing: Voice

Sometimes you are reading a piece of student writing and without even looking at the name, you say something like, "This piece just sounds like Harry!" And when you look, you aren't surprised to find out that you are right. If you have ever written something that shouts, "It's me!" from beginning to end, and your peers, friends, and family members recognize your piece before they see your name, you were writing with voice. It is like a writer's own personal stamp.

When we conduct author studies, we often refer to the author's fingerprints—those aspects of an author's craft that seem to appear over and over in different works, such as Cynthia Rylant's use of parentheses in *An Angel for Solomon Singer*, *The Great Gracie Chase: Stop That Dog!*, or *Little Whistle*, to name a few. Even Rylant's choice of topics lend to her particular voice. If Rylant made a list of writing territories (see Chapter 3), at the top of her list would be family or relatives, pets such as cats and dogs, animals such as whales, home, and a love of the countryside and country living. When you feel that a writer is talking directly to you and understands his or her audience, that's voice, too. If you read Jim Arnosky, a wonderful nonfiction writer who writes picture books for elementary school children, you will hear his voice. Arnosky is an environmentalist and a great optimist. He steps out of third-person writing to talk with his young readers in the first person at the end of many of his survey books such as *All About Frogs*. His friendly, confidential tone helps the reader see what he is seeing. His message is subtle, but even first and second graders will understand what he is saying.

Do you want to continue to read a story or magazine article even when you have more important things that need to get done? Do you ever feel like you "just can't put it down" or that you need to share it with others almost as soon as you finish it? Did the writer seem to understand your needs and interests? That's voice as well. Lynne often talks to her students and her teacher audiences about authors she reads, partly because she likes the genre, but most often because she feels the author understands her and is speaking directly to her. Elizabeth Berg is just such a writer. Lynne says she understands women her age and writes for them. For Lynne it is so magical that she is able to read an entire book in one or two evenings. Audience concern and audience awareness are definitely part of what voice is all about.

One strategy to get students to recognize voice is to use some of their favorite authors who have written the mentor texts the class has been using. Lynne gives one group of students a set of index cards with several sentences and a paragraph on it from an unfamiliar book of a mentor text author. She gives four to eight other students a card with the name of an author on it. The cards are hole-punched with yarn strung through so the students can wear them around their necks. They also carry a mentor text by the same author. Everyone tries to find the mentor author they belong with and congregate in that area of the room. Students compare index cards, read the lines to each other, and listen for the "fingerprints" that are clues to an author's voice. Sometimes they will ask the "author" to read out of the mentor text he or she is holding. For example, one card may contain these lines:

> You can get all hung up
> in a prickle-y perch.
> And your gang will fly on.
> You'll be left in a Lurch.

Or

> They kept paying money. They kept running through
> Until neither the Plain nor the Star-Bellies knew
> Whether this one was that one . . . or that one was this one
> Or which one was what one . . . or what one was who.

Yes, you're right if you said, "That's Dr. Seuss!" There aren't many students who can't recognize his voice. An interesting thing to consider and share with students is the way that *Hooray for Diffendoofer Day* was written. Dr. Seuss died before he was able to complete this story, so Jack Prelutsky and Lane Smith wrote the book with the help of his notes and sketches.

Prelutsky captured his voice so completely that it is almost impossible to believe Dr. Seuss did not write it word for word. And yet, if you reread the book again and again, there is a certain unique quality to it that must be the direct result of three voices blending into one—Prelutsky, Smith (the illustrator), and Seuss. Even if you don't want to consider using the book to teach voice, *Hooray for Diffendoofer Day* has an interesting explanation for how the book came to be and includes some wonderful pages showing Seuss's notes, including sketches and revisions.

Another way that Lynne helps her students understand voice is to talk in the various "voices" of people she knows fairly well by creating a skit or a conversation. The following skit is about work schedules and vacation time. Lynne practices with a group of children who stand in for people other than herself, or she uses different voices so that the students can "hear" the other people. Consider the following skit:

Lynne: *I'll take a vacation later. I know I can fit it all in. I know I can do it. Then I can relax. It's just so hard to say no, and you know what they say about missed opportunities . . .*

Diane (sister):   *That's why we're booking everything in advance—plane tickets, bed-and-breakfasts, hot-air balloon ride, the dinner cruise on Lake Tahoe—just to make sure that you're actually taking this vacation. No backing out!*

Judy (friend):   *I think we are going to have to take bets about whether she will actually get on the plane or not. On Lynne's tombstone it will say, "If I'd only had the time to attend one more meeting, do one more study group, write one more graduate course . . .*

    Later that same day

Auggie (auto mechanic):   *You said you were in a hurry to get to West Chester to do a presentation, so I didn't even ask. I just put new brakes on all the way around. [With raised eyebrows] Been in a hurry a lot lately? You already wore through the brake pads, and there were several hot spots. Lots of miles on the car. This is your summer vacation . . . Working for the Writing Project? Ever hear of the seashore?*

After students get the feel of the different voices in a conversation, they can begin writing conversations as if they were characters they know from mentor texts to help create a sense of voice. For instance, they might create conversations for Kevin Henkes's famous friends, Lilly, Chester, and Wilson. They could also use Ian Falconer's versatile and colorful character, Olivia. Revisit Donald Hall's *I Am the Dog, I Am the Cat* to hear two different voices, or Phillip and Hannah Hoose's *Hey, Little Ant* It is important for students to realize that dialogue in narratives or informational pieces should lend voice to the writing, bringing it to life.

Peter Elbow talks about voice in *Writing with Power* (1981). He describes voiceless writing as dead, mechanical, and faceless:

> *It lacks any sound. Writing with no voice may be saying something true, important, or new; it may be logically organized; it may even be a work of genius. But it is as though the words came through some kind of mixer rather than being uttered by a person. Extreme lack of voice is characteristic of bureaucratic memos, technical engineering writing, much sociology, many textbooks. (287–288)*

Once students begin to develop an understanding of what voice is, it's time to show them how the authors they love are able to create it. Writers achieve voice in many ways. Sometimes they vary the sentence structure as well as sentence length. Students must become aware that their writing sometimes lacks voice because they use the same structures over and over. A good example of an unusual sentence structure can be found in Rylant's *In November*. She offers this description of trees in late fall: "Without their leaves, how lovely they are, spreading their arms like dancers." This structure makes the language sound more like poetry than prose. Another unusual sentence structure can be found in *The Divide* by Michael Bedard: "Summer came, long and hot." Patricia MacLachlan also uses this sentence structure in *Sarah, Plain and Tall*:

> *I looked at the long dirt road that crawled across the plains, remembering the morning that Mama had died, cruel and sunny.*

> *She came through green grass fields that bloomed with Indian paintbrush, red and orange, and blue-eyed grass.*

In the above examples, the adjectives come after the noun, not before it as in the more traditional way. Even the title of MacLachlan's work (*Sarah, Plain and Tall*) uses this unusual placement of adjectives. Other examples of this structure can be found in Fletcher's *Twilight Comes Twice* and MacLachlan's *Skylark*:

> "Trains bring people home, hungry and tired from work."
> (from *Twilight Comes Twice*)

> "Splashes of color in the sky, red, and silver, and green."
> (from *Skylark*)

In examining how authors vary sentence length, consider the following example from *John Henry* by Julius Lester:

> John Henry sang and he hammered and the air danced and the rainbow shimmered and the earth shook and rolled from the blows of the hammer. Finally it was quiet. Slowly the dust cleared.

Lester uses one long sentence followed by two short sentences. This gives the reader the feeling that a great deal of activity is going on and then it suddenly stops. Roald Dahl uses almost this same technique in *James and the Giant Peach* when he talks about the peach breaking free and rolling toward the aunts as they scramble to get out of the way. You can almost feel the peach gaining momentum as the aunts become more and more frantic. Then suddenly it stops. After reading these examples to students, we try to get them to feel the way authors vary their sentences by having them imitate this structure. They can brainstorm situations where there is a lot of activity or commotion going on that suddenly, for some reason, stops, such as the playground right before the whistle signals that recess is over or animals scurrying about in search of food right before the first clap of thunder is heard. Then they can try writing a long sentence followed by two short ones to describe the situation in their writer's notebooks or as a shared writing experience. Remember, it's not enough for students just to notice what authors do; they also need to think about why and try it out for themselves.

Sometimes authors create unusual sentence structures by breaking grammatical rules and writing fragments or run-ons. It is important for students to understand that writers do this purposefully, not because they don't understand how to write sentences correctly. Robert Burleigh uses fragments to create powerful spaces for images and feelings to bubble up inside us in *Langston's Train Ride*:

> *Words and phrases come rushing into my head. The names*
> *of other ancient rivers bubble up. African rivers. The Congo.*
> *The Nile. The Euphrates.*

Michael Bedard does the same thing in *The Divide*:

> *The scattered fields of wheat and corn: dark and light, light and*
> *dark. Treasures laid out on a quilt. Precious things.*

At times, an author chooses to repeat words or phrases to draw out one moment in time so the reader can have the same experience as the character in the story or feel the same things the author is feeling. Laurie Halse Anderson makes her readers fill the heat of an August day, the stillness in the air, in her book *Fever 1793*:

> *It was going to be another hot August day. Another long, hot*
> *August day. Another long, hot, boring, wretched August day.*

Anderson uses effective repetition here, building each time on what came before as well as using sentence fragments to help us experience what her character, Matilda, is thinking and feeling. We can already feel a day that seems to go on without end because there is nothing exciting to do and because the weather is not cooperating either. Connections such as these are powerful.

Jane Yolen's *Nocturne* is built around four elaborate, "stretchy" sentences that use repetitive phrasing while adding on unique adjectives to each successive phrase. The effect is dramatic:

> *In the night,*
> *in the velvet night,*
> *in the quiltdown quietdown velvet night,*
> *moths flutter up, flutter down,*
> *like wind-up toys, without a noise.*

Lynne read *Nocturne* to several fourth-grade classes. She asked the students to jot their thinking about Yolen's unusual sentence structure on the second read, usually the following day. Then Lynne tried it out in her writer's notebook:

> On the day,
> on the thankful day,
> on the cheek-pinching, bear-hugging thankful day,
> the small house becomes even smaller

as friends and family
pour through the door
and spill into the living room, kitchen, and den.

In her description of Thanksgiving Day, Lynne blended the writing of Yolen's book with the descriptions from another familiar mentor text, *The Relatives Came* by Cynthia Rylant. She asked her students to try it again, using the Thanksgiving holiday to inspire their thinking. They were imitating Lynne's writing, Yolen's writing, and Rylant's thinking when they collaborated to create what Katie Wood Ray calls a "taffy sentence." Their shared writing produced a wonderful, stretchy sentence:

On the day,
on the thankful day,
on the delicious feast-filling, belly-rounding thankful day,
couches, chairs, and beds are filled
as silent merrymakers snore and dream
and moms and grandmoms clean and beam.

Later that week, students in a fifth-grade class tried writing "stretchy rubber-band sentences" (what the students decided to name this craft) in their writer's notebooks. Here are two samples from Vanessa's attempts to "play" with language:

Dazzling shoes,
Dorothy-sparkling dazzling shoes,
Paint-the-town-red, dance-all-night shoes . . .
I wore them, I loved them.
I was a shy, quaint princess for a day.

Seeing the moon,
seeing the cratered, unusual, mysterious moon,
the always-punctual-to-come-and-go moon,
that lights the way for dreams to enter your mind at night.
Those dreams, those happy dreams to enter your mind at night.
Those dreams, those happy dreams that tickle babies
like gentle white-as-snow feathers
and make them smile like nothing else . . .
that warm your heart like nothing else.

As you can see, Vanessa went far beyond just experimenting with a rubber-band sentence. She used hyphens to create unusual adjectives, personification, and simile as well. When students are encouraged to play with language, to imitate the mentor texts of their favorite authors, and their writing teacher, they can write in ways they had never even imagined!

One way to achieve a particular voice is to write in the persona of another. Doreen Cronin has had great fun doing this in her books *Diary of a Spider* and *Diary of a Worm*. Writing this way can be very freeing for children, and is a great way to get them thinking outside the box, so to speak, and to have fun at the same time. Recently, we attended the Celebrate Literacy Conference sponsored by the Pennsylvania Writing and Literature Project. One of the keynote speakers was James Howe, author of the *Bunnicula* series. Howe talked about writing as playing and how words can be funny. He noted that some students like to write comic strips, jokes, riddles, or stories that are funny. Often, Howe's stories make us smile or laugh. Even the idea that a sweet little bunny could be a *vampire* bunny that sucks all the juices out of vegetables, leaving them drained of color, is funny. Writing in the voice of an earthworm or spider, as Doreen Cronin does in her books, *Diary of a Worm* and *Diary of a Spider*, could be funny as well.

Many wonderful books use this technique and are also good choices for mentor texts. One book we love to use for this purpose is *Stranger in the Woods* by Carl R. Sams II and Jean Stoick. You can actually hear the many animals talking. Not only is the book a great read-aloud, but it can be used for reader's theater and to teach students how to write vivid descriptions and good conversations. Listen to the voice in the following excerpts:

> "Who-hoo's in the woods?
> Where? Where did the jays say?
> Where is he?" (the owl)

Later . . .

> "Coo-coo-could that be him?" (the mourning dove)

And later . . .

> "I'm-m-m-m the smallest
> and I ca-ca-can scamper quickly." (the field mouse)

Most often, conversations are between characters, but sometimes authors choose to talk directly to the audience. This creates a sense of intimacy, and is often indicated through the use of parentheses. As we said before, this is a fingerprint of Cynthia Rylant, but other authors use it, too. Arthur Howard uses this technique in *When I Was Five* to indicate that something is a secret. Here, the parentheses are almost a signal to the reader to whisper. Madeleine L'Engle uses parentheses a little differently in *The Other Dog*. In this book they are used to hide almost sarcastic remarks (things you might say under your breath because you want to say them but don't want anyone to hear them). In *Little Whistle*, Rylant uses parentheses to give more information about certain characters. Parentheses can be used for many different reasons to help authors create voice. Young writers are often curious about techniques such as this, and once they begin to notice it, they want to try it, too. But as we have said before, it is important to discuss the "why" behind the "what." By doing this, we can help students use techniques purposefully to create voice in their writing. Kyle, a fifth grader, used parentheses to supply confidential information to his reader in "A Magically Magical Christmas Day": "Then Grandmom stops by and gives us a few presents. (We do not always like the presents—they are usually clothes—but hey, it is my grandmom!)" In the following example, Kristy, a second grader, experimented with parentheses. The sentences could have been written without the parentheses, but notice the kind of intimacy she creates with her audience as she chooses to share additional information as an aside.

My Poppop
by Kristy

My favorite ancestor is my Poppop. Poppop is my dad's dad. Poppop gives us candy. (He is always happy to share!) My Poppop loves candy. Kathy got a sweet tooth because of him. My Poppop is big. (The round kind.) When I was little he read me every story that we could find. (Except the scary kind.) My Poppop gives very big hugs. He calls them bear hugs. His favorite color is blue. My Poppop wears glasses only when he reads. My favorite part about my Poppop is his laugh. My Poppop likes to play chess, marbles, dominoes and tick-tack-toe. My Poppop lives in Pennsylvania but he migrates to Florida with my Grandmom for the winter. I love my Poppop!

Avoiding Clichés: Creating Unique Figurative Language

When young writers begin to imitate the writing in mentor texts, they often choose to work with similes and metaphors. Perhaps they do it because figurative language (another technique writers use to create voice) is discussed in both reading and writing workshop, and because comparisons are something we tend to do naturally. The hardest thing about creating a simile or metaphor, however, is to come up with something fresh and interesting *and* appropriate to the text the student is creating. Lynne began to notice the same similes across grade levels and content: *as fast as a cheetah* (a favorite among third, fourth, and fifth graders) or *as deep as the ocean* or *as sweet as candy*. Students were creating comparisons that seemed to be inserted only for the purpose of having a simile or metaphor in their piece, not because it would enhance the writing in any way. It was almost as if the student had considered revision work to "add some style" to his or her writing, and had plucked a simile or metaphor out of thin air, inserting it without any consideration of topic, theme, or appropriateness.

Lynne decided to return to a favorite mentor text to help students understand how similes and metaphors help create vivid pictures in the readers' minds and anchor images and information there as well. Before reading, she asked the students to help her make a list of all the tired, overworked comparisons that they sometimes resorted to just to be able to add a simile. Their list included *as slow as a turtle, as red as a rose, as big as a blue whale, as hungry as a horse, as quick as a bullet, as sly as a fox*. There were many more. Lynne talked about how clichés are simply overworked, overused expressions. They don't lend anything to the writing. Readers don't linger there because they've already heard it—over and over and over. Lynne told her students that they could use a cliché to "hold the spot" until they thought of a better simile, and that a good technique would be to draw a line under the phrase with a pencil or highlighter to help them remember to go back and do some revision. Lynne knew the students needed a great model. It was easy: *Amber on the Mountain*. After she read Tony Johnston's beautiful story, Lynne asked the students to listen to it again, this time jotting down any similes or metaphors they heard. Next, the class shared their notes while Lynne recorded the similes on the board. She checked with the text so she could add or change a word to match Johnston's exact language. Then she distributed paper and colored pencils. She asked her students to choose one of the sentences on the board, copy it onto their paper, and illustrate it as they imagined it. When they were finished, they backed their drawings on colorful squares of construction paper and glued the squares to bulletin-board backing paper to design a quilt. Lynne wanted the class to be able to see the words and images for several weeks before she revisited this lesson.

Three weeks later, Lynne returned to *Amber on the Mountain*. She asked the students to describe the setting of the story and the story's topic and point. Then they looked at the figurative language and discussed how it fit this story. Amber lived high on a mountain. She was surrounded by natural beauty every day and spent a great deal of time outside. The similes fit the text well.

Lynne also used this opportunity to demonstrate how other authors deliberately create figurative language with words that fit the topic of the story. In Chapter 1, we talked about some first graders Rose was working with who began to notice that the similes and metaphors author Linda Oatman High uses in *Barn Savers* match her topic. As it turns out, she does this in her other books as well. In *The Girl on the High-Diving Horse*, she writes, "Summertime gallops by" and "Heart pounding like hooves." In *Beekeepers*, she begins with a beautiful lead that employs a simile to link the weather to her topic immediately: "The springtime sunshine pours like warm honey from the sky." Later she tells the reader, "Goosebumps sting my arms." Notice the unexpected verbs here and in *The Girl on the High-Diving Horse*. Don't we expect goosebumps to pop out or appear? How many of us would use sting? Although summer often flies by much too quickly, it is unlikely we would think of *gallops* to describe that sensation. As Lynne continued the discussion with her students, they readily understood that the author used specific verbs and similes because they matched her topic. Another source that demonstrates the use of words that match the topic is *Chrysanthemum* by Kevin Henkes. In this book, Chrysanthemum is getting used to her unusual flower name. When he describes her feelings, Henkes uses topic-related verbs: "She wilted." "She bloomed."

At this point, the students were asked to look at other mentor texts that have wonderful figurative language. Working in pairs or small groups, they searched for similes and metaphors and copied some into their writer's notebooks, jotting down their thinking about why the author used the literary device, how it seemed to fit with the text, and how it helped the reader. Some good choices are *Twilight Comes Twice* and *Hello, Harvest Moon* by Ralph Fletcher, *One Tiny Turtle* and *Bat Loves the Night* by Nicola Davies, *Owl Moon* by Jane Yolen, *Fireflies!* by Julie Brinckloe, and *Crab Moon* by Ruth Horowitz. *Up North at the Cabin* by Marsha Wilson Chall is particularly good for both similes and metaphors.

One group was excited to report their findings from *Prairie Train*, another book by Chall. "The little girl's taking a train ride to visit her grandma, and the author compares her patent leather shoes to the steel tracks," Matt offered. Lynne wrote the simile on the board: "My patent leather shoes gleam, as smooth as the steel rails below."

"And why do you and Kyle like that?" Lynne asked.

"Because it fits what the author is talking about—it fits the setting," Matt said.

There was more. Kyle said, "She's going to see her grandma in Minnesota, and the book says that the prairie looked like a patchwork quilt."

Another student, Emilie, added, "Like when you're in a plane looking down. Have you ever noticed that? I flew to California and that's what it looked like."

Kyle informed us that quilt-making was something he thought that grandmas would know how to do. But they weren't finished. "She compares the Great Northern Railroad to a frozen buffalo," Matt told us. "It's that quiet. And it's that cold. Besides, I know that the buffalo used to roam the Great Plains."

Other conversations continued and were just as exciting. Then the students were ready to try it out for themselves. They looked through pieces they had already written to exchange a tired or inappropriate metaphor or simile for a better one or looked for a place to try out their newfound knowledge. Nick was writing about a canoe trip down a river. After ending up in the water and struggling to reach the shore, he added a sentence to show how he was feeling as he walked through the woods: "The pain began to rush through my body from being whipped around in the rapids like a rag doll." Lynne nodded. It was a good addition. She could close her eyes and see Nick in the water, arms and legs flailing like the loose limbs on her Raggedy Ann doll. Nick liked the alliteration as well. Sarah had added a metaphor to describe the setting for her story. It was simple, and it worked.

"The April Sunday was warm and cloudy." Sarah added this line to follow her lead: "The trees were all in bloom, standing tall and silent in a curving arc, wearing their white dresses for their outdoor prayer meeting. We, on the other hand, were dressed in comfy, faded jeans, oversized T-shirts, and well worn sneakers—ready to enjoy one of Spring's first warm days." Lynne loved the picture and contrast it created in her mind—the trees dressed in their Sunday best and the people in casual work-or-play clothes.

Amanda balanced her description of a snowy night by adding this sentence to her thumbnail of the setting for a story she was working on: "As the pale moonlight shined a spotlight on tourists wearing fleece-lined jackets while slowly trudging through the heavy-coated street, our Caddy came to a sudden stop." Lynne talked with her about the way she showed that the streets were filled with snow and about her use of the word *spotlight* to describe the moonbeams—so appropriate for a story about performing in a club with her dad.

A student in another fifth-grade classroom was also working on trying out similes and metaphors. Jocelyn had returned to an entry in her writer's notebook. This piece eventually gave birth to a wonderful narrative. It was about her trip to North Carolina with her dad and her best friend, Rachel. Jocelyn had basically written a good lead paragraph. It was nestled in her writer's notebook, all safe and warm and blue, like a tiny robin's egg just waiting to be hatched. It began, "Clear, cool waves crash down onto the sandy beaches in Corolla, North Carolina. My best friend Rachel and I dive through the freeze-blue waves, collecting sand and shells in our dripping hair." Here Jocelyn added, "We wrap ourselves in our warm, sea-green towels with our lips as blue as the ocean—two tiny mermaids gazing out into the water as gray dolphins ride by." A perfect fit. She read her revision to the class, and heads began nodding. Vanessa said she knew Jocelyn had to be talking about the big beach towels that cover you from your shoulders to your feet. She said the towels, the sand and shells clinging to their hair, and the waves crashing all made the mermaid metaphor an excellent choice. Creating similes and metaphors is not easy, but if students study the craft of the mentor authors, have discussions about how it works and what effect it has, and find other examples in their independent reading, they can abandon the clichés and begin to experiment with surprising comparisons.

Discovering Our Writing Voices

Classroom communities are exciting places when they are filled with rich, writerly conversations, especially when those conversations center on style. In *Follow the Moon* by Sarah Weeks, we read the story of a baby sea turtle that hatches at the right time on the night of the full moon. For some reason, he doesn't hear the instinctive voice in his head telling him to follow the moon into the ocean. Sadly, he is left behind. But, a young boy finds him, protects him, encourages him, and, at just the right moment, teaches him how to find the voice inside his head. At the end of the book, we see the little sea turtle swimming off, confident and independent in his new ocean home. Like that young boy, with the help of mentor texts we can show our students how to discover the writing voices inside their heads. We can encourage them to write with confidence, choosing perfect words and arranging them in ways that will reveal their true selves to the reader. When we read their writing, we will hear it. Listen:

The Paleontologist
by Tristyn, Grade 2

One school morning before lunch a paleontologist named Mrs. Gittis came into our classroom. "Hi everyone, how are you doing," she asked. "Good," answered my class. Mrs. Gittis had a big heavy cart she had to pull around. The big cart had fossils in it. The fossils were as gray as an old man's hair. First she took out a triceratop's nose horn. Some people were thinking that the fossil was a plate on a stegosaurus back, but then I, the one and only Tristyn, raised my hand and yelled out, "It's a nose horn from a triceratops!" "Yes," said Mrs. Gittis, "I'm so glad you know what that fossil is!" she exclaimed. "Ya, I know. Aren't I smart!" I said, puffing my hair. Mrs. Gittis passed the fossils around including the triceratops horn. Before we knew it, it was time for Mrs. Gittis to leave. I wish Mrs. Gittis could come again. I had such a good time.

A Dream Come True

by Jocelyn, Grade 5

Dolphins, gray dolphins, gliding, gleaming gray dolphins swam through the clear-blue ocean. Sammi's eyes started to burn as she strained to see the mysterious creatures from her spot on the shore. She wished she was out there on a kayak, so close to them that she could feel them breathe. Little did she know that the thing she dreamed about all her life was about to come true.

"Yo!" Sammi's dad bellowed from behind her, giving her a stampede of chills running down her spine.

"Hi," Sammi whispered, still startled from the surprising appearance of her dad. Sammi looked down at the grainy-soft sand. Her eyes opened as wide as a shark's mouth that is ready to attack. She saw something that was a part of her dream—a kayak.

Sammi's dad carried the firetruck-red kayak down near the ocean to give it a test run. After he pushed it into the water, he pushed off the ocean floor and slid into the boat. Then he sat down on the black cushion and started to paddle deeper, deeper, and deeper into the ocean when it was wave-free. Waves started to come and the sturdy kayak just drifted over them. About ten minutes later, he came out of the ocean with a you-should-try-this smile on his face.

As soon as Sammi's dad had paddled off, Sammi had been anxious to go out on that kayak. She needed no encouragement. "Daddy, may I go out on the kayak with you?" Sammi asked in a wave of words and a sparkle of curiosity in her ocean eyes.

"Sure, I mean it was the best part of this vacation so far," her dad quickly replied. Sammi's heart lifted up with joy. She felt part of her dream come true . . . kayaking.

Together they lifted the heavy kayak off the white sand and headed towards the ocean. Sammi snapped the life jacket closed and plopped onto her dad's lap. She gripped the sides of the kayak and felt the excitement of holding her dream in her grip. Her dad started to paddle farther and farther into the deep ocean.

He stopped the kayak right where the dolphins swam one hour before. Sammi stared out into an ocean of empty blue. Thump! Something bumped into the kayak. Thump!

Sammi shut her eyes and felt her heart start to tremble. What if it was a shark? Surely nothing bad would happen on this short kayak trip! (How could anything interfere with her most passionate dream?)

"Look!" Sammi's dad whispered in a tone filled with raw excitement. When she opened her eyes, she rubbed them so she could see clearly. She looked all around the kayak, twisting her body to take it all in. Then she saw them. Sammi saw her dream. Dolphins, gray dolphins, gliding, gleaming gray dolphins swimming right next to the kayak.

She smiled like she never smiled before. Her heart beat as fast as a tsunami wave rolling to shore. She was so close to the dolphins that she could feel them breathe. Sammi thought to herself, "Dreams really can come true!" She continued watching the dolphins until at last, they left her and disappeared into the ocean mist. Then she fixed them in her mind, turned back to her dad, and smiled. They would remember this trip forever.

Adding Hyphens to Stylize Your Writing

Hook: Michael Bedard's *The Divide* provides an excellent model of the importance of adding hyphens to writing. For this lesson to be effective, this book should be first used as a read-aloud. Return to it and show a few pages on chart paper or an overhead transparency where hyphenated words have been used to create wonderful adjectives. Examine the use of *copper-colored* grass, *weather-beaten* boards, *sunflower-bordered* roads, and *fresh-plowed* soil.

By this time, students should be noticing that the adjective is created by joining two words with a hyphen. Ask students what questions they have about how these adjectives are created.

Options: *Langston's Train Ride* by Robert Burleigh, *Baseball, Snakes, and Summer Squash* by Donald Graves, *Talkin' About Bessie: The Story of Aviator Elizabeth Coleman* by Nikki Grimes, *Twilight Comes Twice* by Ralph Fletcher, *Up North at the Cabin* by Marsha Wilson Chall

Purpose: *Writing without details is boring. But often, we use average adjectives to describe our nouns. If we use adjectives at all, they should be powerful, purposeful, fresh, and interesting. Today I will show you how to create unusual adjectives using the hyphen as you write. Asking questions such as which nouns need more help will guide your thinking about the details you need to add to your writing so that it is clear to the reader. If a hyphenated word can add a precise description, a strong feeling, or a bit of humor to the writing, you might consider using one or more hyphenated words and/or phrases.*

Brainstorm: Ask students to think about a place they are familiar with, or something they recently did, or a person they know very well. Ask them to jot down these ideas in their notebooks, jotting down some adjectives that would describe the place, event, or person. Have them share orally and record some ideas on the board.

Model: Share some of your ideas about the places, people, or events that are important to you. Add the adjectives. Begin to write a paragraph around that place, person, or event. Revise by finding some places that could use an adjective or two. Try to stretch your thinking by finding a place where you could insert a hyphenated word. A variation is to take a piece from your writing portfolio or writer's notebook and revise for hyphenated adjectives. Here is Lynne's example:

> I am standing on the beach and curling my toes into the warm, grainy sand. My grandparents stand on each side of me and each hold a hand tightly. They know I want to run toward the water. I close my eyes and breathe the salty air into my lungs. When I gaze out onto the blue-meets-blue horizon, I catch a glimpse of a gull floating high above me. I think to myself, "I wish I could be that gull and never leave here." The waves roll in and out, in and out, a pulsating rhythm that beats like my heart. It reminds me of life itself. I watch the water stain the sand a dark beige color. The foamy-fingered waves waltz out again to continue their dance from the sea to the shore. My grandparents smile at me, and I cry out to them and the whole world, "It's so beautiful . . . it's so very beautiful!" I catch my breath as the wonder of it all wraps around me like a warm blanket.

Shared/Guided Writing: Ask students to choose one person, place, or event from their brainstormed list. Next, have them write several sentences about their choice in their notebooks, then revise for hyphenated adjectives. Invite one or two students to the front of the room for a guided conversation. Ask them to share their sentences. Write their examples on the board or chart paper. Continue to add to the list as more children share and/or ask children to create more examples from the brainstormed list the two volunteers have shared.

Tell them that when they are writing by themselves they can ask their own questions: What do they think readers would want to know that would help make their writing clearer, that perhaps could be added as a hyphenated adjective? What would add humor? Another feeling? Ask students to examine their independent reading and/or literature circle books for more examples. Hold an open discussion. What do these adjectives do for the reader? Do any examples jump out at you? Why?

Independent Writing: Have students return to their seats and add some adjectives using hyphens to the piece they began until their writing becomes as clear as possible. They can then share again with their partner and receive feedback.

Reflection: Ask writers to reflect on how the strategy worked for them. As a group, discuss how the writing became crisper as their new words were added.

> How could you use this strategy during independent writing time?
>
> Could it be used during partner share?
>
> Could you use this strategy in another type of piece, such as a poem or informational report?

For their writer's notebooks, encourage students to collect examples of hyphenated words from books, magazines, newspapers, and other sources, including the work of their teacher and fellow classmates.

Developing an Understanding of Metaphor

Hook: Read or return to *The Ocean Is . . .* by Kathleen Kranking. List the opening sentence for each page that describes the ocean metaphorically as a garden, a traffic jam, a stage, a galaxy, and a cafeteria, to name a few.

Options: *Tuck Everlasting* by Natalie Babbitt, *Names for Snow* by Judi K. Beach, and *Love Is a Handful of Honey* by Giles Andreae.

Purpose: *We have been talking about ways to add style to our writing through figurative language. You are familiar with similes. Now we are going to explore metaphors, a stronger way to make a comparison. Metaphors, like similes, help to anchor images in the reader's mind.*

Brainstorm: Return to the list of metaphors for *The Ocean Is . . .* and have students add their own thinking to create new ones, such as "The ocean is a circus" or "The ocean is a classroom." Add their suggestions to the list.

Model: Choose one and brainstorm details that support the metaphor. For example, if the ocean is a classroom, you might include schools of fish. If the ocean is a circus, you might talk about clown fish. Then write a short extended metaphor using the details you listed. Here is an example of an extended metaphor comparing the ocean to a circus:

> *The ocean is a circus. Brightly painted black-and-orange clown fish dart in and out of the anemone's poisonous tentacles while the starfish perform acrobatics across the ocean floor. Sea horses prance around the coral reef to the whip of an invisible ringmaster.*

Shared/Guided Writing: Choose another metaphor from the list, brainstorm some details, and write an extended metaphor in a shared writing experience. Encourage students to try writing another extended metaphor with a partner. They can choose another from the list, or make up their own. For example, they might use "The night is a magician," or "Autumn is an artist," "a party-girl," "a masquerader," or "a harvest queen." Circulate around the room, listening in and asking questions that will help students extend their metaphors. Share a few examples in whole group and display some around the room or in a writing center for future reference.

Independent Writing: Have the students return to a piece of writing they are working on, or a previously published portfolio piece and reread the writing to find a spot or two where a metaphor might be appropriate. Have them use their writer's notebooks to brainstorm a simple metaphor, then think of details that might extend it and continue drafting. Or, they can create a new metaphor based on one of the classroom suggestions.

Reflection: Ask students to reflect on how using a metaphor adds style to their writing.

> *When is it appropriate to use a metaphor?*
>
> *What are the best ways you can think of to extend a simple metaphor?*
>
> *Where might you try using a metaphor again?*
>
> *How can you take a simile and change it into a metaphor?*
>
> *How can you use a noun as an adjective to create a metaphor? (for example, describing a dragonfly as a helicopter insect because it pauses to eat its food in the air)*

3

Using Word Pairs to Create Rhythm

Hook: Some authors include word pairs in their descriptions of objects or actions. You can find examples in *Crab Moon* by Ruth Horowitz (*slowly and grandly . . . stepping and pausing*) and *Fireflies!* by Julie Brinckloe (*blinking on, blinking off . . . dipping low, soaring high*). An excellent mentor text to use for word pairs is *Georgia's Bones* by Jen Bryant. There are more than fifteen examples of word pairs in this book. As you reread the book, ask students to listen for the word pairs. Older students can jot them down in a notebook or on a thinking pad.

Purpose: *Writers, sometimes authors use words as pairs. Today we are going to look carefully at that technique and think about why authors might choose to use it. Then I'll give you a chance to try it out for yourself.*

Brainstorm: Ask students to share the word pairs they heard or jotted down as you read *Georgia's Bones* (or a similar mentor text). These can be listed on the board or on chart paper. Return to portions of the text and read sections where the word pairs are used (you could also copy part of the text on an overhead or examine a page of text with a visualizer). For contrast, reread the sections as a list, without the word pairs. Ask students to brainstorm reasons the author might have chosen to use the words in pairs. Students might respond that it "sounds better" that way. Encourage them to think more deeply by asking why it sounds better. This thinking should lead to a discussion of rhythm and its importance as part of style. Then consider how the author did this (use of the word *and*, matching numbers of syllables, and so on). Ask them to consider other words that might go together and add these to the list.

Model: Compose a short piece in front of the class using some word pair examples. Try listing, then combining, as you think aloud about which way adds to the rhythm of what you are writing. You can also return to a previous notebook entry and revise. Here's an example from Rose's journal:

> *The other day I was driving along and I started to notice wildflowers growing by the side of the road. They were all different colors—blue,*

*white, pink. They looked so cheery just blowing in the breeze.
I knew the names of some of them and started to make a list in
my head so I could write about it. I could write, "The other day I
noticed strawflowers, Queen Anne's lace, red clover, and yarrow
growing along the road." Or, I could use word pairs: "The other
day I noticed some wildflowers growing along the road: strawflowers
and Queen Anne's lace, red clover and yarrow, waving and nodding
in the wind."*

Shared/Guided Writing: You could try this technique with the class in at
least two ways. One way might be to compose a shared writing. Once a topic
is decided on, students could pair up to think of word pairs (nouns, adjectives,
verbs, or adverbs) that might be included. This initial brainstorming is a way
to make sure all students are involved. Then you could compose the piece
together. Alternately, you could ask students to search their notebooks for
pieces that could be revised by adding word pairs. You could then hold a
guided conversation with a volunteer in front of the class.

Independent Writing: Ask students to try it out as they go about their work
for the day. If some students are already working on a piece, they can try
adding some word pairs. Others might revisit a notebook entry for revision,
or begin something new. If students have difficulty coming up with a topic,
encourage them to revisit their heart maps or territories, or to do a quick
memory chain—any technique you have already demonstrated to help them
discover topics for writing.

Reflection: Ask students to reflect on this technique in pairs, small groups,
or whole group. The following questions can help guide their thinking:

How did the use of word pairs help your piece?

How did it change your piece?

When is using word pairs effective?

Is this technique appropriate to use all the time?

CHAPTER 9

Walk Around
in the
Author's Syntax

Instead of "drill and kill," instead of the mindless workbook pages,
instead of the vapid test preparation materials, I use powerful
literature and student writing to teach the rules of language.

–Jeff Anderson, *Mechanically Inclined*

Often, you need to examine your students' writing to know what a particular student or class really needs to be able to do. For instance, if your fourth graders are trying to use conversation in their narratives, but they don't use quotation marks and have no idea where to place end punctuation or that they should begin on a new line each time the speaker changes, then it's a good time to take a small group (or the whole group) and do some lessons on writing conversations. Many times these lessons can involve the use of mentor texts, providing far more interesting contexts than the pages of a grammar book or daily edit exercises. Grammar books are excellent references and can be useful during editing conferences with students. In addition, books such as Jeff Anderson's *Mechanically Inclined*, Janet Angelillo's *A Fresh Approach to Teaching Punctuation*, and Donna Topping's and Sandra Hoffman's *Getting Grammar* will help you build the bridge between a traditional approach to the teaching of grammar (syntax and usage) and mechanics (conventions) and a user-friendly, meaningful workshop approach. Mechanics and grammar can be embedded in your daily teaching through the use of mentor texts so that students don't see it as a series of isolated exercises in a workbook but rather in the context of what real authors do.

Analyzing and Modeling Syntax from Mentor Texts

Word study work can include a look at a sentence or paragraph from a novel or picture book. Encourage the students to walk around in the author's shoes, in the syntax of another. It is hard to teach grammar and mechanics without talking about style. It's like reading and writing—they are linked in very specific ways. For example, take this passage from *The Whales' Song* by Dyan Sheldon: "There, enormous in the ocean, were the whales. They leapt and jumped and spun across the moon." Notice that Sheldon begins with an ambiguous word that tells the reader where the whales are. Using commas, she inserts an interrupting phrase that adds nonessential information. It elaborates on exactly where the whales are while adding a description of them. This phrase interrupts the sentence like more common interrupters, such as *after all, in fact, nevertheless,* and *however.* The last part of the sentence is really the subject (*whales*). Notice how the unusual placement of the adjective (*enormous*) makes this sentence sound more like poetry than prose and emphasizes the adjective as well as the noun. In her next sentence, Sheldon describes three consecutive actions and links the verbs with the conjunction *and*, rather than commas, to emphasize each verb and maintain a rhythm. A way to embed this structure into your teaching is to have the students copy her sentences in their writer's notebooks and try it out—in other words, to walk around in Sheldon's syntax. Here are some examples from Rose's notebook:

> There, in the nest, were the baby robins. They screeched and squirmed and opened their beaks wide for their dinner.

> There, low in the sky, were the clouds. They dipped and drifted and danced across the setting sun.

Very often it's best to use the mentor text, imitate it yourself, have your students participate in a shared writing where they imitate it, then ask them to use it independently. After lots of sharing, go back and analyze exactly what the author did. Ask students what they noticed and record their thinking on the board or on a chart. From *The Whales' Song*, the students learned how to combine verbs to create a rhythm, decide on a logical and meaningful order for the three verbs they chose, and use commas to set off an explanation. This is a typical example of how the teaching of style and conventions can be blended. Of course, while you are engaging students in this rich conversation, help them develop the nomenclature of grammar and mechanics. With this specialized vocabulary, they will be able to talk about mentor sentences and passages in more meaningful ways, because everyone will be using the same language.

In a presentation to graduate students, we used the mentor text *Crab Moon* by Ruth Horowitz to provide practice with walking around in an author's syntax. We presented the following sentences:

> *Everywhere they looked, horseshoe crabs crowded and pushed, like restless cobblestones. Under the sandy shuffle of the surf, he could hear the clack of the crabs' shielded backs bumping and scraping together.*

First, the class analyzed the passage to see what exactly the author did, what syntax and punctuation she used. The first sentence starts with a phrase telling where, includes the subject (noun) and two verbs, and ends with a simile. The second sentence starts with a prepositional phrase telling where, uses an apostrophe to show ownership, and again includes two verbs in the rest of the sentence. After brainstorming some possible settings and actions, the class wrote the following passage using Horowitz's syntax:

> Everywhere they hiked, small animals scurried and hid like frightened children. In the freshwater stream, he could see the trouts' silver fins, glistening and reflecting in the sun.

The teacher participants in this class could easily see that the same passage could be used in many different grade levels. What would differ would be the level of sophistication of the writer and the discussion of the grammar and conventions that would follow. For example, younger students could be practicing the rhythm of the sentences and starting sentences with phrases. Older students could be noticing where the subject-noun is and the tense of the verbs.

When students first begin to imitate authors' syntax, their imitation will match more closely. It might even sound very similar, but don't worry. The more you use mentor texts to help students understand language, the more they will move away from a copycat reproduction to make it their own. And it is this ownership that will bridge a writer's notebook playfulness to anything the student is writing—a narrative, persuasive essay, poem, or research piece. Teachers need to tuck in the teaching of mechanics and grammar on a daily basis. It won't take much time, but the rewards will be great.

Many times students get stuck on writing noun-verb or noun-verb-noun sentences, but this is not always bad. Donald Crews uses this sentence structure effectively in *Shortcut*:

> *"I HEAR A TRAIN!"*
> *Everybody stopped.*
> *Everybody listened.*

When you have students use this example to walk around in Crews's syntax, they are learning many things: how to write dialogue, how to use a variety of sentences with appropriate end punctuation, how to build on an emotion with the use of short sentences and effective repetition, and how to make use of print (all caps) to create a sense of urgency or emergency. Crews could have combined many of the short sentences and said, "'I hear a train!' Everybody stopped and listened when we heard the train whistle. We had to decide if we should run ahead to the path home or back to the cut-off." When students have the opportunity to read both versions—as a whisper read and as a choral read—they will soon recognize why Crews chose the sentence structures and the punctuation that he used. After a whole-group discussion where students reflect on the passage, it is easy to move them to the next step: imitate the syntax and mechanics of the mentor text. The teacher can model first, and then the students can participate in a shared writing experience. Here are two examples of how a group of students imitated Crews's syntax:

> "I HEAR A WOLF!"
> Everybody gasped.
> Everybody cringed.
> We all heard the long, low howl.
> Should we run ahead through the thicket
> or back to the campsite?

> "I SEE THE OCEAN!"
> Everybody clapped.
> Everybody smiled.
> We all saw the waves rolling toward the shore.
> Should we dash across the sand to the water's edge
> or stand here to delight in the sunrise?

Sometimes students will begin to use the syntax of a mentor author independently, even combining the syntax of one author with the syntax of another. Hannah, a third grader, did exactly that after working with the lead paragraph from *Amber on the Mountain* by Tony Johnston to experiment with Johnston's syntax (see Your Turn Lesson 1 at the end of the chapter for a more complete explanation). Lynne was surprised to read Hannah's example, since she actually imitated E. B. White's opening paragraph in "Ames Crossing," a chapter in *Stuart Little*. Hannah used a series of dependent clauses to help her reader visualize the setting she created for her character:

> Amber lived on a little island by Hawaii where the
> coconuts grew as big as small pumpkins, where the sea was
> so clear you could see all the way to the bottom, where the
> island people wore brightly colored clothing and the children
> played with Amber every day, where the golden bananas grew

and the sweet scent of flowers lingered in the air. Amber loved it here, for she had so many friends.

At the beginning of the year, start a list of mechanical and grammatical concerns you think you will need to work on with your students. Talk with your grade-level partners. They may have some of the same needs and some different ones. Focus on what is necessary to move the writers forward, not on the individual pieces of writing. Look for examples in the mentor texts you are using that will provide practice in the skills that will give your students a more polished and individualized look to their writing. And please remember—writing cannot be taught in a year! As author George Ella Lyon (1999) so aptly says, "You see, writing is like any other discipline—like dancing, say, or playing a sport. To be good, you have to spend a lot of time practicing, learning the moves, gaining strength and agility" (89). Using a sentence or passages from mentor texts on a daily basis will give your students the strength and agility they need to convey their messages clearly and powerfully to their readers.

Developing a Sense of Sentence

When students are first beginning to write, one of their first needs is to understand where to put the end punctuation. Very young writers might put it at the end of every line, even if the thought continues. Or they might end up with one very long sentence that spans an entire page because they haven't put in any end marks at all. Students need to develop a sense of sentence, and one way to accomplish this is through the sense of hearing. By listening to the sentences of the authors they know well, students can begin to understand where the pauses and stops sound right.

To do this, you first need to find short passages from texts that your students can read fairly well, or that won't be too far beyond their reach through shared reading. The example from *Shortcut* shown above is a good choice for this exercise, as are passages from books such as *Widget* by Lyn Rossiter McFarland or *Crab Moon* by Ruth Horowitz. Display the passage and read it aloud with appropriate phrasing and expression, calling attention to the pauses and stops indicated by commas and periods. (In the beginning, you might want to use passages that contain just periods.) Next, read the passage chorally with the class several times until they can read it fluently. Distribute the passage to the students and instruct them to practice reading it for a few minutes every day. This can be done in pairs for peer support. At the end of the week, have the students work with a partner. While one student reads, the other student's job is to listen carefully and indicate the punctuation with an agreed-upon signal—perhaps a clap for a period, a snap for a comma, and two claps for an exclamation mark.

This activity can be adapted for any level. After students are familiar with this activity, you can vary it by forming two teams using two different passages. The partnerships formed at the end of the week have one student from each team. Each student hears a different passage from the one they practiced, so it raises the importance of reading and listening.

When students read and reread to develop a sense of sentence for writing, they are practicing reading fluency as well. Other activities that link writing and reading fluency are reader's theater, where students are reading directly from the mentor text, the choral reading of poetry, the performance of songs, and the recitation of riddles and jingles. Books such as *You Read to Me, I'll Read to You* by Mary Ann Hoberman, *I Am the Dog, I Am the Cat* by Donald Hall, or *We're Going on a Bear Hunt* by Michael Rosen are all good sources for reader's theater practice.

Word Splash: Building Descriptive Sentences

An interesting way to help your students develop an understanding of both sentence structure and parts of speech is by doing a "word splash." We first learned about this technique from our friend and colleague Sue Mowery and liked it so much we have used it extensively in our classrooms, adapting it and extending it to suit our needs and purposes. Begin by revisiting mentor texts to find illustrations of interesting characters. Some good books to use are *That Magnetic Dog* by Bruce Whatley, *The Recess Queen* by Alexis O'Neill (illustrations by Laura Huliska-Beith), *Olivia* by Ian Falconer, *Mr. George Baker* by Amy Hest (illustrations by Jon J. Muth), and *The Other Dog* by Madeleine L'Engle (illustrations by Christine Davenier). A word splash can also be used to introduce a new mentor text. In fact, sometimes you will get a greater variety of responses if the character is unfamiliar.

FIGURE 9.1 Illustration by Laura Huliska-Beith from *The Recess Queen* by Alexis O'Neill.

The procedure is simple. First, choose a picture and enlarge it to fill a page. Copy it onto an overhead transparency or use a visualizer or smart board; it is important that the picture be large enough to capture and sustain your students' attention. Create a three-column chart for adjectives, nouns, and verbs on the board. You can also use a separate piece of chart paper for each category.

Begin by asking students to brainstorm nouns that name the picture. For example, if it's a picture of a boy, someone in the class might say "friend." You might ask if anyone knows a synonym for that word. Another student might say "buddy" or "pal." Lynne was surprised when one of her students offered the word *chum*. Lynne asked her how she was familiar with that word since it is somewhat old-fashioned. She replied, "It was in a book I was reading and I didn't know what it meant. My mom told me it meant 'friend.'" The next step is to brainstorm verbs. We like to use the *-ing* or *-ed* form when listing verbs, but you can use any form—it depends on what you want to teach. If you know your students need work on the past-tense form of irregular verbs, here is a chance to practice that skill (and get a little practice with spelling in, too). This list should be placed to the right of the list of nouns since verbs typically follow nouns. One of the things you are trying to achieve here is a sense of sentence—a subject and a predicate.

Finally, add adjectives to the chart you are creating. To help students understand what an adjective is, they can test their responses in a short phrase. If it is a picture of a girl, the phrase would be "the _____ girl." Even very young students can easily determine whether the word they are choosing is an adjective if it fits in that frame. You can also add a column for adverbs, adverbial clauses, prepositional phrases, or any other part of speech, depending on grade level and what you expect your students to be able to do. If you are trying to teach sentence combining, you could include a list of conjunctions.

Here is an example of a chart created by second graders for a picture from *The Recess Queen* by Alexis O'Neill. (See Figure 9.1.)

Adjectives		Nouns	Verbs (-ed form)	
nasty	rude	girl	shouted	yakked
mean	bossy	student	screamed	threatened
ugly	loud	classmate	yelled	hissed
mad	horrible	kid	ordered	scared
crazy	terrible	bully	demanded	barked
angry	freaky	sister	commanded	
scary	red-faced	child	told	
frightening		teenager	bossed	
furious		enemy	said	
		meany	growled	

Once the chart is made, examine the list for opportunities to do word work. Sometimes you can ask students to find synonym pairs, antonyms, root words, homophones, compound words, or words that have affixes. Now the children can write one or several sentences using the words from the chart to describe the character, where he or she is, or what he or she is doing. You can even challenge your most gifted students to use some words that are not on the chart. Here are two examples from a shared writing experience with second graders:

The crazy girl screamed.

The loud, angry bully yelled at a little girl and ordered her to leave the kickball game.

The first example can be used to teach students about simple adjective-noun-verb placement. The second sentence lends itself to teaching a compound verb structure. One word of caution: young students love to string adjectives together or try to use as many words as possible to create the longest sentence imaginable. This is where the importance of modeling comes in. Show your students that an effective sentence can be created with just a few words.

You can extend your teaching by having students imitate the basic noun-verb sentence structure as created in the first example, but without the adjective. It is the most basic sentence pattern in our language and will help students develop a sense of sentence. Find mentor texts that use this pattern. Three good books to use are *Shortcut* by Donald Crews, *Roller Coaster* by Marla Frazee, and *Widget* by Lyn Rossiter McFarland. Ask students to create other noun-verb sentence patterns using the words from *The Recess Queen* chart and share with a partner or whole group. Put some of these on sentence strips and post them so that students can have models for creating original sentences for any piece of writing. Students can open their notebooks and jot down a noun-verb sentence. This can be done in a matter of minutes (in fact, you can give students a race-the-clock time limit to challenge them) and can reinforce the grammar and principles you are teaching. If you like, you can pause here to chart precise nouns and powerful verbs, blending the teaching of grammar and mechanics with style.

You might return to this sentence on another day and ask the students to make it grow by adding an *-ly* word (adverb) that tells *how* the girl screamed. For example, the students might give you words such as *loudly, excitedly, happily, angrily*, or even *silently*. You can show your students how these adverbs can be moved to different places in the sentence:

> Angrily the girl screamed.
> The girl screamed angrily.
> The girl angrily screamed.

Here, it might be appropriate to use *Suddenly Alligator: An Adverbial Tale* by Rick Walton or *Suddenly!* by Colin McNaughton as a read-aloud. This knowledge of word placement is important for writing because it shows students how they can vary their sentence patterns.

Building from one simple activity, the teaching possibilities are endless. You can ask your students to tell *what* the girl screamed. This lesson would give practice in writing dialogue. Prepositional phrases could also be taught. Where was the girl when she screamed? Notice how the meaning of the sentence changes simply by changing the prepositional phrase:

In the library, the girl screamed.
At the ballpark, the girl screamed.
On the playground, the girl screamed.

Certainly it is appropriate to use a loud voice on the playground or at the ballpark, but we don't expect screaming in the library. Students can begin to understand and appreciate the power of words as well as how to make sentences grow with prepositional phrases.

Another lesson that illustrates the power of the single word is a look at adjectives. Changing the adjective in the sentence "The crazy girl screamed" gives students practice placing adjectives in a correct position in a sentence, but it also shows how one word can make a big difference. "The frightened girl screamed" is very different from "The crazy girl screamed."

We have found that once students are predisposed to the context of the mentor text, they give you only the words that were used by the author rather than stretching to use their own. Therefore, if you are doing a word splash, offer the mentor text as a read-aloud to your students at its conclusion. The students will listen with a heightened interest, eagerly waiting to hear which of the words they offered were used by the author. When you are finished, you can return to the original chart to add any nouns, verbs, and adjectives the students heard in the entire text. In *The Recess Queen* students might add *Mean Jean, Katie Sue, Queen Jean, growled, howled, snarled, quick, clean,* and *teeny.* Word splashes build vocabulary, develop syntax, and provide a way to investigate language on a weekly or monthly basis. They can also be conducted with pictures of scenes. This will help students build the vocabulary necessary to describe setting.

Studying One Author's Use of Conventions

One of the best ways to study the use of conventions is through author study. By gathering the works of a particular author and examining the texts for different purposes, students can come to a deeper understanding of craft and conventions. Whose books do your students love to read? Whose works have you already examined for other purposes such as crafting a good beginning or studying the use of a repeated refrain? The authors whose words have found their way into the hearts and minds of your students are those you can return to for the study of conventions. One such author is Kevin Henkes, author of *Lilly's Purple Plastic Purse*, *Chrysanthemum*, *Chester's Way*, and *Wemberly Worried*, to name a few. His books can be used to study a variety of conventions, including end punctuation, dialogue, dashes, parentheses, use of italics, talking captions, capitalization, variation of print size, and ellipses.

One of Henkes's unique fingerprints as an author is what we refer to as "talking captions." His illustrations often contain the thoughts or words of the character, but they are not written in traditional speech bubbles, just simply printed next to or above the picture of the character, more like a caption. The first step in examining mentor texts for craft or conventions is to guide students to notice what the author is doing. As students begin studying Henkes's books, they may discover these talking captions themselves, or you can simply show several pages from his books and ask them what they notice. But as Katie Wood Ray (1999) reminds us, we must go beyond the noticing, helping our students develop a deeper understanding by questioning why a particular technique was used, and then guiding students to envision its use in their own writing.

If you were studying these talking captions, you might conduct a whole-class discussion about why Henkes added them to his illustrations. Have your students think about how they add to the story, and perhaps question why he chose not to use traditional speech bubbles. A class of first graders had the following ideas about why Henkes uses this technique in almost all of his books:

> *"I think he wants us to know what Lilly was thinking."*
> *"Sometimes it adds more words that they said."*
> *"It makes the story better because it adds more details."*
> *"Maybe he doesn't like to draw bubbles."*
> *"I think he wanted his books to look different."*

If the technique you are studying has a name (such as ellipses or dashes), make sure you provide your students with the correct term. If not, work together to come up with a name the class will recognize and use. (The first graders coined the term *talking captions* to distinguish them from *speech bubbles*.) Finally, ask your students to think about how they might use the technique in their own writing. See Figure 9.2 for an example of one student trying it out. This would be an excellent time to build in some guided writing as suggested in the Your Turn lessons.

Chapter 6- Ashley's Imaginary Friend

Don't tease Ashley. When you were little you had one too,

Ashley has an imaginary friend. Her name is Nikki. She takes her everywhere. She even has to eat with her. Sometimes Kevin teases her, but then he gets yelled at.

FIGURE 9.2 Annie experiments with talking captions.

Lucy Calkins (2003), Debbie Miller (2002), and Janet Angelillo (2002) remind us that charting the thinking that occurs in the classroom makes the work you do together permanent and visible. It allows the conversations to extend to other days and fosters connections to other areas of instruction. Charting, which can be conducted in the brainstorming part of the Your Turn lessons, helps students build their thinking gradually as new thoughts, ideas, and examples are added.

A chart developed for the thinking surrounding the talking captions and other conventions studied in the books of Kevin Henkes might look something like the one that follows. It was adapted from the work of Katie Wood Ray (1999) and Lucy Calkins (2003).

Of course there are some conventions, such as capitalizing names and using appropriate end marks, that we want students always to use. But other things, such as dashes, dialogue, or talking captions, require more thinking when considering appropriate use. You might find that students tend to overuse a particular technique when they first discover it. Through the reflections that take place at the end of the Your Turn lessons or during individual conferences, you can guide your students into thinking about when and how often the technique is appropriate to use. Reflection is a key ingredient in trying out any new skill. By making their thinking visible and getting feedback from the community of writers, students can more deeply internalize the power of words and conventions.

Conventions Kevin Henkes Uses				
Books	What Did We Notice?	Why/When Is It Used?	It's Called...	Who Else Uses It?
Lilly's Purple Plastic Purse *Wemberly Worried* *Jessica* *Chester's Way*	There are words in the illustrations.	To add details. To tell what a character thinks. It adds more to what characters say.	Talking captions	(Use this space to add the names of the students who tried it out in their own writing— include a specific example if possible.)
Chrysanthemum *Lilly's Purple Plastic Purse*	Names of people, some places, and some things begin with a capital letter.	Names begin with capitals. Places and things can have names just like people.	Capitalizing proper nouns.	
Lilly's Purple Plastic Purse *Kitten's First Full Moon* *Grandpa and Bo*	There are lines in the middle of a sentence then more words.	Sometimes it's used before a list. It tells there are more words coming to explain something.	Dashes	

The works of Linda Oatman High and other authors offer an interesting study in the use of the colon. In *Barn Savers*, there are many examples of the use of a colon followed by a listing:

> *I shiver as I dress:*
> *soft flannel shirt,*
> *long johns,*
> *cracks.*
> *jeans,*
> *hard hat,*
> *boots,*
> *and scratchy leather gloves.*

> *Soon we see the barn:*
> *red paint peeling like sunburn,*
> *and old boards, splintered with*

High uses this same technique in *Beekeepers*:

> *We dress:*
> *long-sleeved white overalls,*
> *boots,*

gloves,
and straw hats with
veils of mesh.

Kyle, a fifth grader, had just finished looking at *Beekeepers* and *Barn Savers*. He was in the middle of writing a piece about holiday traditions. His piece, titled "A Magically Magical Christmas Day . . ." did not originally include a list. After reading High's books, he revised it to include the following paragraph:

> Soon all my relatives (mostly children) are boasting about what awesome presents they were given. When the house gets quite quiet and bellies start to rumble, my grandmom fixes up a light snack before the three-course meal. When we finally sit down to eat, we can almost hear the table moan and groan with the weight of the Christmas feast:
>
> salad drowned in ranch dressing,
> mashed potatoes piled with gravy,
> sweet cranberry sauce,
> juicy honeyed ham,
> roasted turkey with stuffing,
> creamy, sweet corn,
> yuck, slender asparagus,
> soft, warm rolls,
> a three-layer chocolate "moose" cake.
> (It's big enough to satisfy a moose!)

Other examples of a colon followed by a list can be found in *Twilight Comes Twice* by Ralph Fletcher, *Up North at the Cabin* by Marsha Wilson Chall, *Dad and Me* by Peter Catalanotto, and *Wallace's Lists* by Barbara Bottner and Gerald Kruglik. In *The Girl on the High-Diving Horse*, High again uses the colon, but this time what follows is less like a listing and more like an explanation:

> *It's like flying: the horse and rider suspended high in silent air . . . dropping.*

Farther on in the text she writes this sentence:

> *Red Lips jumps, and it's like flying: wind in my hair and sunshine in my eyes.*

Other authors also use the colon to indicate that what follows further explains their ideas. Examples of this kind of colon use can be found in *Mud* by Mary Lyn Ray, *The Divide* by Michael Bedard, and *Arthur, For the Very First Time* by Patricia MacLachlan. Sometimes authors use the colon to set off dialogue as in *Preston's Goal!* by Colin McNaughton or *Wolf!* by Becky Bloom.

The important thing to remember is that we want to get students not only to notice a particular craft, or in this case, convention use, but to consider why the author might have chosen to use it, and to examine its use across texts. This reflection will lead to a much deeper understanding, and will help students consider many more opportunities for using it in their own writing.

In Chapter 8, we discuss the use of proper nouns as a way to help students add style to their writing. One way to further this discussion of noun specificity is to introduce the epithet. An epithet is a descriptive name or title used to enhance a description of a character. Sometimes it is humorous, as in *Olivia Saves the Circus* by Ian Falconer. Olivia describes herself as "Olivia the Tattooed Lady," "Olivia the Tight-rope Walker," the "Flying Olivia," and "Queen of the Trampoline," among others. Judy Schachner does the same thing in *Skippyjon Jones* when she has his mother refer to him as "Mr. Kitten Britches," "Mr. Fuzzy Pants," "Mr. Flutternutter," and "Mr. Cocopugs." During his imagined adventure, Skippyjon Jones refers to himself as "Skippito Friskito," and "El Skippito." Students can notice the use of capitalization here, but also how the epithet breathes humor into the piece.

The use of the epithet is not limited to humor, however. In *Barefoot: Escape on the Underground Railroad*, Pamela Duncan Edwards uses epithets to show how the animals separate and describe the runaway slaves (the "Barefoot") from the slave catchers (the "Heavy Boots"). *In Stranger in the Woods*, Carl R. Sams II and Jean Stoick describe the Owl as the "Owl of Many Questions." This specific naming of a character helps the reader focus on a characteristic. In *The Recess Queen* by Alexis O'Neill, the personality of one of the main characters is appropriately summed up in her epithet "Mean Jean." Authors also use the epithets of historic figures in biographies. For example, Robert Burleigh refers to Babe Ruth as "the Babe" in his book *Home Run*. In another book, he and coauthor Ed Young use the epithet for the historical figure Tenzing Norgay as their title: *Tiger of the Snows*. They also give Mount Everest the epithet "Mother Goddess of the Earth." In *Snowflake*

Bentley, a book about photographer Wilson Bentley, Jacqueline Briggs Martin uses "Snowflake Bentley" and "the Snowflake Man" when she refers to him. Jean Fritz teaches us in *Bully for You, Teddy Roosevelt* that "Teddy's Terrors" and "Roosevelt's Rough Riders" were epithets for Theodore Roosevelt's regiment.

By studying the use of epithets across texts, students can gain a deeper understanding of the rules of capitalization. As they read books that use epithets, including historical texts, they can come to realize exactly what an epithet is. They can easily see that if an epithet is used in place of a name, all the important words (just like a book title) are capitalized. In addition, they can discover another way to add style to their writing.

Hey, Study Those Interjections

Interjections are fun to explore with your students. They certainly have changed over time. In Ruth Heller's *Fantastic! Wow! And Unreal!: A Book About Interjections and Conjunctions*, Heller shares interjections that were used by people who lived in the Middle Ages, such as "Alas!" and "Alack!" that we sometimes come across in the literature we read but never hear in our spoken language. Our grandmothers probably said things such as "Goodness gracious!" and "For goodness' sake!" or "Good grief!" as interjections. When we were growing up, we used "Cool!" and "Jive!" and "Wow!" or even "Groovy!" to declare how we felt about something. Students today often use "Awesome!" or "Gross!" as interjections. We use interjections to express emotions. Sometimes they show worry or concern: "Uh-oh" or "Whoa!" Other times, they express our delight: "Yeah!" They can also be used to show our contempt or disgust: "Yuck!" Sometimes, they are trying to draw attention to something: "Hey!" Many times, your students will use them to show surprise: "What!" or "Wow!" or "Awesome!" Interjections can stand alone, or commas can set them off. When they are strong, they are followed by an exclamation point. Mild interjections are followed by a comma.

There are many wonderful examples in children's picture books. A good place to start is Heller's book about interjections and conjunctions, perhaps as a read-aloud. The book has many colorful illustrations and can continue to serve as a resource for your students. (Ruth Heller has many books about parts of speech. Some are listed in Chapter 10, "A

Treasure Chest of Books.") Return to a mentor text to explore the use of interjections. In *The Recess Queen* by Alexis O'Neill, several sentences use interjections. Sometimes, she uses capital letters to shout at the reader. Here are some examples from the text:

> *"Oh! Katie Sue was one quick kid."*
> *"Say YOU!" she snarled and grabbed Katie Sue by the collar.*
> *"Well, Mean Jean bullied through the playground crowd."*
> *"'Hey, Jeanie Beanie," said Katie Sue.*
> *"WELL—now when recess rolls around*
> *the playground's one great place."*

The author ends her book with an interjection set apart from the rest of the text by its size, color, and position on the page. The author helps the reader emphasize it even more by extending the sound of the word with the letter s. It's written in all capital letters: "YESSSSSS!" It might be a good idea to place this page on a visualizer or overhead transparency and give the students time to talk about how the author emphasizes the interjection and how effective it is at the close of this particular story. You could simply ask your students what effect it has on the reader, what feelings they are left with.

Another text that could be used as a model for interjections is *Moo Who?* by Margie Palatini. The use of punctuation, print size, and conversation can be studied for conventions, but it is Palatini's humor that students can't seem to get enough of. In the lead paragraph of this story, Palatini chooses to use a mild interjection. "Oh boy, could Hilda let loose with the tra-la-las." (The main character is a cow, Hilda Mae Heifer.) A little later, the author uses an interjection we might consider slang: "Yup. It was lights out for Hilda Mae Heifer." Here is another example of her use of interjections: "'Hey!' cried the chick. 'Stop peeping at us!'" And again, she puts voice into her writing when another character speaks, also using an interjection: "'You mean, me and you? Heavens no,' said the cat." Students can take turns reading the dialogue aloud to talk about what effect the interjections have. They certainly help to give a text voice and to breathe life into a piece of writing. Students can continue to find examples in other mentor texts and copy them into their writer's notebooks. Next, they can try to use them, either in a new piece of writing or a previously published piece. It is a good idea to keep writing folders or portfolios where students can store some of their work. This way they have easy access to try out new strategies they are learning in pieces that are already complete. It is difficult to ask students to begin a new piece of writing every time you want them to take a risk and try something on for size. As we said before, sometimes students overuse something new. Palatini's story works well with many interjections embedded throughout. One word of caution to young writers: the overuse of interjections can give a piece of writing a nervous-and-jerky, breathless quality.

There are so many great examples of the use of interjections that teachers of any grade level will be able to examine their use. In *Chrysanthemum* by Kevin Henkes, the interjections are fresh and appealing. They are also intended to be mild. "'Oh, pish,' said her mother. 'Your name is beautiful.'" "'Oh, pish,' said her mother. 'They're just jealous.'" Henkes also uses an interjection to express Chrysanthemum's joy on her first day of school: "'Hooray!' said Chrysanthemum. 'School!'"

Other fun examples include *Preston's Goal!* by Colin McNaughton, *Dad and Me* by Peter Catalanotto, *We're Going on a Bear Hunt* by Michael Rosen, and *Pigs in the Mud in the Middle of the Rud* by Lynn Plourde. One of our favorite examples is in Pam Muñoz Ryan's *Mice and Beans*. It is written in Spanish and immediately translated into English so the reader will not misunderstand: "'¡Fíjate! Imagine that!' she said." She also uses an interjection that can stand for the thing she is talking about as well as serve as the familiar interjection "Rats!"

> But as Rosa María swept out the cupboard, she discovered
> the telltale signs of mice!
> "¡Ratones!" she cried. "Where are my mousetraps?
> I will set them all!"

Bravery Soup by Maryann Cocca-Leffler is another great book for students of all ages. It contains many interjections and opportunities to create skits for reader's theater to practice reading fluency to gain writing fluency. Print size and end punctuation will help the youngest readers understand exactly how the author intended the words to be spoken. The use of interjections helps us understand exactly what the characters are feeling in this wonderful story about facing our greatest fears.

When you study parts of speech in an interesting way through the use of mentor texts, eventually it spills over into the students' own writing. They become mentors for each other during peer conferences and shared readings. In Francisco's story, "It's Only a Dream," the fifth grader uses interjections to put his voice into the piece of writing:

"Great!" I whispered to myself. "It seems I'm either being punked or I'm Harry in *Harry Potter and the Secret Chamber*." (Either way, could I explain the window thing? It restored itself? No way!)

Dylan, another fifth grader, inserts his voice by using interjections as well. He begins his piece about an experience at Disney World with an interjection that serves to pull the reader right in: "Whoa! This is incredibly awesome!" Later in the piece, he writes, "'Uh Oh!!' I heard a six-year-old say in a baby type of voice. That must be one tall six-year-old. Or maybe I'm just small . . . SHEESH!" Brielle, another student in this class, used an interjection to speak in the voice of her toddler sister: "'Ooooo . . . pretty colors!' we heard Jenna shout excitedly."

Embedding Grammar Study in Writing Work

We can teach grammar and mechanics in interesting, fun ways that will help students listen attentively, want to hear more, and try things out. Exercises that teach students the traditional rules of grammar are best learned within the context of real reading and writing so that students understand the "why" as well as the "how." We also know that students will learn something when they need it—when they are going to use it in their own writing. In this case, necessity is truly the mother of invention.

The best way to encourage students to take risks with grammar and mechanics, as well as develop an understanding of sentence, is to embed this teaching into daily practice. We are not speaking of the widespread use of a daily editing activity. Here, students are given sentences or passages with grammatical and/or mechanical errors to correct. Unfortunately, the students who can correct with ease are not challenged to take risks and try out new structures and conventions. The students who have difficulty with the daily edit are not growing either. After all, they are seeing things incorrectly, sometimes copying them down incorrectly, and then are expected to take this out-of-context experience and transfer it to their personal writing. From our observations, it doesn't happen that way. What we have found is that instruction in grammar and mechanics must be part of our everyday teaching. The easiest way to tuck in these skills is through the use of sentences or passages from mentor texts. This work will stretch students as writers through imitation, and eventually, through adaptation and playfulness with language; it will allow them to *own* these skills. However, on our bookshelves, we should have many grammar reference books that will help us understand how to analyze passages with students or work through grammar and mechanics issues during conferences. Some students will be able to consult these references independently, but it should be part of the work they are doing with real writing, not as isolated exercises.

According to Schuster (2003), teachers are often looking for simple formulas for correctness. He says we do this because teaching writing is perhaps the hardest thing we do. Then he tells us to remember to let the students break the "rules" if it leads them to better writing. Using passages or even just a sentence from mentor texts, students can study a variety of syntactic structures and punctuation rules. This practice will lead to an understanding of why the experts (the authors of the mentor texts) sometimes break the rules; it helps them bring their voices to the writing experience. Finally, it will help your students make their voices heard as well.

The teaching of grammar and mechanics *is* important. It is through these avenues that we teach our writers how to interact with their readers—their target audience—and make their message clear. Students will begin to understand that the rules for syntax and mechanics are the writer's tools for developing this relationship with the reader.

Scaffolds

Scaffolds are writers' shoes:
Shoes of poets. Shoes of wordsmiths. Shoes of mentors.
Shoes waiting to be tried on for size; that will hug your feet
and guide your path if you'll only slip inside.

This poem was written by Heather Lovelace, a first-grade teacher and participant in a Pennsylvania Writing and Literature Project graduate course. She borrowed the syntax that Charlotte Otten used in her poem "February."

Using the Syntax of an Author

Hook: *Amber on the Mountain* by Tony Johnston is a wonderful model of how an author brings readers into a book by helping them visualize the setting and experience the mood created by the description. By imitating the author's flow of language, or syntax, students can get a feel for how the author uses words. After sharing *Amber on the Mountain* as a read-aloud, reread the lead paragraph.

Options: *Alejandro's Gift* by Richard E. Albert, *One Tiny Turtle* by Nicola Davies, "Ames Crossing" in *Stuart Little* by E. B. White, and *The Days Before Now* by Margaret Wise Brown. For middle school writers, also use *The Winter Room* or other books by Gary Paulsen.

Purpose: *One important strategy to build content is to create descriptions for the setting and characters. Setting gives the reader a sense of place (where) and time (when) and helps create a mood. Today we will walk around in the shoes of Tony Johnston. We will use her syntax, or flow of language, to create interesting descriptions of setting while at the same time creating a mood.*

Brainstorm: Ask students to turn and talk with a partner or small group about settings they are familiar with in real life or ones they can vividly recall from books. Have them jot down ideas for settings in their notebooks. In whole group, record them on chart paper or on the board.

Model: *I am going to use the lead paragraph from* Amber on the Mountain *to write my own lead paragraph, but I am going to choose a setting that is familiar to me and place Amber in it. As I write, I am going to think about what sensory experiences such as sights, sounds, and smells come to mind and the feelings I associate with that place.*

Amber lived in a city so big it took hours to drive through traffic-snarled avenues from one side to the other. Skyscrapers loomed like granite mountains against a hazy blue sky. And the air made you sick— it was that thick and soured with pollutants. Still, for all that man-made ugliness, Amber was content. For city people had parks, museums, theaters, and libraries where she could be transported to other worlds.

Shared/Guided Writing: Ask students to choose something from the class list of settings or something else they think of and write a lead paragraph that places Amber in a new setting. Make sure all the students can see the lead paragraph from *Amber on the Mountain* on a chart stand or blackboard or a transparency on the overhead projector. Students can share their drafts with a partner and talk about how their sentences matched those of the mentor text and your model. Share a few in whole group on an overhead or visualizer. For struggling or younger writers, ask them to first orally write by talking about their ideas with a partner. You can model this technique with another student. Another helpful strategy is to get the students to draw their settings before they begin to write.

Independent Writing: Ask students to revisit a draft or a finished portfolio piece. Revise the lead paragraph to include a vivid snapshot of setting, using a favorite mentor text as a model. Students can also place Amber in a number of different settings as additional practice and post their lead paragraphs on the writing bulletin board. If they are ready, students can begin a new draft for a narrative. Furthermore, students can use this strategy to begin an informational essay or research piece with a snapshot of setting where it is applicable. For example, informational reports about endangered animals could begin with a description of the animal's disappearing habitat. It is always a good idea to have young writers share their writing with a partner, a small response group, or in the general sharing session of writing workshop.

Reflection: Students can turn and talk with a partner about their lead paragraph.

> *How did the language of the author help you write a better paragraph?*
>
> *What strategies did the author use that you were able to imitate?*
>
> *How did the language in the mentor text and your paragraph create a mood through setting?*
>
> *How did the description of setting help your readers (peer response group/teacher) visualize it?*
>
> *How can you use the show, not tell strategy here?*
>
> *When could you use this again?*

2

Using a Variety of End Punctuation

Once students have developed a sense of what a sentence is, it is time to help them understand the various types of sentences and the end punctuation that goes with each. It is also important for them to understand how meaning can be conveyed through various types of sentences.

Hook: *Yo! Yes?* by Chris Raschka comprises one- and two-word sentences through which two boys carry on a conversation. Meaning is conveyed through the use of periods, question marks, and exclamation points. This is a great mentor text to use for reader's theater. After your students are familiar with the content and have practiced how to use expression to convey the meaning indicated by the end punctuation, you can return to it to discuss end punctuation in more depth. You can also use short passages from other texts that contain a variety of sentence types. Good choices include *Kitten's First Full Moon* by Kevin Henkes, *Shortcut* by Donald Crews, and *Mr. George Baker* by Amy Hest.

Purpose: *Writers, we know it is important to use punctuation marks at the end of a sentence. We've seen how authors sometimes use a period, sometimes a question mark, and sometimes an exclamation point. Today we will practice writing a variety of different sentences with different end marks and talk about when it is appropriate to use each one.*

Brainstorm: Together with your students, think of some familiar situations or places that are familiar to them and record the list on the board or chart paper. This list could include things such as opening your lunch bag to see what Mom packed, picking teams at recess, arriving at a surprise birthday party, losing a tooth, or finally getting to your vacation destination.

Model: Pick one and, using a think-aloud, create some different types of sentences that might be associated with that situation. Make this thinking visible by jotting the sentences down on the board or in your notebook. For example, if you choose "opening up your lunch bag to see what Mom packed," the sentences could be

"What's inside?" I wondered.
Do you want to trade?
It's peanut butter and jelly again!
Time for lunch!
I wondered what surprise my mom packed today.
Slowly and carefully, I opened my lunch bag.

Then, in front of the students, put the sentences together in a way that might make sense, adding others as needed. Share your thinking as you write. Talk about why you are putting the sentences in the order you did and also why you used certain end marks. The sentences above might end up like this:

Finally, it was time for lunch! As I entered the cafeteria, I wondered what surprise my mom had packed today. My mouth watered as I thought of the possibilities. Could it be tuna fish? Could it be ham and cheese? Slowly and carefully, I opened my lunch bag. Ugh! It was peanut butter and jelly again! I looked over at my best friend. "Do you want to trade?" I asked hopefully.

Shared/Guided Writing: Have students choose another situation from the brainstormed list and create different types of sentences that might be associated with that situation. This can be done in whole group as a shared writing, or students can work in pairs. Have them jot down at least two examples for each type of sentence, then use them in writing a small vignette.

Independent Writing: Students can return to a previous notebook entry or a piece they are currently working on to revise for appropriate end punctuation. They could also choose a different situation, brainstorm some sentences, and write another vignette. Yet another alternative could be to rewrite one of the models with different sentences that change the meaning. In other words, the example given could be rewritten so that peanut butter and jelly is a welcomed lunch.

Reflection: As students share their work, ask them to share their thinking about why they used periods, question marks, and exclamation points with certain sentences.

How does thinking about end punctuation help you convey the meaning you want?

Would the meaning change if you used a different sentence type?

Why is it important to vary your sentence types?

Option: Students who understand basic sentence structure might return to the modeled example or the example they wrote and rewrite some of the sentences into fragments so that they sound more natural (Tuna fish? Ham and cheese? Peanut butter and jelly again! Want to trade?) This would add another dimension to the writing. Students can reflect on which way sounds better and why.

Exploring Variations in Print

Hook: With your students, explore mentor texts for unusual print style. This could be the use of italics, bold print, underlining, variations in size, or use of all uppercase. Some good examples of print variations can be found in *Roller Coaster* by Marla Frazee, *Chameleons Are Cool* by Martin Jenkins, *The Recess Queen* by Alexis O'Neill, *Mice and Beans* by Pam Muñoz Ryan, and *Muncha! Muncha! Muncha!* by Candace Fleming.

Purpose: *Writers, we've been exploring the way authors sometimes write words in a different way. Today, we will think about the reasons why they make some words bigger or smaller, underline them, or make them stand out in some way. Then, we'll try out that technique for ourselves.*

Brainstorm: With your students, list the different types of variations in print that you noticed in the mentor texts you explored together. Remember to list specific examples. If you are working with younger students, you can limit the variations to one or two and perhaps just discuss writing some words bigger, or making the letters all uppercase. Ask students to consider the reasons they think the authors might have chosen to write the words as they did. An excellent way to do this is to create a chart that can be added to as students make new discoveries. Here's a short example:

Title and Author	Print Variation	Why did the author do this?	When could we use it?
Muncha! Muncha! Muncha! by Candace Fleming	*furious* is all uppercase, bigger, and darker	She wanted to show that Mr. McGreely was very angry; the reader should say the word loudly.	If we want the reader to say the word loudly.
	happy is bigger	To show that the word is important—his feelings finally changed.	For very important words that we want to stand out.

The categories of any chart can be changed to suit your purposes. You could also have a section for student examples.

Model: Return to a previous notebook entry or compose a short piece in front of the students. When you are finished, think aloud about how you could use some variation in print (take one word and make it bigger or smaller, underlined, and so on) and why you would do that. It is important for students to understand why certain words could be written differently, and also that if this technique is overused, it will lose its effectiveness.

Shared/ Guided Writing: Ask students to return to a previous notebook entry and revise for print variation. As you circulate, conference with students about how and why they chose to make the revision. An alternative is to write a whole-class shared piece about a common experience (a recent class field trip, activity, or event) and decide together where it would be appropriate to vary the print in some way.

Independent Writing: Ask students to consider print variations as they work on individual pieces. They might also want to return to previous notebook entries or published pieces to revise for effective print variations.

Reflection: As students share their work, ask them to reflect on how this strategy worked for them.

> *What kind of print variations did you use?*
>
> *How did this technique make your writing better?*
>
> *What other variations in print could you use to accomplish the same thing?*
>
> *What other variations would you like to try?*

CHAPTER 10

A Treasure Chest
of Books

Come to the Library

Nichole H., Grade 5

Come to the library . . . come!
The silence creeps in, but no one notices,
I feel the soft brush of air from the turning of a page,
I gulp in the words like a refreshing glass of water,
I picture myself waving to subjects of my kingdom or fighting a pirate.
Come to the library . . . come!
Nonfiction, Biographies, Fiction, Mysteries,
Colorful covers and perfect pictures,
Silent movies, sitting and waiting to be read,
Come to the library . . . come!
Forgotten stories only known to books,
I find new things in the treasure hunt,
It is silent again, everyone is reading.
Come to the library . . . come!

Our goal now is to share our library with you. The books we referenced, as well as some others we didn't mention, are organized around the chapters. You will notice that many books are listed more than once. These are our true mentor texts, the ones we go back to again and again and use for many different purposes. We have added brief annotations so that you will have some idea of what to look for or how the book can be used for a specific purpose. If you have already started your own library and have some of the titles mentioned, we hope you might look at them through new eyes and find additional ways to use them in your classroom. If you are just starting to build a library, start small and pick the books that you love and that can be used in many different ways. The treasure chest is not an exhaustive list by any means! There are always new discoveries to make, and we encourage you to make your own, to find your own mentors and keep growing.

In *A Hope in the Unseen*, Ron Suskind talks about the journey of one determined young African American man who dreams of attending an Ivy League university even though he comes from a high school in Washington, D.C., where many of his peers do not have his same hopes and dreams. After reading the book one can conclude that it is also the story of a young man's ability to find the right mentors in his life at the right time. We believe this sense of timing and need is true of mentor texts in the writing workshop.

Sometimes we need to find a new mentor. As we grow as writers and teachers of writing, our mentors can change. We are using the same skills and strategies; however, our level of sophistication and understanding changes. Some mentors will remain tried and true throughout your years as a teacher of writing. Others will serve as good friends who have perhaps moved away but with whom you still keep in touch from time to time. And then there are the new friends who come into your life who can teach you something you never even thought about before.

It is our hope that this book along with the treasure chest of books we have provided in this chapter will help you lay a strong foundation for your literacy house. Each year you will find new books, and perhaps you will need to build an additional room or two (we say that both figuratively and literally!) as you add books to your collection. Like all good literacy lessons, mentor texts should be revisited often. When you read them again as you grow as a writer, you make new discoveries that were there all along—you just weren't ready for them yet.

Chapter 2   Digging for Treasure: Discovering Personal Stories by Connecting with Read-Alouds

Connections to books can take many directions. The following books are rich stories for read-alouds that writers can easily relate to in some way. Although possible connections are listed, students might relate in a variety of other ways that lead to an awareness of the writing treasures in their lives.

Ackerman, Karen. 1988. *Song and Dance Man*. New York: Alfred A. Knopf.
>   Special time with grandfather.

Alexander, Martha. 1992. *Where Does the Sky End, Grandpa?* Orlando, FL: Harcourt Brace Jovanovich Publishers.
>   Child asks grandfather questions about the world; an example of writing about things you might wonder about.

Anderson, Laurie Halse. 1996. *Turkey Pox*. Morton Grove, IL: Albert Whitman and Co.
>   Memories of holidays or illnesses.

Bradby, Marie. 1995. *More Than Anything Else*. New York: Orchard Books.
>   Connections to important things in your life.

Brinckloe, Julie. 1985. *Fireflies!* New York: Simon and Schuster.
>   Special times with friends; catching fireflies; conflicted feelings—feeling happy and sad at the same time.

Brunelle, Nicholas. 2005. *Snow Moon*. New York: Penguin Young Readers Group.
>   A "What if . . . ?" story based on an event from the author's childhood.

Bryant, Jen. 2006. *Call Me Marianne*. Grand Rapids, MI: Wm. B. Eerdmans Publishing Co.
>   An example of how authors use writer's notebooks.

Bunting, Eve. 1989. *The Wednesday Surprise*. New York: Clarion Books.
>   Tells about a special time with grandmother who has learned how to read. Writers can connect to things that they have accomplished, and how that accomplishment was shared with others.

————. 1991. *Night Tree*. Orlando FL: Harcourt Brace and Co.
>   Memories connected to holidays.

————. 1996. *Secret Place*. New York: Clarion Books.
>   Connections to writing about secret places.

————. 1999. *Butterfly House*. New York: Scholastic.
>   Learning how to do something with grandfather's help; also connections to setting something free.

————. 2000. *The Memory String*. New York: Houghton Mifflin Co., Clarion Books.
>   Using objects to spark memories.

Catalanotto, Peter. 1995. *The Painter*. New York: Orchard Books.
>   Connections to "being old enough" to do something; can also be used to connect to feelings.

————. 2001. *Emily's Art*. New York: Simon and Schuster Children's Publishing Division.
>   Connections to feelings, especially in illustrations.

————. 2002 *Matthew A.B.C.* Simon and Schuster Children's Publishing Division.
>   An example of "What if . . .?": What if all the students in a class had the same name?

Cisneros, Sandra. 1984. *The House on Mango Street*. New York: Random House, Vintage Books.
>   This book is probably most appropriate for older students. The story is told in a series of vignettes that can be used to help students make connections to the stories in their own lives. A particularly useful vignette is "My Name" that can help students start thinking about their own names.

Cooper, Elisha. 2006. *Beach*. New York: Orchard Books.
>   Rich in thumbnail sketches that provide seeds of ideas.

Crews, Donald. 1991. *Bigmama's*. New York: Greenwillow Books.
>   Memories built around places and objects.

————. 1992. *Shortcut*. New York: Greenwillow Books.
>   A close call—recalling a time of excitement and danger.

Evans, Richard Paul. 1993. *The Christmas Box*. New York: Simon and Schuster.
> Excerpts can be used to demonstrate how senses can trigger memories.

Fox, Mem. 1985. *Wilfrid Gordon McDonald Partridge*. New York: Kane/Miller Book Publishers.
> Demonstrates how objects can spark memories.

Golenbock, Peter. 1990. *Teammates*. Orlando, FL: Harcourt, Inc.
> Uses photographs of real people and places to tell the story.

Henkes, Kevin. 1991. *Chrysanthemum*. New York: Greenwillow Books.
> Writers can make connections to name

———. 1996. *Lilly's Purple Plastic Purse*. New York: Greenwillow Books.
> Connections to special people or things, also "getting in trouble."

———. 2000. *Wemberly Worried*. New York: Greenwillow Books.
> Young writers can relate to things they worry about; beginning suggestions for a "What If . . .?" list.

High, Linda Oatman. 1998. *Beekeepers*. Honesdale, PA: Boyds Mills Press.
> Special time with grandfather who is teaching how to do something.

———. 1999. *Barn Savers*. Honesdale, PA: Boyds Mills Press.
> Special time with dad; connections can also be made to souvenirs and how they help us remember special times or places.

Hoberman, Mary Ann. 2002. *Right Outside My Window*. New York: MONDO Publishing.
> Can be used to spark connections and writing ideas about things "right outside the window."

Horowitz, Ruth. 2000. *Crab Moon*. Cambridge, MA: Candlewick Press.
> Connections to special places and events; can be used to dig up memories connected to feelings.

Houston, Gloria. 1992. *My Great Aunt Arizona*. New York: Harper Collins Publishers.
> Connections to special people in our lives.

Howard, Elizabeth Fitzgerald. 1991. *Aunt Flossie's Hats (and Crab Cakes Later)*. New York: Clarion Books.
> Memories built around objects—in this case, hats.

Johnson, Angela. 1989. *Tell Me a Story, Mama*. New York: Orchard Books.
> A series of memories told as nighttime stories in a conversation between a mother and child.

———. 1990. *Do Like Kyla*. New York: Orchard Books.
> Connections to trying to be like an older sister or brother; can lead to thinking about special things sisters or brothers do together.

Johnston, Tony. 1994. *Amber on the Mountain*. New York: Penguin Books Inc.
> Can be used to connect to stories about friends or learning how to do something.

Joyce, William. 1985. *George Shrinks*. New York: Harper Collins Publishers.
A "What if . . . ?" story. Can be used to inspire more what-ifs.

Keats, Ezra Jack. 1962. *The Snowy Day*. New York: Penguin Books.
A special time in the snow.

Kroll, Steven. 2001. *Patches Lost and Found*. New York: Winslow Press.
Connections to stories about pets; great demonstration of story mapping.

Krupinski, Loretta. 1998. *Best Friends*. New York: Hyperion Books for Children.
Can be used as an example of using photographs to spark a story.

Laminack, Lester. 2004. *Saturdays and Teacakes*. Atlanta: Peachtree Publishers.
Spending time with grandmother.

Lillie, Patricia. 1993. *When This Box Is Full*. New York: William Morrow and Company.
Memories associated with objects for each month of the year.

Lowry, Lois. 2002. *Gooney Bird Greene*. New York: Houghton Mifflin Co.
An excellent read-aloud to encourage students to tell the stories of their lives; helps students understand that ordinary events can be told and written in an extraordinary way.

MacLachlan, Patricia. 1991. *Journey*. New York: Bantam Doubleday Dell Publishing.
Use of photographs for finding writing topics; connections can also be made to names.

———. 1994. *All the Places to Love*. New York: Harper Collins Publishers.
Can be used to spark memories about special places.

McKissack, Patricia. 2001. *Goin' Someplace Special*. New York: Atheneum Books.
Connections to special places.

McLerran, Alice. 1991. *Roxaboxen*. New York: William Morrow and Co.
An imaginary place created during children's play; use to make connections to playtime adventures.

Moss, Marissa. 1990. *Regina's Big Mistake*. New York: Houghton Mifflin Co.
Young writers can relate to mistakes they have made and how those mistakes might have been fixed.

Newsome, Jill. 1999. *Shadow*. New York: DK Publishing.
Connections to moving, pets, meeting new friends.

Nolen, Jerdine. 1999. *In My Momma's Kitchen*. New York: William Morrow and Company.
A collection of stories that occur in the same place; connections to memories about special places.

Polacco, Patricia. 1994. *My Rotten Redheaded Older Brother*. New York: Simon and Schuster.
Use of photographs—finding the story behind the picture; connections to special people.

————. 1995. *My Ol' Man*. New York: Philomel Books.

Use of photographs—finding the story behind the picture; connections to special people.

————. 2001. *Betty Doll*. New York: Philomel Books.

Using objects to spark memories.

Rappaport, Doreen, and Lyndall Callan. 2000. *Dirt on Their Skirts: The Story of the Young Women Who Won the World Championship*. New York: Penguin Putnam, Dial Books for Young Readers.

Can be used as an example of starting with photographs to write a story.

Ray, Mary Lyn. 1996. *Mud*. New York: Harcourt.

Connections to things.

Ryan, Pam Muñoz. 2001. *Hello Ocean*. Watertown, MA: Charlesbridge Publishing.

Use of the senses to describe a special place; can be used to connect memories to a special place, particularly the seashore.

Rylant, Cynthia. 1985. *The Relatives Came*. New York: Macmillan Publishing Co.

Visits from relatives.

————. 1986. *Night in the Country*. New York: Simon and Schuster.

Use of sounds to spark memories; connections to places.

————. 1992. *An Angel for Solomon Singer*. New York: Orchard Books.

Connections to special places and people as well as wishes and dreams.

Schachner, Judith Byron. 1999. *The Grannyman*. New York: Penguin Putnam.

Connections to stories about pets.

Sheldon, Dyan. 1990. *The Whales' Song*. New York: Dial Books for Young Readers.

Connections to feelings.

Small, David. 1985. *Imogene's Antlers*. New York: Crown Publishers.

A "What if . . . ?" story. Can be used to inspire more what-ifs.

Spinelli, Eileen. 2004. *In Our Backyard Garden*. New York: Simon and Schuster.

A series of story poems that occur in one place; connections to memories about special places.

Swanson, Susan Marie. 1998. *Letter to the Lake*. New York: DK Publishing.

Memories triggered by objects.

Tripp, Nathaniel. 2001. *Snow Comes to the Farm*. Cambridge, MA: Candlewick Press.

Remembering a special time with a sibling or a particular snowstorm.

Van Allsburg, Chris. 1984. *The Mysteries of Harris Burdick*. New York: Houghton Mifflin Co.

The book is a collection of drawings, each accompanied by a title and a caption. Students can write the stories that go with the drawings.

Williams, Vera. 1982. *A Chair for My Mother*. New York: William Morrow and Company.

> Connections can be made to times writers have saved money for something special.

Wood, Douglas. 2006. *Nothing to Do*. New York: Penguin Group.

> Brainstorming lists of things to do, which can be seeds of writing ideas.

Wyeth, Sharon Dennis. 1998. *Something Beautiful*. New York: Bantam Doubleday Dell Publishing Group.

> Everyone has "something beautiful" in his or her life. What's yours?

Yolen, Jane. 1987. *Owl Moon*. New York: Philomel Books.

> Connections to special outings with father or other relative.

Zolotow, Charlotte. 1992. *The Seashore Book*. New York: Harper Collins Publishers.

> Can be used to spark connections to special places, particularly the seashore.

Chapter 3   What Are You Really Writing About? Discovering the Inside Story

Ackerman, Karen. 1988. *Song and Dance Man*. New York: Alfred A. Knopf.

> Can be used to stimulate thinking about territories, in this case relatives or grandpa.

Aruego, Jose, and Ariane Dewey. 2002. *Weird Friends*. New York: Harcourt, Gulliver Books.

> This book is a series of small descriptions of animals who help each other survive. Each small story makes the point stated in the title.

Bang, Molly. 2004. *My Light*. New York: Scholastic, Blue Sky Press.

> First-person narrative written in the voice of the sun.

Baylor, Byrd. 1986. *I'm in Charge of Celebrations*. New York: Simon and Schuster.

> Can be used to stimulate thinking about territories, then narrowing the territory to very specific things.

Beach, Judi K. 2003. *Names for Snow*. New York: Hyperion Books.

> Begins with an author's note that explains the inspiration for the book.

Brinckloe, Julie. 1985. *Fireflies!* New York: Simon and Schuster.

> Can provide a stimulus for connecting with emotions to find topics for writing—feelings of being happy and sad at the same time.

Browne, Anthony. 1998. *Voices in the Park*. New York: DK Publishing.

> Examples of different points of view.

Bryant, Jen. 2005. *Music for the End of Time*. Grand Rapids, MI: Eerdmans Books for Young Readers.

> Contains an author's note that provides more information and reveals the inspiration for the book.

Bunting, Eve. 1991. *Night Tree*. New York: Voyager, Harcourt Brace & Co.
> Illustrates narrowing the topic—the book describes one holiday tradition, not the whole holiday.

Catalanotto, Peter. 1999. *Dad & Me*. New York: DK Publishing.
> Can be used to stimulate thinking about territories, in this case relatives or dad.

Crews, Donald. 1992. *Shortcut*. New York: Greenwillow Books.
> Can provide a stimulus for connecting with emotions to find topics for writing.

———. 1998. *Night at the Fair*. New York: Greenwillow Books.
> Can be used to stimulate thinking about territories, perhaps summer fun, then narrowing the territory to something more specific.

Curtis, Jamie Lee. 1993. *When I Was Little: A Four-Year-Old's Memoir of Her Youth*. New York: Harper Collins.
> Good stimulus for thinking about heart maps, especially for younger students.

Davies, Nicola. 2001. *Bat Loves the Night*. Cambridge, MA: Candlewick Press.
> Narrowing the topic (one specific kind of bat); information on the flap gives information about the author and indicates that the book came from personal experience.

———. 2001. *One Tiny Turtle*. Cambridge, MA: Candlewick Press.
> The introduction provides a wonderful example of narrowing the topic, especially for a nonfiction piece.

Hoose, Phillip, and Hannah Hoose. 1998. *Hey, Little Ant*. Berkeley, CA: Tricycle Press.
> An excellent model for explaining point of view.

Horowitz, Ruth. 2000. *Crab Moon*. Cambridge, MA: Candlewick Press.
> Can provide a stimulus for connecting with emotions to find topics for writing—feelings of excitement, surprise, fear, or nervousness.

Howard, Arthur. 1996. *When I Was Five*. New York: Voyager Books, Harcourt Brace & Co.
> A clear example of making a point—the point is stated in the last line.

Jenkins, Martin. 1997. *Chameleons Are Cool*. Cambridge, MA: Candlewick Press.
> The introduction is an example of narrowing the topic; the point is made in the title.

Karas, G. Brian. 2002. *Atlantic*. New York: G. P. Putnam's Sons.
> First-person narrative written in the voice of the Atlantic Ocean.

Ketterman, Helen. 1998. *I Remember Papa*. New York: Penguin Putnam.
> Can provide a stimulus for connecting with emotions to find topics for writing.

Kilborne, Sarah S. 1994. *Peach & Blue*. New York: Alfred A. Knopf.
> A book about friendship that helps illustrate point of view.

L'Engle, Madeleine. 2001. *The Other Dog*. New York: SeaStar Books.
> Can be used to explain point and point of view; contains an author's note that explains how the story originated.

Little, Jean. 1986. *Hey World, Here I Am!* New York: Harper Trophy.
> A collection of individual stories with common characters; can be used to stimulate emotions for hand maps.

Lyon, George Ella. 2000. *One Lucky Girl*. New York: DK Publishing.
> Can be used to stimulate thinking about territories.

———. 2003. *Mother to Tigers*. New York: Atheneum Books for Young Readers.
> Contains an author's note that provides additional information and reveals the source of the idea for the book.

McKissack, Patricia C. 2001. *Goin' Someplace Special*. New York: Atheneum Books.
> A good stimulus for thinking about heart maps; contains an author's note that provides more information on the origin of the story.

Murphy, Frank. 2000. *The Legend of the Teddy Bear*. Chelsea, MI: Sleeping Bear Press.
> Contains an author's note that provides more information and reveals the inspiration for the book.

Nolen, Jerdine. 1999. *In My Momma's Kitchen*. New York: William Morrow and Co.
> Can be used as an example of places as territories for writing topics.

Rappaport, Doreen. 2004. *John's Secret Dreams*. New York: Hyperion Books for Children.
> Contains a note from the author as well as the illustrator (Bryan Collier) that explains the process, research, and thinking each went through to create the book.

Rylant, Cynthia. 2002. *Best Wishes*. Katonah, NY: Richard C. Owen.
> Helps identify the author's writing territories.

Scieszka, Jon. 1989. *The True Story of the 3 Little Pigs!* New York: Viking Penguin.
> An example of telling a story from a different point of view.

Siebert, Diane. 1988. *Mojave*. New York: Crowell.
> Written in first-person narrative from the point of view of the desert.

———. 1989. *Heartland*. New York: Crowell.
> Written in first-person narrative from the point of view of the American Midwest.

———. 1991. *Sierra*. New York: Harper Collins.
> Written in first-person narrative from the point of view of the mountain.

Swinburne, Stephen. 1999. *Safe, Warm, and Snug*. New York: Harcourt, Voyager Books.
> Uses rhyming couplets to explain how animals protect their young; the point is found in the title; contains explanations of each animal in the back.

Tripp, Nathaniel. 2001. *Snow Comes to the Farm*. Cambridge, MA: Candlewick Press.

>An example of narrowing the topic—the book is about one time it snowed, not all experiences with snow.

Whatley, Bruce. 1994. *That Magnetic Dog*. New York: Harper Collins.

>A clear example of making a point. In this case the point is made in the title—the dog has a magnetic personality.

Whitcomb, Mary E. 1998. *Odd Velvet*. San Francisco, CA: Chronicle Books.

>Can be used as an example of topic and point.

White, E. B. 1952. *Charlotte's Web*. New York: Harper and Row.

>The first chapter can lead to a discussion of the emotions that are revealed. Connections made can be used in creating a hand map.

Winer, Yvonne. 2002. *Birds Build Nests*. Watertown, MA: Charlesbridge.

>Can be used as an example of making a clear and stated point—the point is found in the title.

The following books, all by Cynthia Rylant, can be used to explore some of her writing territories. This is just a sampling of Rylant's many books that help us know something about her and where she gets her writing ideas:

When I Was Young in the Mountains. 1982. New York: Dutton Children's Books.

The Relatives Came. 1985. New York: Macmillan Publishing Co.

Night in the Country. 1986. New York: Simon and Schuster.

Henry and Mudge: The First Book. 1987. New York: Simon and Schuster.

>This is the first in a series of books about the big dog Mudge. Rylant also wrote the *Mr. Putter and Tabby* series about the adventures of a cat and her owner.

Tulip Sees America. 1988. New York: Scholastic.

Dog Heaven. 1995. New York: Scholastic.

The Whales. 1996. New York: Scholastic.

The Great Gracie Chase: Stop That Dog! 2001. New York: Scholastic.

The following books by Judy Schachner can be used to explore her territories of pets and family:

Mr. Emerson's Cook. 2002. Akron, PA: Reading Matters.

>This book contains an afterword that provides factual information about Ralph Waldo Emerson and also reveals some of Schachner's family history that inspired the book.

The Grannyman. 1999. New York: Dutton Children's Books.

Yo, Vikings! 2002. New York: Dutton Children's Books.

>This book contains an author's note that explains how the story came from a personal experience.

Skippyjon Jones. 2003. New York: Dutton Children's Books.

Skippyjon Jones in the Doghouse. 2005. New York: Dutton Children's Books.

Chapter 4   When Writers Use a Magnifying Lens

Bottner, Barbara, and Gerald Kruglik. 2004. *Wallace's Lists.* New York: HarperCollins.
Contains examples of thoughtshots.

Brinckloe, Julie. 1985. *Fireflies!* New York: Simon and Schuster.
The whole book provides details surrounding a small moment in time.

Bryant, Jen. 2006. *Call Me Marianne.* Grand Rapids, MI: Wm. B. Eerdmans Publishing Co.
Descriptions of an object to build content.

Bunting, Eve. 1996. *Secret Place.* New York: Clarion Books.
Appeal to the senses—sights and sounds—to add description for building content.

———. 2000. *The Memory String.* New York: Houghton Mifflin, Co., Clarion Books.
Examples of show, not tell.

———. 2006. *One Green Apple.* New York: Clarion Books.
A sprinkling of dialogue, and rich descriptions of people, places, and objects.

Burleigh, Robert. 1991. *Flight: The Journey of Charles Lindbergh.* New York: Philomel Books.
Contains an example of slowing down the action to add specific details that explode a small moment in time.

———. 1998. *Home Run.* New York: Harcourt Brace & Co.
Contains an example of slowing down the action to add specific details that explode a small moment in time.

———. 2004. *Langston's Train Ride.* New York: Orchard Books.
Written in the first person; contains examples of exploding a moment.

Burleigh, Robert, and Ed Young. 2006. *Tiger of the Snows: Tenzing Norgay: The Boy Whose Dream Was Everest.* New York: Atheneum Books.
Contains examples of thoughtshots, sensory details, and exploding a moment in time.

Catalanotto, Peter. 1995. *The Painter.* New York: Orchard Books.
Use of show, not tell through illustration.

———. 1999. *Dad & Me.* New York: DK Publishing.
Use of show, not tell to reveal the feelings of the characters in the words as well as the illustrations.

Chall, Marsha Wilson. 1992. *Up North at the Cabin.* New York: Lothrup, Lee, & Shepard Books.
Appeal to the senses to build content.

———. 2000. *Sugarbush Spring.* New York: Lothrup, Lee & Shepard Books.
Use of dialogue with description to build content.

Dahl, Roald. 1983. *The Witches*. New York: Puffin Books.

> Examples of snapshots of character; show, not tell (the chapter "The Meeting" is especially good for "fear").
> **Note:** Many of Roald Dahl's books (listed in the "Treasure Chest of Books" under Chapter 5) provide examples of snapshots of character.

Falconer, Ian. 2001. *Olivia Saves the Circus*. New York: Atheneum Books.

> Examples of show, not tell—we learn about Olivia by the things she says and does; this is also an example of snapshot of character.

Farris, Christine King. 2003. *My Brother Martin: A Sister Remembers Growing Up with the Rev. Dr. Martin Luther King, Jr.* New York: Simon and Schuster.

> Contains examples of anecdotes to build interesting content.

Fletcher, Ralph. 1997. *Twilight Comes Twice*. New York: Clarion Books.

> Appeal to the senses to build content.

Gardiner, John Reynolds. 1979. *Stone Fox*. New York: Crowell.

> Includes examples of character snapshots.

Giff, Patricia Reilly. 2002. *Pictures of Hollis Woods*. New York: Random House, Dell.

> Travels back and forth between time; examples of exploding a moment.

Grimes, Nikki. 2002. *Talkin' About Bessie: The Story of Aviator Elizabeth Coleman.* New York: Scholastic, Orchard Books.

> Contains many examples of the use of anecdote to provide interesting information about a character and build content; snapshots of character and setting; some examples of exploding a moment.

Henkes, Kevin. 1991. *Chrysanthemum*. New York: Greenwillow Books.

> Show, not tell through use of illustration.

———. 1996. *Lilly's Purple Plastic Purse*. New York: Greenwillow Books.

> Examples of adding content through the use of descriptions and details. Henkes's style is to use "the power of three" in his explanations, most often adding three details to elaborate on something; some examples of show, not tell.

Hesse, Karen. 1999. *Come On, Rain!* New York: Scholastic.

> Appeal to the senses to build content.

High, Linda Oatman. 2003. *The Girl on the High-Diving Horse*. New York: Philomel Books.

> Exploding a moment—slowing down the action and adding more detail; uses appeal to the senses and examples of show, not tell.

Horowitz, Ruth. 2000. *Crab Moon*. Cambridge, MA: Candlewick Press.

> Exploding a moment—slowing down the action and adding more detail; examples of show, not tell.

Howard, Elizabeth Fitzgerald. 1991. *Aunt Flossie's Hats (and Crab Cakes Later)*. New York: Clarion Books.

> Rich descriptions; appeal to the senses.

Howell, Will C. 1999. *I Call It Sky*. New York: Walker and Co.
> Uses appeal to the senses to build content; has an afterword that gives facts about the atmosphere.

Johnston, Tony. 1994. *Amber on the Mountain*. New York: Penguin Putnam.
> Vivid description to build content; examples of thoughtshots and dialogue.

Ketterman, Helen. 1998. *I Remember Papa*. New York: Penguin Putnam.
> Examples of show, not tell.

Laminack, Lester. 2004. *Saturdays and Teacakes*. Atlanta: Peachtree Publishers.
> Use of dialogue to build content. The dialogue is written in italics.

Lyon, George Ella. 2003. *Mother to Tigers*. New York: Atheneum Books for Young Readers.
> Use of anecdote to build content; use of explanations to elaborate and add details.

MacLachlan, Patricia. 1994. *All the Places to Love*. New York: Harper Collins.
> Appeal to the senses to build content.

MacLachlan, Patricia, and Emily MacLachlan. 2003. *Painting the Wind*. New York: Harper Collins.
> Descriptions of objects to build content.

McFarland, Lyn Rossiter. (Illustrated by Jim McFarland.) 2001. *Widget*. New York: Farrar Straus & Giroux.
> Snapshot of character in the beginning; often adds details in threes; example of show, not tell through illustration.

Miller, William. 1997. *A House by the River*. New York: Lee and Low Books.
> Use of the senses to build content.

Naylor, Phyllis Reynolds. 1991. *Shiloh*. New York: Dell.
> Written in the first person, this book helps students understand what it means to "be in the moment," assisting them in visualizing the details.

Paulsen, Gary. 1999. *Canoe Days*. New York: Random House.
> Appeal to the senses to build content.

Polacco, Patricia. 2001. *Betty Doll*. New York: Philomel Books.
> Use of anecdotes to build content; rich descriptions of objects and people; use of dialogue to reveal more about a character.

Raschka, Chris. 1993. *Yo! Yes?* New York: Orchard Books.
> Use of show, not tell through illustrations.

Raven, Margot Theis. 1997. *Angels in the Dust*. New York: Troll, BridgeWater Books.
> Rich descriptions of the setting that provide information about the time period or era.

Reese, Barbara. 2005. *Storm Angels*. West Chester, PA: Stargazer Publishing, LLC.
> Use of thoughtshots to add content.

Rotner, Shelley, and Ken Kreisler. 1992. *Nature Spy*. New York: Simon and Schuster.
    Provides examples of looking at things in nature to see all the details and patterns—like looking at something under a magnifying lens; this concept can be linked to writing.

Ryan, Pam Muñoz. 2001. *Hello Ocean*. Watertown, MA: Charlesbridge Publishing.
    Use of the senses to build content.

———. 2001. *Mice and Beans*. New York: Scholastic.
    Use of thoughtshots to add content.

Rylant, Cynthia. 1985. *The Relatives Came*. New York: Bradbury Press, Macmillan Publishing.
    Rich descriptions; appeal to the senses.

———. 1992. *An Angel for Solomon Singer*. New York: Orchard Books.
    Rich descriptions; examples of thought shots; snapshots of setting and character.

Sierra, Judy. 2006. *Thelonius Monster's Sky-High Fly Pie*. New York: Alfred A. Knopf.
    Includes a sprinkling of dialogue and lists to build content.

Smith, Doris Buchanan. 1973. *A Taste of Blackberries*. New York: Harper Collins.
    Slowing down the action to explode a small moment in time by adding specific details; contains snapshots of character.

Tripp, Nathaniel. 2001. *Snow Comes to the Farm*. Cambridge, MA: Candlewick Press.
    Appeal to the senses to build content.

Van Wright, Cornelius. 1997. *A House by the River*. New York: Lee and Low Books.
    Appeal to the senses to build content; also contains anecdotes and examples of show, not tell.

Wells, Rosemary. 2002. *Wingwalker*. New York: Hyperion Books for Children.
    Provides examples of snapshots of character.

Whatley, Bruce. 1994. *That Magnetic Dog*. New York: Harper Collins.
    The whole book provides an example of a snapshot of character.

Whitcomb, Mary E. 1998. *Odd Velvet*. San Francisco: Chronicle Books.
    Combines dialogue and descriptions to build content and provide information about the main character.

White, E. B. 1952. *Charlotte's Web*. New York: Harper and Row.
    Provides examples of snapshots of character; characters are revealed by what they say and do.

Wyeth, Sharon Dennis. 1998. *Something Beautiful*. New York: Bantam Doubleday Dell Publishing Group.
    Use of dialogue to build content; appeal to the senses; rich descriptions.

Yolen, Jane. 1987. *Owl Moon*. New York: Philomel Books.
    Appeal to the senses to build content.

———. 1991. *All Those Secrets of the World*. New York: Little, Brown and Co.

> Can be used to explain to young writers how looking at something from close up makes it bigger, providing more of the details—just what we want them to do when they write.

Zolotow, Charlotte. 1992. *The Seashore Book*. New York: Harper Collins.

> Appeal to the senses to build content.

Chapter 5   Creating Powerful Beginnings and Satisfying Endings

Agee, Jon. 2001. *Milo's Hat Trick*. New York: Hyperion Books for Children.

> An example of a surprise ending.

Albert, Richard E. 1994. *Alejandro's Gift*. Needham Heights, MA: Silver Burdett Ginn, a division of Simon and Schuster.

> Opens with a description of setting that creates the mood of loneliness; the ending describes a decision reached and resolves the feeling of loneliness planted in the beginning.

Allen, Janet. 2005. *Best Little Wingman*. Honesdale, PA: Boyds Mills Press.

> The ending is a wish for the future; also ends with dialogue—what the girl imagines her father to be saying.

Applebaum, Diana. 1997. *Cocoa Ice*. New York: Orchard Books.

> This book has two separate stories that are linked through the thoughts of the characters. Each story opens with a description of weather; the endings describe the thoughts of the characters.

Bedard, Michael. 1997. *The Divide*. New York: Bantam Doubleday Dell Publishing Group.

> The ending is an example of a lesson learned or decision reached.

Bogart, Jo Ellen. 1997. *Jeremiah Learns to Read*. New York: Orchard Books.

> The beginning is a snapshot of character focusing on what the main character, Jeremiah, was able to do. The ending reflects a wish for the future. The seed for the ending can be found in the beginning when Juliana tells Jeremiah he can read to her once he learns how.

Bradby, Marie. 1995. *More Than Anything Else*. New York: Orchard Books.

> Begins with a description of setting combined with action; ending describes an accomplishment and self-discovery as it reflects the seed planted in the beginning of the story—Booker's desire to learn to read.

Brinckloe, Julie. 1985. *Fireflies!* New York: Simon and Schuster.

> Helps writers understand time—the beginning is not too far away from the main event; ends with a final action where the feelings of the main character are revealed.

Bunting, Eve. 1991. *Fly Away Home*. New York: Houghton Mifflin, Clarion Books.
The ending describes a memory that lingers.

———. 1991. *Night Tree*. New York: Harcourt Brace & Co.
The ending describes what the main character is thinking.

———. 1993. *Someday a Tree*. New York: Houghton Mifflin, Clarion Books.
Begins and ends with dialogue; the ending dialogue is from an inanimate object.

———. 1997. *On Call Back Mountain*. New York: Scholastic, Blue Sky Press.
The beginning of this book (description of the character Bosco and the setting) is reflected in the ending.

———. 2000. *The Memory String*. New York: Houghton Mifflin Co., Clarion Books.
Ends with a self-discovery.

Burleigh, Robert. 1991. *Flight: The Journey of Charles Lindbergh*. New York: Philomel Books.
The first and last lines are the same—an example of a bookend structure.

———. 1998. *Home Run*. New York: Harcourt Brace & Co.
An example of bookends—the beginning and the end mirror each other.

Cannon, Janell. 1993. *Stellaluna*. New York: Harcourt Brace & Co.
Ends with what the characters are thinking as they describe a lesson learned.

Carter, Anne. 1999. *From Poppa*. Montreal: Lobster Press Limited.
Opens with a description of the weather; can be used as an example of a book where the seed of the ending is planted in the beginning.

Chall, Marsha Wilson. 1992. *Up North at the Cabin*. New York: Lothrup, Lee & Shepard Books.
The ending describes a memory that lingers.

———. 2000. *Sugarbush Spring*. New York: Lothrup, Lee & Shepard Books.
Opens with a description of weather.

Crews, Donald. 1992. *Shortcut*. New York: Greenwillow Books.
Provides an example of establishing a beginning, middle, and end with one small moment in time; the ending is a decision that reflects the problem revealed in the beginning.

Cronin, Doreen. 2000. *Click, Clack Moo: Cows That Type*. New York: Simon and Schuster Books for Young Readers.
The ending combines a decision with a final action. Part of the ending is revealed in the final illustration by Betsy Lewin.

Dahl, Roald. 1961. *James and the Giant Peach*. New York: Puffin Books.
Physical descriptions of character.

———. 1982. *The BFG*. New York: Puffin Books.
Physical descriptions of character.

———. 1983. *The Witches*. New York: Puffin Books.
Physical descriptions of character.

———. 1988. *Matilda*. New York: Puffin Books.
Excellent examples of physical descriptions of character (note especially "The Trunchbull").

Davies, Nicola. 2001. *One Tiny Turtle*. Cambridge, MA: Candlewick Press.
The beginning of this lyrical nonfiction book is a snapshot of setting. The words from the opening line appear again in the ending—an example of a bookends book.

Duke, Kate. 1992. *Aunt Isabel Tells a Good One*. New York: Penguin Books.
As Aunt Isabel tells a story, she provides an example of how to craft a beginning, middle, and end.

Fleming, Candace. 2002. *Muncha! Muncha! Muncha!* New York: Simon and Schuster, Atheneum Books for Young Readers.
The ending combines a decision with a final action and is shown in the final illustration by G. Brian Karas.

Gray, Libba Moore. 1995. *My Mama Had a Dancing Heart*. New York: Orchard Books.
An example of bookends—the last line of the book repeats the first line.

Henkes, Kevin. 1988. *Chester's Way*. New York: Penguin Books.
A here-we-go-again ending indicates that the events might start all over again.

———. 1989. *Jessica*. New York, Greenwillow Books.
An example of a bookends book, in which the beginning and the end are the same.

———. 1996. *Lilly's Purple Plastic Purse*. New York: Greenwillow Books.
Begins with a description of what the main character, Lilly, loves; the ending shows how Lilly is feeling combined with an action.

Hest, Amy. 2004. *Mr. George Baker*. Cambridge, MA: Candlewick Press.
Beginning combines a description of character and setting. The book ends with onomatopoeia.

High, Linda Oatman. 2003. *The Girl on the High-Diving Horse*. New York: Philomel Books.
Begins with a snapshot of setting; the ending includes the book title and describes an accomplishment.

Hoffman, Mary. 1991. *Amazing Grace*. New York: Dial Books for Young Readers.
Begins with a description of the main character in the form of describing what she loves.

Horowitz, Ruth. 2000. *Crab Moon*. Cambridge, MA: Candlewick Press.
> Helps writers understand how they can transition quickly between events to get to the main focus of the story. The beginning is a snapshot of setting that quickly sets the stage for the main event of finding the marooned horseshoe crab. The ending describes a final action and includes dialogue.

Howard, Arthur. 1996. *When I Was Five*. New York: Harcourt Brace & Co.
> The ending (the last line) describes a discovery made.

Johnston, Tony. 1994. *Amber on the Mountain*. New York: Penguin Putnam.
> This book begins with a snapshot of setting; the ending includes the thoughts and feelings of the main characters as well as the final action of writing the letter; an excellent example of planting the seed for the ending in the beginning—Amber's loneliness in the beginning is resolved at the end.

Ketterman, Helen. 1998. *I Remember Papa*. New York: Penguin Putnam.
> Ends with a memory that lingers.

Kroll, Steven. 2001. *Patches Lost and Found*. New York: Winslow Press.
> Clear beginning, middle, and end; has a satisfying ending in the form of a final action; an excellent example of story mapping—using pictures to plan a story.

Laminack, Lester. 1998. *The Sunsets of Miss Olivia Wiggins*. Atlanta: Peachtree Publishers.
> An example of a bookends book, in which the beginning and the end are the same.

L'Engle, Madeleine. 2001. *The Other Dog*. New York: Sea Star Books.
> The ending is an example of self-discovery.

Lyon, George Ella. 2003. *Mother To Tigers*. New York: Atheneum Books for Young Readers.
> Illustrator Peter Catalanotto set up the beginning of this book as a prologue, much like you might find in a movie before the credits role; there are two pages of text before the title page. The last line includes the title of the book.

McFarland, Lyn Rossiter. 2001. *Widget*. New York: Farrar Straus & Giroux.
> Written with a clear beginning, middle, and satisfying ending that are easily identified; beginning combines description of character and setting; ends with a description of what the character is thinking and feeling; an excellent example of how the ending is most often tied to the beginning.

McNaughton, Colin. 1994. *Suddenly!* Orlando, FL: Harcourt Brace & Co.
> An example of a surprise ending.

Miller, Debbie S. 2003. *Arctic Lights, Arctic Nights*. New York: Walker and Co.
> This is a nonfiction book that describes a year in the Arctic region. Each page is written as a snapshot of setting, describing what is happening from month to month. Each snapshot also begins with onomatopoeia; includes an introduction and a glossary.

Mitchell, Margaree King. 1997. *Granddaddy's Gift*. BridgeWater Books.

> An example of a beginning that combines a description of setting and character.

Mora, Pat. 1997. *Tomás and the Library Lady*. New York: Alfred A. Knopf.

> The beginning combines a description of setting with how the main character is feeling.

O'Neill, Alexis. 2002. *The Recess Queen*. New York: Scholastic.

> Beginning is a description of a trait of the main character.

Paulsen, Gary. 1999. *Canoe Days*. New York: Random House.

> The ending line reflects the title of the book.

Penn, Audrey. 1993. *The Kissing Hand*. New York: Scholastic.

> Ends with dialogue from an inanimate object.

Polacco, Patricia. 2001. *Betty Doll*. New York: Philomel Books.

> Ends with a memory that lingers.

Raven, Margot Theis. 1997. *Angels in the Dust*. New York: Troll Communications, BridgeWater Books.

> Opens with a snapshot of setting.

Rylant, Cynthia. 1985. *The Relatives Came*. New York: Macmillan Publishing, Bradbury Press, Publishing.

> An example of a book where the ending indicates that things will start all over again (sometimes called a circular text). The first line of the book sets the stage for the story that happens in the summer. In the end, the relatives are dreaming of the next summer, when things will start all over again.

———. 1992. *An Angel for Solomon Singer*. New York: Orchard Books.

> The ending combines a decision with a final action; final illustration by Peter Catalanotto enhances the ending.

———. 1998. *Tulip Sees America*. New York: Scholastic.

> Opens with a snapshot of setting; the entire book is a series of rich descriptions of setting; the ending reveals a decision reached.

———. 2001. *The Great Gracie Chase: Stop That Dog!* New York: Scholastic.

> The beginning combines a description of character and setting.

———. 2001. *Little Whistle's Dinner Party*. Orlando, FL: Harcourt.

> An example of a beginning that combines a snapshot of character and setting.

Sams II, Carl R., and Jean Stoick. 2000. *Stranger in the Woods*. Milford, MI: Carl R. Sams II Photography.

> This book begins with a description of weather.

Schachner, Judith Byron. 1999. *The Grannyman*. New York: Dutton Children's Books.

> Begins with a physical description of the main character; the last line of the ending includes the book title.

Sheldon, Dyan. 1990. *The Whales' Song*. New York: Dial Books for Young Readers.

Ends with what the main character, Lilly, is thinking in the form of dialogue—she thinks the whales are calling her name.

Small, David. 1985. *Imogene's Antlers*. New York: Crown Publishers.
A here-we-go-again ending indicates that the story might start all over again.

Smith, Doris Buchanan. 1973. *A Taste of Blackberries*. New York: Harper Collins.
The title appears in the ending.

Soto, Gary. 1993. *Too Many Tamales*. New York: G. P. Putnam's Sons.
Interesting beginning sentence that describes the weather.

Spinelli, Jerry. 1990. *Maniac Magee*. Boston: Little, Brown, and Co.
Begins with a description of the main character in the form of what other people say about him.

Vizurraga, Susan. 2000. *Miss Opal's Auction*. New York: Henry Holt and Co.
Opens with dialogue; ends with a memory that lingers.

Wells, Rosemary. 1997. *Bunny Cakes*. New York: Penguin Putnam, Dial Books for Young Readers.
A good mentor text to demonstrate the beginning, middle, and end of a story to very young writers.

———. 2002. *Wingwalker*. New York: Hyperion Books for Children.
Opens with a snapshot of setting that extends into a snapshot of character.

White, E. B. 1952. *Charlotte's Web*. New York: Harper and Row.
Begins with a question. Students might try a different beginning—snapshot of setting, character sketch, etc.—just as E. B. White did, then talk about why this was such a powerful beginning. The book ends with the thoughts and feelings of Wilbur as he remembers Charlotte.

Wood, Douglas. 2006. *Nothing To Do*. New York: Penguin Group.
An example of a book where the seed of the ending can easily be found in the beginning.

Wyeth, Sharon Dennis. 1998. *Something Beautiful*. New York: Bantam Doubleday Dell Publishing Group.
Begins with a description of setting; ends with a final action in which the character makes a self-discovery.

Yolen, Jane. 1987. *Owl Moon*. New York: Philomel Books.
Opens with a snapshot of setting.

———. 1997. *Miz Berlin Walks*. New York: Philomel Books.
An example of a bookends book, in which the beginning and the end are the same.

Chapter 6   Using Scaffolds to Organize Texts

Aardema, Verna, reteller. 1975. *Why Mosquitoes Buzz in People's Ears: A West African Tale*. New York: Dial Press.
> A folktale that can easily be adapted for reader's theater.

———, reteller. 1981. *Bringing the Rain to Kapiti Plain*. New York: Dial Press.
> A folktale that can easily be adapted for reader's theater.

Bang, Molly. 2004. *My Light*. New York: Blue Sky Press, Scholastic.
> First-person narrative written in the voice of the sun.

Baskwill, Jane. 1996. *Somewhere*. New York: MONDO Publishing.
> Repeated refrain, moving through different places.

Bauer, Caroline Feller. 1981. *My Mom Travels a Lot*. New York: Puffin Books.
> Whole-book seesaw scaffold: "The good thing about it is . . ."; "The bad thing about it is . . ."

Bouchard, David. 1995. *If You're Not from the Prairie . . .* New York: Simon and Schuster Children's Publishing Division.
> Use of the repeated refrain "If you're not from the prairie . . ."

Brown, Margaret Wise. 1949. *The Important Book*. New York: HarperCollins.
> A useful scaffold for writing text innovations.

Bunting, Eve. 1997. *I Am the Mummy: Heb-Nefert*. New York: Harcourt.
> First-person narrative written in the voice of the mummy.

Catalanotto, Peter. 2001. *Emily's Art*. New York: Simon and Schuster/Atheneum.
> Organized around days of the week; the first few pages of the book appear before the title page, serving as a preface.

———. 2002 *Matthew A.B.C.* Simon and Schuster Children's Publishing Division.
> ABC text structure.

———. 2003. *Daisy 1, 2, 3*. New York: Atheneum Books.
> Number scaffold.

Chall, Marcia Wilson. 1992. *Up North at the Cabin*. New York: William Morrow and Co.
> Contains the repeated refrain "Up north at the cabin . . ." to open small vignettes. This technique can be adapted by students and used as a structure for similar pieces such as "Down at the seashore . . ." or "Up at the lake . . ."

Charlip, Remy. 1964. *Fortunately*. New York: Simon and Schuster.
> Whole-book seesaw scaffold: "Fortunately . . ."; "Unfortunately . . ."

Cherry, Lynne. 1990. *The Great Kapok Tree*. New York: Harcourt Brace.
> Can be adapted for use in reader's theater.

Cisneros, Sandra. 1994. *Hairs/Pelitos*. New York: Alfred A. Knopf.
> Written in English and Spanish; organized around descriptions of each family member's hair.

Cooper, Elisha. 2006. *Beach*. New York: Orchard Books.
> Organized around a day at the beach from morning until sunset.

Crimi, Carolyn. 1995. *Outside, Inside*. New York: Simon and Schuster Books for Young Readers.
> Whole-book seesaw scaffold; the inside structure shows the passing of time.

Cronin, Doreen. 2003. *Diary of a Worm*. New York: Joanna Cotler Books.
> Diary format; an example of writing in the persona of another.

———. 2005. *Diary of a Spider*. New York: Joanna Cotler Books.
> Diary format; an example of writing in the persona of another.

Curtis, Jamie Lee. 1993. *When I Was Little: A Four-Year-Old's Memoir of Her Youth*. New York: Harper Collins.
> Seesaw scaffold; good for writing a text innovation: "When I was . . ." "Now I'm . . . ," or "When it was . . ." "Now it's . . ."

Cuyler, Margery. 1991. *That's Good! That's Bad!* New York: Henry Holt and Company.
> Seesaw scaffold.

Danneburg, Julie. 2003. *First Year Letters*. Watertown, MA: Charlesbridge Publishing.
> The book is a series of letters from students to their teacher.

De Coteau Orie, Sandra. 1995. *Did You Hear Wind Sing Your Name? An Oneida Song of Spring*. New York: Walker and Company.
> The entire book is written as a series of questions.

Edwards, Pamela Duncan. 2001. *Boston Tea Party*. New York: G. P. Putnam's Sons.
> Cumulative text structure.

———. 2003. *The Wright Brothers*. New York: Hyperion Books.
> Cumulative text structure.

Fox, Mem. 1985. *Wilfrid Gordon McDonald Partridge*. New York: Kane/Miller Book Publishers.
> Text is organized around objects.

———. 1992. *Tough Boris*. New York: Harcourt Brace and Co.
> Seesaw scaffold.

George, Jean Craighead. 1990. *One Day in the Tropical Rain Forest*. New York: Harper Collins.
> A series of short descriptions of the rain forest at different times throughout the day.

———. 1995. *Everglades*. New York: HarperCollins.
> Story within a story; use of print to define the scaffold.

———. 1997. *Look to the North: A Wolf Pup Diary*. New York: Harper Collins.
> This book is written as a diary detailing the growth of a litter of wolf pups at intervals from one day to ten and a half months; contains the repeated refrain "Look to the North . . ."

Gilman, Phoebe. 1992. *Something from Nothing*. New York: Scholastic.

> Contains a parallel story in the illustrations; several repeated refrains.

Granowsky, Dr. Alvin. 1996. *Help Yourself, Little Red Hen!* Orlando, FL: Steck-Vaughn.

> A fairy tale told through the eyes of another character. This is a two-for-one book—contains the original tale as well.

Gray, Libba Moore. 1995. *My Mama Had a Dancing Heart*. New York: Orchard Books.

> Bookend structure, in which the first line of the book is repeated at the end.

Hall, Donald. 1994. *I Am the Dog, I Am the Cat*. New York: Dial Books.

> Seesaw scaffold used to express point of view of the dog and the cat; written in a play format.

High, Linda Oatman. 2001. *Under New York*. New York: Holiday House.

> Repeated refrain ("Under New York . . .") used to organize information.

Hoose, Phillip, and Hannah Hoose. 1998. *Hey, Little Ant*. Berkeley, CA: Tricycle Press.

> A good choice for reader's theater; written in play format.

Howard, Arthur. 1996. *When I Was Five*. New York: Harcourt Brace and Co.

> Seesaw scaffold: "When I was five . . ."; "Now I'm six . . ."

Howard, Elizabeth Fitzgerald. 1991. *Aunt Flossie's Hats (and Crab Cakes Later)*. New York: Clarion Books.

> Organized around objects; includes small anecdotes about several different hats.

Janeczko, Paul B., ed. 2001. *Dirty Laundry Pile: Poems in Different Voices*. New York: Harper Collins.

> A collection of poems by many authors written in the voice of objects or animals.

Jenkins, Martin. 1997. *Chameleons Are Cool*. Cambridge, MA: Candlewick Press.

> Seesaw scaffold used in opening.

Karas, G. Brian. 2002. *Atlantic*. New York: G. P. Putnam's Sons.

> First-person narrative written in the voice of the Atlantic Ocean.

Kimmel, Eric. 1998. *Anansi and the Moss-Covered Rock*. New York: Holiday House.

> A folktale that can easily be adapted for reader's theater.

Krupinski, Loretta. 1994. *A New England Scrapbook: A Journey Through Poetry, Prose, and Pictures*. New York: Harper Collins Publishers.

> An unusual scaffold offering explanatory text, poetry and pictures.

Laminack, Lester. 1998. *The Sunsets of Miss Olivia Wiggins*. Atlanta: Peachtree Publishers.

> Bookend structure—the first line of the book is repeated at the end; moves back and forth across time.

Lobel, Anita. 2000. *One Lighthouse, One Moon*. New York: HarperCollins/Greenwillow.

> A series of three stories using days of the week, months, and counting as organizational structures.

Lowry, Lois. 2002. *Gooney Bird Greene*. New York: Houghton Mifflin Co.

> Use of print to define the scaffold.

MacLachlan, Patricia. 1994. *All the Places to Love*. New York: Harper Collins.

> The text is composed of a series of memories about the places on a farm.

Mannis, Celeste Davidson. 2002. *One Leaf Rides the Wind: Counting in a Japanese Garden*. New York: Penguin.

> Examples of haiku inspired by a Japanese garden; organized like a counting book.

Martin, Bill, Jr. 1983. *Brown Bear, Brown Bear, What Do You See?* New York: Henry Holt and Co.

> Whole-book scaffold useful for writing text innovations.

Martin, Bill, Jr., and John Archambault. 1966. *Knots on a Counting Rope*. New York: Henry Holt and Company.

> The entire book is written as a dialogue between the two main characters, which is shown in the way the words are placed on the page.

McFarland, Lyn Rossiter. 2001. *Widget*. New York: Farrar, Straus & Giroux.

> Seesaw scaffold used in part of the text.

McGrath, Barbara Barbieri, and Peter Alderman. 2003. *Soccer Counts!* Watertown, MA: Charlesbridge Publishing, Inc.

> Number scaffold.

Melmed, Laura Krauss. 2003. *Capital! Washington D.C. from A to Z*. New York: Harper Collins.

> Nonfiction ABC text; contains nonfiction features such as time lines, captions, and labels.

Miller, Debbie S. 2003. *Arctic Lights, Arctic Nights*. New York: Walker and Company.

> Passing of time—describes what is happening in a certain place on a particular day of each month.

Nolan, Jerdine. 1999. *In My Momma's Kitchen*. New York: William Morrow and Co.

> A series of small chapters organized around events that happen in one particular place—the kitchen.

Numeroff, Laura. 1994. *If You Give a Mouse a Cookie*. New York: Scholastic.

> Circular text organization.

Polacco, Patricia. 2001. *Betty Doll*. New York: Philomel Books.
Organized around one object, the doll.

Ryan, Pam Muñoz. 2001. *Mice and Beans*. New York: Scholastic.
Text is organized around days of the week.

Rylant, Cynthia. 1982. *When I Was Young in the Mountains*. New York: Dutton Children's Books.
Repeated refrain used to link small vignettes.

———. 1985. *The Relatives Came*. New York: Macmillan Publishing Co.
Circular text.

———. 1998 *Tulip Sees America*. New York: Scholastic.
A series of snapshots of setting; repeated refrain.

———. 2000. *In November*. New York: Harcourt.
Repeated refrain: "In November . . ."

Scieszka, Jon. 1989. *The True Story of the 3 Little Pigs!* New York: Penguin.
A retelling of a fairy-tale that can be adapted for use in reader's theater.

Sendak, Maurice. 1963. *Where the Wild Things Are*. New York: Harper Collins.
Home-adventure-home structure.

Siebert, Diane. 1991. *Sierra*. New York: Harper Collins.
First-person narrative structure written in the voice of the mountains; a companion book by the same author, *Mojave*, is about the desert.

Sierra, Judy. 2006. *Thelonius Monster's Sky-High Fly Pie*. New York: Alfred A. Knopf.
Borrows a familiar scaffold ("There was an old lady who swallowed a fly . . .").

Spinelli, Eileen. 2004. *In Our Backyard Garden*. New York: Simon and Schuster Books for Young Readers.
A collection of poems about events that all happen in one place—the backyard; moves through the seasons from spring to winter.

Thomson, Sarah L. 2003. *Imagine a Night*. New York: Atheneum Books for Young Readers.
Repeated refrain "Imagine a night . . ." begins each page.

———. 2005. *Imagine a Day*. New York: Atheneum Books for Young Readers.
Repeated refrain "Imagine a day . . ." begins each page.

Van Allsburg, Chris. 1988. *Two Bad Ants*. New York: Houghton Mifflin.
Home-adventure-home structure.

Williams, Sue. 1989. *I Went Walking*. New York: Harcourt Brace and Co.
Whole-book scaffold for writing text innovations.

Williams, Vera. 1982. *A Chair for My Mother*. New York: William Morrow and Company.
Contains a flashback describing the fire in the middle of the story about acquiring the chair.

Wood, Audrey. 1984. *The Napping House*. New York: Scholastic.
>   Cumulative text structure.

Woodruff, Elvira. 1994. *Dear Levi—Letters from the Overland Trail*. New York: Alfred A. Knopf.
>   Letter format.

Yolen, Jane. 1981. *Sleeping Ugly*. New York: Coward, McCann, and Geoghegan.
>   A retelling of a fairy-tale that can be adapted for reader's theater.

Chapter 7   Poetry: Everybody Can Be a Writer

Ackerman, Karen. 1988. *Song and Dance Man*. New York: Alfred A. Knopf.
>   This book is a character sketch of a grandfather; can be used to stimulate thoughts about special people.

Aska, Warabe. 1990. *Seasons*. New York: Bantam Doubleday Dell.
>   A collection of poems to match illustrations about the seasons.

Baylor, Byrd. 1986. *I'm in Charge of Celebrations*. New York: Macmillan Publishing Co.
>   An example of prose that sounds and looks like poetry and reflects the beauty of the Southwest.

Brinckloe, Julie. 1985. *Fireflies!* New York: Simon and Schuster.
>   Prose that contains poetic language.

Brown, Margaret Wise. 2002. *My World of Color*. New York: Hyperion Books for Children.
>   Descriptions of colors written as similes.

Carlstrom, Nancy White. 1993. What Does the Rain Play? New York: Macmillan.
>   Uses a repeated refrain to provide snapshots; use of onomatopoeia throughout.

Chall, Marsha Wilson. 2003. *Prairie Train*. New York: Harper Collins.
>   Poetic language; excellent for use with found poetry.

Collins, Pat Lowery. 1992. *I Am an Artist*. Brookfield, CT: The Millbrook Press.
>   Describes how artists observe the world in special ways; uses a repeated refrain "I am an artist . . ." to create poetic prose.

Crimi, Carolyn. 1995. *Outside, Inside*. New York: Simon and Schuster Books for Young Readers.
>   Use to stimulate thoughts about rain before writing poetry about rain.

Fleming, Denise. 1993. *In the Small, Small Pond*. New York: Henry Holt and Co.
>   Uses a word scaffold (verb-verb-noun-verb) to describe the activities of the pond animals in rhyme.

———. 2001. *Pumpkin Eye*. New York: Henry Holt and Co.

Describes the sights and sounds of Halloween in rhyme; provides a useful word scaffold (adjective-noun) and examples of a repeated refrain.

Fletcher, Ralph. 1997. *Twilight Comes Twice*. New York: Clarion Books.

Poetic language; excellent for use with found poetry.

———. 2005. *A Writing Kind of Day: Poems for Young Poets*. Honesdale, PA: Boyds Mills Press.

A collection of poems that provide especially good models for students.

Freedman, Russell. 1980. *They Lived with the Dinosaurs*. New York: Holiday House.

Short nonfiction text that can be used to create found poetry.

George, Christine O'Connell. 1997. *The Great Frog Race*. New York: Houghton Mifflin.

Rhymed and unrhymed about simple pleasures of country life.

Goldstein, Bobbye S. 1992. *Inner Chimes: Poems on Poetry*. Honesdale, PA: Boyds Mills Press.

A collection of poems about poems and poets.

Graham, Joan Bransfield. 1994. *Splish Splash*. New York: Ticknor & Fields.

A collection of mostly unrhymed, concrete poems about water in its many forms.

Graves, Donald. 1996. *Baseball, Snakes, and Summer Squash: Poems About Growing Up*. Honesdale, PA: Boyds Mills Press.

Unrhymed poetry that tells stories of childhood with heartfelt voice.

Heard, Georgia. 1992. *Creatures of Earth, Sea, and Sky*. Honesdale, PA: Boyds Mills Press.

Poetry for two voices; examples of unrhymed poems.

Heard, Georgia, ed. 2006. *This Place I Know: Poems of Comfort*. Cambridge, MA: Candlewick Press.

A collection of poems that can be used to provide comfort after a difficult time.

Hirschi, Ron. 1990. *Spring*. New York: Penguin Books.

Lyrical language written as prose to describe the season of spring; this author has written a similar book for each season.

Hoberman, Mary Ann. 1959. *Hello and Good-by*. Boston: Little, Brown and Co.

A collection of miscellaneous poems.

Horowitz, Ruth. 2000. *Crab Moon*. Cambridge, MA: Candlewick Press.

Poetic language; excellent for use with found poetry.

Hughes, Langston. 1994. *The Dream Keeper and Other Poems*. New York: Alfred A. Knopf.

A collection of free-verse poems by the author.

Hummon, David. 1999. *Animal Acrostics*. Nevada City, CA: Dawn Publications.

> A collection of acrostics poems about animals; includes factual information and a glossary of wonderful words.

Janeczko, Paul B., ed. 2001. *Dirty Laundry Pile: Poems in Different Voices*. New York: Harper Collins.

> A collection of poems by many authors written in the voice of objects or animals.

————, ed. 2005. *A Kick in the Head: An Everyday Guide to Poetic Forms*. Cambridge, MA: Candlewick Press.

> A collection of twenty-nine poems that illustrate different forms with explanations.

Levy, Constance. 2002. *Splash! Poems of Our Watery World*. New York: Orchard Books, Scholastic.

> A collection of rhymed and unrhymed poems about water in its varied forms.

Little, Jean. 1986. *Hey World, Here I Am!* New York: HarperCollins.

> A collection of poems and vignettes from a young girl's view point.

Livingston, Myra Cohn. 1997. *Cricket Never Does: A Collection of Haiku and Tanka*. New York: Margaret K. McElderry.

> Original haiku and tanka about the four seasons.

London, Jonathan. 1997. *Puddles*. New York: Penguin Putnam.

> A story about the day after a night rainstorm; written in poetic form with lyrical language; many examples of onomatopoeia.

Lotz, Karen E. 1993. *Snowsong Whistling*. New York: Penguin Putnam.

> A celebration in rhyme of the coming of winter; word scaffold (noun-verbing).

Mannis, Celeste Davidson. 2002. *One Leaf Rides the Wind: Counting in a Japanese Garden*. New York: Penguin.

> Examples of haiku inspired by a Japanese garden; organized like a counting book; use of personification and appeal to the senses.

Martin, Bill, Jr., and John Archambault. 1988. *Listen to the Rain*. New York: Henry Holt and Company.

> Poetic language used to describe the progression of a rainstorm.

Nibenegenasabe, Jacob. 2000. "Quiet Until the Thaw." In *Americans' Favorite Poems*. Robert Pinsky and Maggie Dietz, ed. New York: W.W. Norton and Co.

> Poetry scaffold.

O'Neill, Mary. 1961. *Hailstones and Halibut Bones*. New York: Bantam Doubleday Dell Publishing Group.

> A collection of poems about colors that invoke all of the senses.

Otten, Charlotte. 1997. *January Rides the Wind*. New York: William Morrow and Co.
> Short poems about each month; examples of personification, exact nouns, and specific verbs.

Paolilli, Paul, and Dan Brewer. 2001. *Silver Seeds*. New York: Viking.
> Acrostic nature poetry that spans daybreak to night.

Partridge, Elizabeth. 2002. *Moon Glowing*. New York: Dutton Children's Books.
> Describes autumn to winter in rhythmic verse; useful scaffold.

Pinkney, Sandra L. 2000. *Shades of Black: A Celebration of Our Children*. New York: Scholastic.
> Uses poetic language to describe physical features.

Polacco, Patricia. 1994. *My Rotten Redheaded Older Brother*. New York: Simon and Schuster.
> Can be used to stimulate thoughts about special people.

———. 1995. *My Ol' Man*. New York: Philomel Books.
> Can be used to stimulate thoughts about special people.

Roseliep, Raymond. 1984. *The Earth We Swing On*. Minneapolis, MN: Winston Press.
> A book of haiku most often not written in the five-seven-five syllable pattern; use of three lines to describe a very small moment in time; appeal to emotions and sensory experiences.

Sandburg, Carl. 1998. *Grassroots*. New York: Harcourt Brace and Company.
> A collection of poems that illustrate strategies such as effective repetition and use of proper nouns; unrhymed poetry.

Serio, John, ed. 2005. *The Seasons*. New York: Sterling Publishing Co.
> A book of poems organized around the seasons. Each season is introduced with haiku; rhymed and unrhymed; beautiful illustrations and information about each poet.

Seuss, Dr. 1996. *My Many Colored Days*. New York: Alfred A. Knopf.
> Rhyming text that links colors to feelings.

Sheldon, Dyan. 1990. *The Whales' Song*. New York: Dial Books for Young Readers.
> Poetic language; excellent for use with found poetry.

Singer, Isaac Bashevis. 1967. *The Fearsome Inn*. New York: Scribner.
> Examples of poetic language.

Spinelli, Eileen. 1998. *When Mama Comes Home Tonight*. New York: Simon and Schuster Books for Young Readers.
> Rhythmic prose that sounds more like a poem; can be used to stimulate thoughts about special people.

Tripp, Nathaniel. 2001. *Snow Comes to the Farm*. Cambridge, MA: Candlewick Press.
> Poetic language; excellent for use with found poetry.

Viorst, Judith. 1981. *If I Were in Charge of the World*. New York: Simon and Schuster Children's Publishing Division.

> A collection of poems that can be used as scaffolds.

Yolen, Jane. 1987. *Owl Moon*. New York: Philomel Books.

> Poetic language; excellent for use with found poetry.

———. 2000. *Color Me a Rhyme*. Honesdale, PA: Boyds Mills Press.

> Poems about the colors in nature accompanied by photographs.

Young, Judy. 2005. *R Is for Rhyme: A Poetry Alphabet*. Chelsea, MI: Sleeping Bear Press.

> A collection of poems to illustrate scaffolds and poetic literary devices; includes explanations of each device or form.

Zolotow, Charlotte. 1992. *The Seashore Book*. New York: Harper Collins.

> Poetic language; excellent for use with found poetry.

Chapter 8   Choice, Voice, and All That Jazz

Anderson, Laurie Halse. 2000. *Fever, 1793*. New York: Simon and Schuster Books for Young Readers.

> Contains an example of a rubber-band (stretchy, or taffy) sentence.

Andreae, Giles. 2001. *Love Is a Handful of Honey*. Wilton, CT: Tiger Tales.

> Provides a good example of metaphor for younger students.

Arnosky, Jim. 2002. *All About Frogs*. New York: Scholastic.

> This book is written in a friendly, confidential tone that helps the reader hear the voice of the author.

Babbitt, Natalie. 1975. *Tuck Everlasting*. New York: Farrar, Straus, & Giroux.

> Contains examples of metaphors.

Baylor, Byrd. 1982. *The Best Town in the World*. New York: Macmillan Publishing Co.

> Use of hyphenated adjectives to create a description of setting.

Bedard, Michael. 1997. *The Divide*. New York: Bantam Doubleday Dell Publishing Group.

> Use of hyphenated adjectives and adjectives in unusual placement; fragments; proper nouns.

Brinckloe, Julie. 1985. *Fireflies!* New York: Simon and Schuster.

> Use of unexpected verbs; word pairs.

Brown, Margaret Wise. Ed. Joan Blos. 1994. *The Days Before Now*. New York: Simon and Schuster.

> Rich descriptions through use of color words.

Bryant, Jen. 2005. *Georgia's Bones*. Grand Rapids, MI: Eerdmans Books for Young Readers.

> Use of word pairs to create rhythm.

Bunting, Eve. 2006. *One Green Apple*. New York: Clarion Books.

    Appeal to the senses; use of onomatopoeia; effective repetition; strong verbs; hyphenated adjectives; variety of sentence length.

Burleigh, Robert. 1998. *Home Run*. New York: Harcourt Brace & Co.

    Use of fragments.

———. 2004. *Langston's Train Ride*. New York: Orchard Books.

    Written in the first person to create a friendly, conversational tone; use of unexpected adjectives; use of fragments; hyphenated adjectives.

Burleigh, Robert, and Ed Young. 2006. *Tiger of the Snows: Tenzing Norgay: The Boy Whose Dream Was Everest*. New York: Atheneum Books.

    Contains hyphenated adjectives, similes and metaphors, unexpected nouns and verbs, parentheses, and exact language.

Carle, Eric. 2002. *"Slowly, Slowly, Slowly," said the Sloth*. New York: Scholastic.

    A great book to introduce word choice; contains a page of factual information on sloths.

Chall, Marsha Wilson. 1992. *Up North at the Cabin*. New York: Lothrop, Lee & Shepard Books.

    Examples of specialized vocabulary, hyphenated adjectives, and strong verbs; figurative language; personification.

———. 2003. *Prairie Train*. New York: Harper Collins.

    Use of figurative language.

Cooper, Elisha. 2006. *Beach*. New York: Orchard Books.

    Excellent word choice—strong verbs, exact nouns, and specific adjectives; use of metaphor and simile; appeal to the senses.

Crews, Donald. 1991. *Bigmama's*. New York: Greenwillow Books.

    Variety of sentence length and beginnings; use of proper nouns.

Crimi, Carolyn. 1995. *Outside, Inside*. New York: Simon and Schuster Books for Young Readers.

    Use of strong verbs.

Cronin, Doreen. 2003. *Diary of a Worm*. New York: Joanna Cotler Books.

    An example of writing in the persona of another to create voice.

———. 2005. *Diary of a Spider*. New York: Joanna Cotler Books.

    An example of writing in the persona of another to create voice.

Dahl, Roald. 1961. *James and the Giant Peach*. New York: Puffin Books.

    Variation of sentence length; rich language.

Davies, Nicola. 2001. *Bat Loves the Night*. Cambridge, MA: Candlewick Press.

    An example of narrative nonfiction; use of figurative language; strong verbs and adjectives.

————. 2001. *One Tiny Turtle.* Cambridge, MA: Candlewick Press.

    An example of narrative nonfiction; use of figurative language; strong verbs and adjectives.

Edwards, Pamela Duncan. 1996. *Some Smug Slug.* New York: Harper Collins.

    Can be used to introduce alliteration.

Fleming, Candace. 2002. *Muncha! Muncha! Muncha!* New York: Atheneum Books for Young Readers.

    Use of hyphenated words; fragments; word choice.

Fletcher, Ralph. 1997. *Twilight Comes Twice.* New York: Clarion Books.

    Use of hyphenated adjectives and unusual placement of adjectives; strong and unexpected verbs used to create powerful images; figurative language.

————. 2003. *Hello, Harvest Moon.* New York: Clarion Books.

    Figurative language; word pairs; alliteration.

Fox, Mem. 1989. *Night Noises.* New York: Harcourt Brace & Co.

    Contains examples of similes and onomatopoeia; strong verbs; repeated refrain.

Frazee, Marla. 2003. *Roller Coaster.* New York: Harcourt, Voyager Books.

    Use of parentheses.

Graves, Donald. 1996. *Baseball, Snakes, and Summer Squash: Poems About Growing Up.* Honesdale, PA: Boyds Mills Press.

    Use of hyphenated adjectives; strong sense of voice.

Gray, Libba Moore. 1995. *My Mama Had a Dancing Heart.* New York: Orchard Books.

    Use of hyphenated adjectives and color words.

Grimes, Nikki. 2002. *Talkin' About Bessie: The Story of Aviator Elizabeth Coleman.* New York: Orchard Books, Scholastic.

    Contains examples of hyphenated adjectives; written in the voice of different characters; examples of use of dialect.

Hall, Donald. 1994. *I Am the Dog, I Am the Cat.* New York: Dial Books.

    Use of dialogue to hear different voices.

Henkes, Kevin. 1991. *Chrysanthemum.* New York: Greenwillow Books.

    Use of unexpected verbs that match the topic, in this case, flowers.

————. 1996. *Lilly's Purple Plastic Purse.* New York: Greenwillow Books.

    Use of strong verbs and adjectives; alliteration.

Hesse, Karen. 1999. *Come On, Rain!* New York: Scholastic.

    Examples of unexpected verbs.

Hest, Amy. 2004. *Mr. George Baker.* Cambridge, MA: Candlewick Press.

    This book is a wonderful example of voice created with word choice (some invented words) and by writing in a very conversational tone; some fragments.

High, Linda Oatman. 1998. *Beekeepers*. Honesdale, PA: Boyds Mills Press.
Choice of words to match the topic.

———. 1999. *Barn Savers*. Honesdale, PA: Boyds Mills Press.
Use of similes that match the topic.

———. 2003. *The Girl on the High-Diving Horse*. New York: Philomel Books.
Some hyphenated words; use of words that match the topic; contains both an author's note and an illustrator's note.

Hirschi, Ron. 1990. *Winter*. New York: Penguin Books.
Examples of the use of color words and figurative language (similes and metaphors); other books in this series on the seasons have similar examples.

Hoose, Phillip, and Hannah Hoose. 1998. *Hey, Little Ant*. Berkeley, CA: Tricycle Press.
Use of dialogue to hear different voices.

Hornby, Nick. 2001. *How to Be Good*. New York: Penguin Putnam.
A book written for adults that contains many examples of hyphenated adjectives.

Horowitz, Ruth. 2000. *Crab Moon*. Cambridge, MA: Candlewick Press.
Use of figurative language; examples of strong verbs, alliteration, and word pairs.

Hosta, Dar. 2003. *I Love the Night*. Flemington, NJ: Brown Dog Books.
"Adjective-ly adjective" structure, for example, "perfectly perfect."

Howard, Arthur. 1996. *When I Was Five*. New York: Harcourt, Voyager.
Use of parentheses to whisper a secret.

Janeczko, Paul B., ed. 2001. *Dirty Laundry Pile: Poems in Different Voices*. New York: Harper Collins.
A collection of poems by many authors written in the voice of objects or animals.

Jenkins, Martin. 1997. *Chameleons Are Cool*. Cambridge, MA: Candlewick Press.
An example of nonfiction writing with voice; strong verbs and adjectives; hyphenated adjectives.

Johnston, Tony. 1994. *Amber on the Mountain*. New York: Penguin Putnam.
Powerful similes and metaphors; some use of dialect to create voice; examples of good word choice with vivid verbs and adjectives.

Kranking, Kathleen. 2003. *The Ocean Is . . .* New York: Henry Holt.
A good mentor text for extended metaphor.

Laminack, Lester. 2004. *Saturdays and Teacakes*. Atlanta: Peachtree Publishers.
Use of repeated refrains and fragments; written in a conversational tone that adds voice; use of parentheses to add more information; use of proper nouns specific to a certain era.

Leedy, Loreen, and Pat Street. 2003. *There's a Frog in My Throat!: 440 Animal Sayings a Little Bird Told Me*. New York: Henry Holt and Co.
>A collection of similes, metaphors, idioms, and proverbs that relate to animals; meanings are explained.

L'Engle, Madeleine. 2001. *The Other Dog*. New York: SeaStar Books.
>Use of parentheses to add sarcasm.

Lester, Julius. 1994. *John Henry*. New York: Dial Books, a Division of Penguin Books.
>Variation of sentence length.

Lyon, George Ella. 2003. *Mother to Tigers*. New York: Atheneum Books for Young Readers.
>Alliteration; strong verbs and adjectives; word pairs.

MacLachlan, Patricia. 1980. *Through Grandpa's Eyes*. New York: Harper Collins.
>Use of personification; unexpected verbs.

———. 1985. *Sarah, Plain and Tall*. New York: Harper and Row.
>Unusual placement of adjectives.

———. 1991. *Journey*. New York: Bantam Doubleday Dell Publishing.
>Use of personification; unexpected verbs.

———. 1994. *Skylark*. New York: Harper Collins.
>Unusual placement of adjectives.

McFarland, Lyn Rossiter. 2001. *Widget*. New York: Farrar, Straus & Giroux.
>Contains examples of vivid verbs.

Miller, Debbie S. 2003. *Arctic Lights, Arctic Nights*. New York: Walker and Company.
>An excellent example of voice in nonfiction text; onomatopoeia; word choice.

Mitchell, Margaree King. 1997. *Granddaddy's Gift*. BridgeWater Books.
>Contains examples of hyphenated adjectives.

Murphy, Frank. 2000. *The Legend of the Teddy Bear*. Chelsea, MI: Sleeping Bear Press.
>Contains examples of word pairs and alliteration.

O'Neill, Alexis. 2002. *The Recess Queen*. New York: Scholastic.
>Word choice; rhythm.

Palatini, Margie. 1997. *Moosetache*. New York: Hyperion Books for Children.
>Strong verbs and adjectives for vocabulary building; use of "perfectly perfect."

———. *Mooseltoe*. New York: Hyperion Books for Children.
>Use of "perfectly perfect."

Pattou, Edith. 2001. *Mrs. Spitzer's Garden*. New York: Harcourt.
>Can be used with older students to explain metaphor—the book uses gardening as an extended metaphor for teaching.

Paulsen, Gary. 1999. *Canoe Days*. New York: Random House.
>Use of figurative language.

Pinkney, Sandra L. 2000. *Shades of Black: A Celebration of Our Children*. New York: Scholastic.

      Creative use of unique color words; personification.

———. 2002. *A Rainbow All Around Me*. New York: Scholastic.

      Descriptions of color—leads to understanding of how color can be used to create rich descriptions.

Reese, Barbara. 2005. *Storm Angels*. West Chester, PA: Stargazer Publishing, LLC.

      Contains examples of onomatopoeia, strong verbs, personification, extended metaphor, and hyphenated adjectives.

Rylant, Cynthia. 1986. *Night in the Country*. New York: Simon and Schuster.

      Variation in sentence length; fragments; onomatopoeia.

———. 1992. *An Angel for Solomon Singer*. New York: Orchard Books.

      Use of parentheses to indicate wishes or dreams.

———. 1998. *Tulip Sees America*. New York: Scholastic.

      Use of color words.

———. 2000. *In November*. New York: Harcourt.

      Unusual sentence structures to make prose sound like poetry; figurative language.

———. 2001. *The Great Gracie Chase: Stop That Dog!* New York: Scholastic.

      Use of parentheses.

———. 2001. *Little Whistle*. Orlando, FL: Harcourt, Voyager Books.

      Use of parentheses to add extra information.

Sams II, Carl R., and Jean Stoick. 2000. *Stranger in the Woods*. Milford, MI: Carl R. Sams II Photography.

      An example of writing in the persona of another, in this case, the animals.

Seuss, Dr. 1961. *The Sneetches*. New York: Random House.

      An example of a distinctive voice.

———. 1990. *Oh, the Places You'll Go!* New York: Random House.

      An example of a distinctive voice.

———. 1996. *My Many Colored Days*. New York: Alfred A. Knopf.

      Descriptions of colors linked to feelings.

Seuss, Dr., with Jack Prelutsky and Lane Smith. 1998. *Hooray for Diffendoofer Day*. New York: Random House.

      Blending of the voices of Seuss, Prelutsky, and Smith; includes pages of original notes and sketches made by Theodore Geisel; shows revision process.

Sierra, Judy. 2006. *Thelonius Monster's Sky-High Fly Pie*. New York: Alfred A. Knopf.

      Examples of powerful verbs, exact nouns, super (unexpected or unusual) and hyphenated adjectives; made-up words; parentheses.

Steinberg, Laya. 2003. *Thesaurus Rex*. Cambridge, MA: Barefoot Books.

> Can be used as an introduction to word choice, especially synonyms.

Tripp, Nathaniel. 2001. *Snow Comes to the Farm*. Cambridge, MA: Candlewick Press.

> Repeated words; poetic language; variety of sentence patterns.

Weeks, Sarah. 1995. *Follow the Moon*. New York: HarperCollins, Laura Geringer.

> This book is an extended metaphor for teaching and learning. It can be used as an example to students of how finding the voice inside their heads allows them to add style to their writing.

Wells, Rosemary. 1997. *Bunny Cakes*. New York: Penguin Putnam, Dial Books for Young Readers.

> Includes examples of specific word choice and proper nouns; especially good as a mentor text for emergent writers.

Wood, Douglas. 2006. *Nothing to Do*. New York: Penguin Group.

> Use of parentheses to provide more information.

Yolen, Jane. 1987. *Owl Moon*. New York: Philomel Books.

> Use of figurative language and onomatopoeia.

———. 1996. *Welcome to the Sea of Sand*. New York: G. P. Putnam's Sons.

> Use of color words; strong word choice; hyphenated adjectives.

———. 1997. *Nocturne*. New York: Harcourt Brace.

> Examples of rubber-band (stretchy, or taffy) sentences.

Zolotow, Charlotte. 1992. *The Seashore Book*. New York: Harper Collins Publishers.

> Use of color to provide rich descriptions of setting.

Chapter 9 Walk Around in the Author's Syntax

Albert, Richard E. 1994. *Alejandro's Gift*. Needham Heights, MA: Simon and Schuster, Silver Burdett Ginn.

> The opening paragraph is a snapshot of setting. It can be used to help students create other snapshots of setting by borrowing the structure of the author.

Beach, Judi K. 2003. *Names for Snow*. New York: Hyperion Books.

> The book is a collection of epithets for snow written in poetic form.

Bedard, Michael. 1997. *The Divide*. New York: Bantam Doubleday Dell Publishing Group.

> Contains examples of the use of a semicolon, colon, and dashes.

Bloom, Becky. 1999. *Wolf!* New York: Orchard Books.

> Use of the colon for explanations; variations in print type.

Bottner, Barbara, and Gerald Kruglik. 2004. *Wallace's Lists*. New York: Harper Collins Publishers.

> Use of colon for listing; use of italics to emphasize a word.

Brown, Margaret Wise. Ed. Joan Blos. 1994. *The Days Before Now*. New York: Simon and Schuster.

> Passages from this book can be used to help students create snapshots of setting by borrowing the author's syntax.

Bryant, Jen. 2005. *Georgia's Bones*. Grand Rapids, MI: Eerdmans Books for Young Readers.

> Examples of dashes; use of colon followed by a list.

———. 2005. *Music for the End of Time*. Grand Rapids, MI: Eerdmans Books for Young Readers.

> Italics used to signify thoughts; examples of ellipses and dashes.

Bunting, Eve. 1996. *Secret Place*. New York: Clarion Books.

> Use of colons for lists.

Burleigh, Robert. 1991. *Flight: The Journey of Charles Lindbergh*. New York: Philomel Books.

> Use of colons for a variety of reasons; examples of dashes; use of epithets.

———. 1998. *Home Run*. New York: Harcourt Brace & Co.

> Use of italics; epithet, "the Babe."

Burleigh, Robert, and Ed Young. 2006. *Tiger of the Snows: Tenzing Norgay: The Boy Whose Dream Was Everest*. New York: Atheneum Books.

> Uses colons and dashes for various reasons; italics to signify thoughts; capitalization of myriad proper nouns; contains examples of epithets and a variety of sentence types.

Catalanotto, Peter. 1999. *Dad and Me*. New York: DK Publishing.

> Use of colon for listing; use of ellipses, type and size of print; interjections.

Chall, Marsha Wilson. 1992. *Up North at the Cabin*. New York: Lothrup, Lee & Shepard Books.

> Examples of dashes, ellipses, and use of colon followed by a list.

Cocca-Leffler, Maryann. 2002. *Bravery Soup*. Morton Grove, IL: Albert Whitman & Company.

> A good text to use for reader's theater; includes interjections, different types of sentences, and a variety of conventions.

Crews, Donald. 1991. *Bigmama's*. New York: Greenwillow Books.

> Variation of print size; use of all caps to indicate shouting; dashes and ellipses; punctuation for dialogue.

———. 1992. *Shortcut*. New York: Mulberry Books, William Morrow and Co.

> Simple noun-verb sentence structures for sentence sense and punctuation for dialogue; use of all caps to indicate shouting.

Davies, Nicola. 2001. *Bat Loves the Night*. Cambridge, MA: Candlewick Press.
>   Examples of dashes and ellipses.

———. 2001. *One Tiny Turtle*. Cambridge, MA: Candlewick Press.
>   The beginning of this lyrical nonfiction book is a snapshot of setting.
>   It can be used to help students create other snapshots of setting by
>   borrowing the author's structure.

Edwards, Pamela Duncan. 1997. *Barefoot: Escape on the Underground Railroad*.
New York: Harper Collins Publishers.
>   Use of epithets; includes an author's note about the Underground Railroad.

Falconer, Ian. 2000. *Olivia*. New York: Atheneum Books for Young Readers.
>   Short sentences that can be used to develop sentence sense; use of illustrations
>   for word splash.

———. 2001. *Olivia Saves the Circus*. New York: Atheneum Books for Young
Readers.
>   Use of epithets; variation in print size.

Fleming, Candace. 2002. *Muncha! Muncha! Muncha!* New York: Atheneum Books
for Young Readers.
>   Variation in print size; interjections.

Fletcher, Ralph. 1997. *Twilight Comes Twice*. New York: Clarion Books.
>   Contains examples of the use of a colon followed by a list.

———. 2003. *Hello, Harvest Moon*. New York: Clarion Books.
>   Use of italics, dashes, ellipses, and colon.

Fox, Mem. 1989. *Night Noises*. New York: Harcourt Brace & Co.
>   Contains examples of ellipses and speech bubbles; variation of print style
>   and size.

Frazee, Marla. 2003. *Roller Coaster*. New York: Harcourt, Inc., Voyager Books.
>   Simple noun-verb sentence; varying print type and size.

Fritz, Jean. 1991. *Bully for You, Teddy Roosevelt*. New York: G. P. Putnam's Sons.
>   Contains the use of epithets, parentheses, and commentary dashes.

Hall, Donald. 1994. *I Am the Dog, I Am the Cat*. New York: Dial Books.
>   Written in play format, this book easily lends itself to reader's theater.

Heller, Ruth. 1987. *A Cache of Jewels and Other Collective Nouns*. New York:
Grosset & Dunlap.
>   Excellent examples of different types of nouns accompanied by rich
>   illustrations.

———. 1989. *Many Luscious Lollipops: A Book About Adjectives*. New York:
Grosset & Dunlap.
>   Many examples of the use of adjectives combined with rich illustrations.

————. 1998. *Fantastic! Wow! And Unreal!: A Book About Interjections and Conjunctions*. New York: Grosset & Dunlap.

Contains many examples of interjections and the different kinds of conjunctions in context as well as in lists; beautiful illustrations are appealing to students.

Henkes, Kevin. 1991. *Chrysanthemum*. New York: Greenwillow Books.

Use of mild interjections; simple noun-verb sentences; capitalization of proper nouns; use of varying print size and italics.

The following Kevin Henkes books can be used to study a variety of conventions, including end punctuation, dialogue, dashes, parentheses, use of italics, talking captions, capitalization of proper nouns, variety of print size, and ellipses.

Chester's Way. 1988. New York: Penguin Books.

Jessica. 1989. New York, Greenwillow Books.

Lilly's Purple Plastic Purse. 1996. New York: Greenwillow Books.

Wemberly Worried. 2000. New York: Greenwillow Books.

Grandpa and Bo. 2002. New York: Greenwillow Books.

Kitten's First Full Moon. 2004. New York: Scholastic.

Hest, Amy. 2004. *Mr. George Baker*. Cambridge, MA: Candlewick Press.

Use of dashes and semicolons; illustrations by Jon J. Muth can be used for a word splash.

High, Linda Oatman. 1998. *Beekeepers*. Honesdale, PA: Boyds Mills Press.

Use of the colon followed by a list.

————. 1999. *Barn Savers*. Honesdale, PA: Boyds Mills Press.

Use of the colon followed by a list.

————. 2003. *The Girl on the High-Diving Horse*. New York: Philomel Books.

Use of the colon followed by an explanation.

Hoberman, Mary Ann. 2001. *You Read to Me, I'll Read to You*. New York: Little, Brown and Co.

Short poems written for two voices—can be used for reader's theater.

Horowitz, Ruth. 2000. *Crab Moon*. Cambridge, MA: Candlewick Press.

Short passages lend themselves to trying out the author's syntax.

Jenkins, Martin. 1997. *Chameleons Are Cool*. Cambridge, MA: Candlewick Press.

Use of ellipses and dashes; variation in print size.

Johnston, Tony. 1994. *Amber on the Mountain*. New York: Penguin Putnam.

The opening paragraph is a snapshot of setting. It can be used to help students create other snapshots of setting by borrowing the structure of the author.

Laminack, Lester. 1998. *The Sunsets of Mrs. Olivia Wiggins*. Atlanta: Peachtree Publishers.

Uses italics to distinguish Mrs. Olivia Wiggins's memories from the present-day dialogue.

———. 2004. *Saturdays and Teacakes*. Atlanta: Peachtree Publishers.
> Dialogue written in italics without quotation marks; examples of dashes and ellipses.

L'Engle, Madeleine. 2001. *The Other Dog*. New York: SeaStar Books.
> Variation in print size; dashes, ellipses; use of illustrations by Christine Davenier for word splash.

Lyon, George Ella. 2003. *Mother to Tigers*. New York: Atheneum Books for Young Readers.
> Use of dashes and ellipses; colon followed by a list as well as use of colon to further explain.

MacLachlan, Patricia. 1980. *Arthur, For the Very First Time*. New York: Harper Collins Publishers.
> Use of colon to offer explanation or definition; use of bold print to indicate writing in a journal; use of italics to indicate the character's thinking.

———. 1994. *All the Places to Love*. New York: Harper Collins.
> Use of the colon followed by a list; also contains examples of semicolons and dashes.

Martin, Jacqueline Briggs. 1998. *Snowflake Bentley*. New York: Houghton Mifflin.
> Use of epithets.

McFarland, Lyn Rossiter. 2001. *Widget*. New York: Farrar, Straus & Giroux.
> Simple noun-verb sentence structures for developing sentence sense and punctuation for dialogue; ellipses.

McNaughton, Colin. 1994. *Suddenly!* New York: Harcourt Brace & Co.
> Variation of print size and style; use of word placement; variety of sentence types; use of speech bubbles.

———. 1997. *Preston's Goal!* New York: Harcourt Brace & Company
> Contains examples of the use of a colon to set off dialogue; also contains ellipses, speech bubbles, examples of exclamatory sentences, and interjections.

Most, Bernard. 1990. *The Cow That Went Oink*. New York: Harcourt.
> Use of speech bubbles that are integral to an understanding of the text.

O'Neill, Alexis. 2002. *The Recess Queen*. New York: Scholastic.
> Illustrations by Laura Huliska-Beith can be used for word splash; variation of print size; use of epithets.

Otten, Charlotte. 1997. *January Rides the Wind*. New York: William Morrow and Co.
> Use of the colon followed by a list in the poem "February."

Palatini, Margie. 1997. *Moosetache*. New York: Hyperion Books for Children.
> Variations in print; ellipses.

———. 2004. *Moo Who?* New York: Katherine Tegan Books.
> Use of interjections and dialogue.

Paulsen, Gary. 1989. *The Winter Room*. New York: Orchard Books.

> Passages from this book can be used to help middle school students create other snapshots of setting by borrowing the structure of the author.

———. 1999. *Canoe Days*. New York: Random House.

> Interesting use of *and* to connect a series of objects without the use of a comma, like a rewind in the character's mind, recalling all the things he saw that day.

Plourde, Lynn. 1997. *Pigs in the Mud in the Middle of the Rud*. New York: Scholastic, Blue Sky Press.

> Simple noun-verb sentences; use of *and* to begin sentences for a list effect; use of ellipses; varying print size; conventions for conversation; interjections.

Pulver, Robin. 2003. *Punctuation Takes a Vacation*. New York: Holiday House.

> Explains the importance of using punctuation marks in a very engaging way. Ellipses; use of different sizes and arrangement of print.

Rappaport, Doreen. 2004. *John's Secret Dreams*. New York: Hyperion Books for Children.

> Variations in print size and style.

Raschka, Chris. 1993. *Yo! Yes?* New York: Orchard Books.

> Can be used for examples of end punctuation.

Ray, Mary Lyn. 1996. *Mud*. New York: Harcourt.

> Use of colon to offer an explanation; simple noun-verb sentences.

Reese, Barbara. 2005. *Storm Angels*. West Chester, PA: Stargazer Publishing, LLC.

> Use of ellipses; conventions for dialogue; variety of print size; variation of sentence structures; interjections.

Rosen, Michael. 1989. *We're Going on a Bear Hunt*. New York: Simon and Schuster.

> A good text to use for reader's theater; includes interjections and variation of sentence types and print size.

Ryan, Pam Muñoz. 2001. *Mice and Beans*. New York: Scholastic.

> Use of variations in print style and size; ellipses; interjections.

Rylant, Cynthia. 1982. *When I Was Young in the Mountains*. New York: Dutton Children's Books.

> Use of commas in compound sentences.

———. 1986. *Night in the Country*. New York: Simon and Schuster.

> Dashes; ellipses; use of colon.

Sams II, Carl R., and Jean Stoick. 2000. *Stranger in the Woods*. Milford, MI: Carl R. Sams II Photography.

> Use of epithets.

Schachner, Judy. 2003. *Skippyjon Jones*. New York: Dutton Children's Books.

> Use of ellipses and variety of print size; examples of epithets.

Schertle, Alice. 2004. *All You Need for a Beach*. New York: Harcourt.

> Contains examples of ellipses, dashes, and variations in print; a variety of different types of sentences for examples of different end punctuation.

Shapiro, Karen Jo. 2005. *Because I Could Not Stop My Bike and Other Poems*. Watertown, MA: Charlesbridge.

> A collection of parodies written in the style of well-known poems; demonstrates how to use the syntax and mechanics of another author.

Sheldon, Dyan. 1990. *The Whales' Song*. New York: Dial Books for Young Readers.

> Short passages lend themselves to trying out the author's syntax. Examples of print size; interjections; ellipses; dashes; punctuation for dialogue; apostrophes.

Steinberg, Laya. 2003. *Thesaurus Rex*. Cambridge, MA: Barefoot Books.

> Use of colon followed by a list.

Tripp, Nathaniel. 2001. *Snow Comes to the Farm*. Cambridge, MA: Candlewick Press.

> Commas used in a variety of ways.

Truss, Lynne. 2006. *Eats, Shoots and Leaves: Why, Commas Really DO Make a Difference!* New York: G. P. Putnam's Sons.

> A visual example of the use of commas; includes explanations written in simple language.

Walton, Rick. 2004. *Suddenly Alligator: An Adverbial Tale*. Layton, UT: Gibbs Smith.

> Provides examples for using adverbs.

Whatley, Bruce. 1994. *That Magnetic Dog*. New York: Harper Collins.

> Wonderful illustrations that can be used for a word splash activity.

Whitcomb, Mary E. 1998. *Odd Velvet*. San Francisco: Chronicle Books.

> Variations in print.

White, E. B. 1945. *Stuart Little*. New York: Harper & Row.

> Examples of a variety of sentence types; the opening to "Ames Crossing" is useful for trying out the author's syntax.

Wood, Douglas. 2006. *Nothing to Do*. New York: Penguin Group.

> Use of ellipses and commentary dashes; fragments as part of a list; variety of print size and type; use of italics.

Yolen, Jane. 1996. *Welcome to the Sea of Sand*. New York: G. P. Putnam's Sons.

> Use of commas, semicolons, and colons.

We continue to be inspired and grow as writers through the study of mentor texts and their authors. Our association with the many wonderful teachers we meet in graduate courses and conferences, as well as those with whom we work closely on a daily basis, is the extended writing community that sustains us and supports our work. When the classroom teacher reads aloud regularly to the students and becomes the model for writing along with the mentor texts, something quite magical happens in classrooms. Students express themselves as writers in extraordinary and unexpected ways. They develop a passion for writing and become mentors for their peers, and even for their teachers. What happens, in fact, is that a writing community is built with a strong foundation of mentor texts that allows the teacher to start constructing the walls for many rooms using scaffolds from the mentor texts, adding windows, doors, and crown molding, like craft. At first the students are only apprentices, but eventually they become master masons and carpenters. Just like Fred and Lulu, characters in *The Magic Toolbox* by Mie Araki, students can dream big and imagine something new if they have the right tools. The mentor texts and the teacher will provide them with just that—the tools they need to grow as writers.

Bruce Bloome, a fourth-grade teacher at the Upper Moreland Intermediate School in Hatboro, PA, recently rediscovered the power of the read-aloud, mentor texts, and the reading-writing connection in his classroom. He was continually inspired and challenged by his students' work. He shared his writing and often asked for their help when he got stuck. He encouraged his students to discover new mentor texts and share them with others. As his students searched for books that would help them move forward as writers, their love for reading also grew. It produced an incredible snowball effect, quickly gaining momentum, and is best described in Bruce's letter to his students at the end of the year:

> The room was silent . . . library-silent . . . don't-make-a-sound-unless-it-is-absolutely-necessary library-silent, with occasional whispers crawling across the ceiling and the floor, and the graphite scrapings of pencil against paper spelling out a message of writing in progress.

The teacher sat low to the floor in his reading chair, reflecting and remembering.

Had it really been nine months?

That first day had been one that was much like all the other first days he had been through over the past twenty years. They seemed to be always the same, full of rules, responsibilities, reminders, and refreshers; the unknown.

That fear had been there, that nagging little voice of doubt that kept taunting and torturing him, telling him that he would never learn their names, and the students would spend the year in anonymous fog, led by an absent-minded professor.

He was sure that one of these years, if not this one, would find him no longer able to do that thing that he loved doing more than any other, teaching. That thought frightened him more than he could imagine.

He had doubled his efforts to match names with faces, and had quickly begun the yearly routine, rushing toward that zone of comfort where he was confident and ready to conquer.

It began with the writer's notebook, a treasure chest of ideas, beginnings, middles, and endings,

Together they visited and shared the authors:

Yolen,
Rylant,
Burleigh,
Paterson,
Bunting,
Paulsen,
Fletcher,
Davies,
Spinelli.

They had embraced these writers' craft, and made it theirs.

Each craft became a tool added to their toolbox, to be used to carve, shape, and finely sand each piece of writing, so that it would be smooth to the ear and pleasing to the eyes.

Then, like a field of varying and vigorous wildflowers, they burst into bloom, each at their own time, each with their own pattern of beauty, each with their own unique nectar and sensory sensation to share and spread around, creating future compositions of words and wonder for the world.

And they became the authors, adding their names to the list, and they became the mentors for those future students who would enter his classroom.

Now the year was almost over, and he was not ready to let go. He held on to each passing day, trying to squeeze every last bit of creative juice out of the plentiful orchard they had proven to be.

Their gifts had proven to be abundant, taking him to levels that he had only imagined.

They were writers. They were readers and writers. They were all-consuming readers and prolific writers, amazingly amazing in their abilities to awe and astound with an abundance of articulation.

He had watched them grow and proliferate.

They had conferenced and created together. They had collaborated and composed together. They had conquered and celebrated together.

And they were all better for it.

There are many ways to stretch ourselves as writers. Shelly Harwayne (2005) has created writing lessons inspired by the children in the adult fiction she reads. Harwayne clearly demonstrates the importance of teacher as reader to do the job of teacher as writer. She encourages teachers to use the titles from her book *Novel Perspectives* for staff book clubs. In this way teachers are reading like writers on two levels—with picture books and adult books as mentor texts. We find ourselves doing this all the time. Right now, we are reading two different books,

The History of Love by Nicole Krauss and *The Year of Pleasures* by Elizabeth Berg. Both of these authors make use of the colon in different ways, a craft we have discussed with our students many times. We believe that examining the craft of adult authors will enrich your understanding and help you notice the same thing in the books you use in your classroom, promoting deeper and more interesting conversations with your students. It also brings a real-world connection to the writing workshop.

Using mentor texts to help us live the writing journey with our students exemplifies what the reading-writing connection is all about. When you begin using mentor texts, the teaching possibilities are endless. You do not have to limit yourself to the mentor texts we have used here, but we invite you to start here with many of our favorites. We wish you good fortune as you embark on your writing journey, walking in the shoes of many different authors, trying them on for size, for aesthetic appeal, for comfort. We'd like to close with the words of Heather Lovelace, a first-grade teacher at Fern Hill Elementary School in West Chester, PA, who participated in our Writing and Children's Literature course at West Chester University.

> The power of the reading-writing connection is clear, and now it's a matter of recognizing my responsibility to use this knowledge. Scaffolds are just the invitation I needed to make writing instruction a foundation in my classroom. What will I look for to feel as if I've succeeded? . . . What I really want to see is children who have lots of ideas for their writing. Children who begin to read like writers. Children who are excited about writing and confident that they can write. And, glimpses of another author—or of craft—in a child's writing. This year I want them to try on lots of shoes. I want them to walk around in all the shoes they want, for as long as they like, until they begin to find shoes of their own.

REFERENCES

Anderson, Jeff. 2005. *Mechanically Inclined: Building Grammar, Usage, and Style into Writer's Workshop*. Portland, ME: Stenhouse Publishers.

Angelillo, Janet. 2002. *A Fresh Approach to Teaching Punctuation*. New York: Scholastic.

Araki, Mie. 2003. *The Magic Toolbox*. San Francisco, CA: Chronicle.

Atwell, Nancie. 1998. *In the Middle: New Understanding About Writing, Reading, and Learning*. Portsmouth, NH: Heinemann.

Berg, Elizabeth. 2005. *The Year of Pleasures*. New York: Random House.

Calkins, Lucy McCormick. 2001. *The Art of Teaching Reading*. New York: Addison-Wesley.

———. 2003. *Units of Study for Primary Writing: A Yearlong Curriculum Grades K–2*. Portsmouth, NH: Heinemann.

Dunning, Stephen, and William Stafford. 1992. *Getting the Knack: 20 Poetry Writing Exercises*. Urbana, IL: NCTE.

Elbow, Peter. 1981. *Writing with Power*. New York: Oxford University Press.

Esbensen, Barbara Juster. 1995. *A Celebration of Bees: Helping Children Write Poetry*. New York: Henry Holt and Co.

Fletcher, Ralph. 1993. *What a Writer Needs*. Portsmouth, NH: Heinemann.

Fletcher, Ralph, and JoAnn Portalupi. 2001. *Writing Workshop: The Essential Guide*. Portsmouth, NH: Heinemann.

Gay, Carol. 1976. "Reading Aloud and Learning to Write." *The Elementary School Journal* 77: 87–93.

Graves, Donald. 1994. *A Fresh Look at Writing*. Portsmouth, NH: Heinemann.

Harwayne, Shelley. 1992. *Lasting Impressions: Weaving Literature into the Writing Workshop*. Portsmouth, NH: Heinemann.

———. 2005. *Novel Perspectives: Writing Minilessons Inspired by the Children in Adult Fiction*. Portsmouth, NH: Heinemann.

Heard, Georgia. 1999. *Awakening the Heart: Exploring Poetry in Elementary and Middle School*. Portsmouth, NH: Heinemann.

Keene, Ellin, and Susan Zimmerman. 1997. *Mosaic of Thought: Teaching Comprehension in a Reader's Workshop*. Portsmouth, NH: Heinemann.

Krauss, Nicole. 2005. *The History of Love*. New York: W.W. Norton.

Lancia, Peter J. 1997. "Literary Borrowing: The Effects of Literature on Children's Writing." *The Reading Teacher* 50: 470–475.

Lane, Barry. 1993. *After THE END: Teaching and Learning Creative Revision*. Portsmouth, NH: Heinemann.

———. 1993. *Writing as a Road to Self-Discovery*. Shoreham, VT: Discover Writing Press.

Lyon, George Ella. 1999. *Where I'm From, Where Poems Come From*. Spring, TX: Absey & Co.

MacLachlan, Patricia, and Emily MacLachlan. 2003. *Painting the Wind*. New York: Harper Collins.

Miller, Debbie. 2002. *Reading with Meaning: Teaching Comprehension in the Primary Grades*. Portland, ME: Stenhouse.

Morgan, Bruce. 2005. *Writing Through the Tween Years: Supporting Writers, Grades 3–6*. Portland, ME: Stenhouse.

Murphy, Pamela. 2003. "Discovering the Ending in the Beginning." Language Arts 80:461–469.

Portalupi, JoAnn, and Ralph Fletcher. 2001. *Nonfiction Craft Lessons: Teaching Information Writing K–8*. Portland, ME: Stenhouse.

Ray, Katie Wood. 1999. *Wondrous Words: Writers and Writing in the Elementary Classroom*. Urbana, IL: NCTE.

———. 2002. *What You Know By Heart: How to Develop Curriculum for Your Writing Workshop*. Portsmouth, NH: Heinemann.

Ray, Katie Wood, with Lester Laminack. 2001. *The Writing Workshop: Working Through the Hard Parts (And They're All Hard Parts)*. Urbana, IL: NCTE.

Routman, Regie. 2005. *Writing Essentials*. Portsmouth, NH: Heinemann.

Schuster, Edgar H. 2003. *Breaking the Rules: Liberating Writers Through Innovative Grammar Instruction*. Portsmouth, NH: Heinemann.

Spandel, Vicki. 2005. *The 9 Rights of Every Writer*. Portsmouth, NH: Heinemann.

Suskind, Ron. 1998. *A Hope in the Unseen: An American Odyssey from the Inner City to the Ivy League*. New York: Broadway Books.

Topping, Donna, and Sandra Hoffman. 2006. *Getting Grammar: 150 New Ways to Teach an Old Subject*. Portsmouth, NH: Heinemann.

Vygotsky, L. S. 1978. *Mind in Society: The Development of Higher Psychological Processes*. Cambridge, MA: Harvard University Press.